Philanthropy in India

Philanthropy in India

PROMISE TO PRACTICE

Meenaz Kassam
Femida Handy
Emily Jansons

SSAGE   www.sagepublications.com
Los Angeles • London • New Delhi • Singapore • Washington DC

First published in 2016 by

 SAGE Publications India Pvt Ltd
B1/I-1 Mohan Cooperative Industrial Area
Mathura Road, New Delhi 110 044, India
www.sagepub.in

SAGE Publications Inc
2455 Teller Road
Thousand Oaks, California 91320, USA

SAGE Publications Ltd
1 Oliver's Yard, 55 City Road
London EC1Y 1SP, United Kingdom

SAGE Publications Asia-Pacific Pte Ltd
3 Church Street
#10-04 Samsung Hub
Singapore 049483

Published by Vivek Mehra for SAGE Publications India Pvt Ltd, typeset in 10/12 pt Sabon by PrePSol Enterprises Pvt Ltd and printed at Chaman Enterprises, New Delhi.

Library of Congress Cataloging-in-Publication Data Available

ISBN: 978-93-515-0752-9 (HB)

The SAGE Team: Aditi Chopra, Saima Ghaffar and Ritu Chopra

To all anonymous philanthropists, small and big,
especially RAC and MK

Thank you for choosing a SAGE product!
If you have any comment, observation or feedback,
I would like to personally hear from you.
Please write to me at **contactceo@sagepub.in**

Vivek Mehra, Managing Director and CEO,
SAGE Publications India Pvt Ltd, New Delhi

Bulk Sales

SAGE India offers special discounts
for purchase of books in bulk.
We also make available special imprints
and excerpts from our books on demand.

For orders and enquiries, write to us at

Marketing Department
SAGE Publications India Pvt Ltd
B1/I-1, Mohan Cooperative Industrial Area
Mathura Road, Post Bag 7
New Delhi 110044, India

E-mail us at **marketing@sagepub.in**

Get to know more about SAGE

Be invited to SAGE events, get on our mailing list.
Write today to **marketing@sagepub.in**

This book is also available as an e-book.

Contents

List of Abbreviations

AIF	American India Foundation
APPI	American Association of Physicians of Indian Origin
ASIE	American Society of Indian Engineers
B.CLIP	B.PAC Civic Leadership Incubation Program
B.PAC	Bangalore Political Action Committee
BAIF	Bharat Agro India Foundation
BAPS	Bochasanwasi Shri Akshar Purushottam Swaminarayan Sanstha
BHEL	Bharat Heavy Electrical Limited
BM	Bala Mandir
BMRF	BM Research Foundation
CAF	Charities Aid Foundation
CAP	Centre for Advancement of Philanthropy
CFI	Cultural Festival of India
CIA	Central Intelligence Agency
CIDA	Canadian International Development Agency
CORD	Chinmaya Organization for Rural Development
COVA	Confederation of Voluntary Associations
CPSE	Central Public Sector Enterprise
CRM	Customer Relationship Management
CRO	Contract Research Organization
CRY	Child Rights and You
CSR	Corporate Social Responsibility
DFAIT	Department of Foreign Affairs and International Trade
DOS	Disk Operating System
FCRA	Foreign Contributions Regulation Act
GDP	Gross Domestic Product
HNWI	High Net-worth Individual
ICCC	Indo-Canada Chamber of Commerce
ICI	Imperial Chemical Industries
IDRC	International Development Research Centre
IIT	Indian Institute of Technology

IMF	International Monetary Fund
INC	Indian National Congress
IT	Information Technology
MCGM	Municipal Corporation of Greater Mumbai
MFI	Microfinance Institution
MOIA	Ministry of Overseas Indian Affairs
MSCC	Mazumdar-Shaw Cancer Center
MSCTR	Mazumdar-Shaw Center for Translational Research
MSSR	Multistate Societies Registration
MWS	Mijwan Welfare Society
NGO	Nongovernmental Organization
NIMDAC	Northern Indian Medical & Dental Association of Canada
NPI	Nonprofit Institution
NTPC	National Thermal Power Corporation Limited
ONGC	Oil and Natural Gas Corporation
PBD	Pravasi Bharatiya Divas
PHFI	Public Health Foundation of India
PPP	Public–Private Partnership
PSU	Public Sector Unit
PTI	Press Trust of India
ROC	Registrar of Companies
SAJA	South Asia Journalists Association
SC	Swaminarayan Chapter
SDTT	Sir Dorabji Tata and Allied Trusts
SHG	Self-help Group
SIFPSA	State Innovations in Family Planning Services Agency
SKDRDP	Shri Kshetra Dharmasthala Rural Development Project
SOSVA	Society for Service to Voluntary Agencies
SRTT	Sir Ratan Tata Trust
TISS	Tata Institute of Social Sciences
TRAI	Telecom Regulatory Authority of India
TTD	Tirumala Tirupathi Devasthanams
USAID	United States Agency for International Development
USIG	United States International Grantmaking
VLSI	Very Large-scale Integration
WDL	Winding Down Lodge

Foreword

Researching philanthropy in a country as diverse and culturally rich as India is a daunting task. The roots go back many millennia. There is a chapter devoted to charity in the *Rig Veda* (one of the oldest Hindu religious texts), where *Daan* (giving or charity) is divided into three classes—*Satvik, Rajasi,* and *Tamasi.* Satvik giving would entail making the right contribution for the right cause at the right time. Rajasi giving could be for personal aggrandizement while Tamasi giving could be for destructive purposes.

The world, as we know it today, has moved on from charity to philanthropy, and now venture philanthropy. Venture philanthropy, also known as 'Philanthro-capitalism,' takes concepts and techniques from venture capital finance and high-technology business management and applies them to achieving philanthropic goals. Venture philanthropy is characterized by a willingness to experiment and try new approaches and focus on measurable results. This has resulted in the growth of several social entrepreneurs and social enterprises across the country.

The Indian tradition of *Shresthdharma* recommends that the better-off one is in the society, the higher should be one's sense of responsibility. The number of high net-worth individuals (HNWIs), especially in Asian countries, including India, is booming. The number of millionaires in India has surged to a record high. The BNP Paribas 'Individual Philanthropy Index' reveals that philanthropy is growing worldwide, increasing by five points on an average in 2015. However, the question remains: Does more wealth automatically lead to increased giving? Conventionally, this has been true. Ford and Carnegie 'gave' only because they had the wealth in the first place. Wanting to give is easy. But, giving wisely is challenging. Today, philanthropists are not just looking for the 'feel good factor.' They are looking for measurable impact and a sound return on their social investment. They are looking for innovation and are willing to provide 'risk capital.'

Mandating CSR under the new Indian Companies Act 2013 has also opened up several more opportunities. One still observes a lot of excitement and hope, but the impact of mandating CSR in India will be known only after a few more years. However, there is no doubting the fact that we are living in exciting times where philanthropy is concerned.

This book, *Philanthropy in India: Promise to Practice,* is the result of a three-year study on the many aspects of philanthropy in India and a reflection of the interests of three authors. This book takes a wide-angle view of current religious and secular practices of philanthropy and its influences, including the range of public charitable organizations, both religious and secular, through which donations as well as volunteer efforts are channeled. It is a laudable effort and I offer my hearty congratulations to Meenaz Kassam, Femida Handy, and Emily Jansons.

Noshir H. Dadrawala

Acknowledgments

As with all books, this book would not have been possible without the help and support of many people. We gratefully acknowledge the partial support provided by Global Engagement Fund of the University of Pennsylvania to the second author along with support from the International Development Research Centre (IDRC) to the third author. It would not have been possible to write this book without the generosity of the many individuals who appeared in our book, directly and indirectly. Despite their busy lives, they shared with us their knowledge and insights and allowed us to survey, interview, probe, and question them. We hope that our words have done justice to them and the philanthropy they engage in.

Our editors, Aditi Chopra and Saima Ghaffar, at SAGE wisely steered us when we most needed it. We are also grateful to the student assistant, Eunice Lim, who did a careful and most intelligent review of our work, taking care of the many details involved in writing this manuscript. We thank, as with our other books, Adam at the café in Toronto, where we wrote many parts of this book, for graciously keeping us caffeinated and fed. Our families provided moral and emotional support which helped us persevere. They believed in this project and encouraged us from the very beginning and tolerated our long absences as we conducted our research and spent many days together in India, Toronto, Dubai, and Philadelphia.

Introduction

India is at an interesting crossroads, as its poorest and wealthiest populations grow at each end of the spectrum. On the one hand, there are tens of millions of Indians who lack basic necessities such as food, shelter, and health care—and this population is expected to grow exponentially. On the other hand, and in between the spectrum, multitudes of Indians are mobilizing to reduce extreme poverty to great success. The official poverty rate decreased almost to half from 45 percent in 1994 to 22 percent in 2012. Although the task of improving the lot of the poor is monumental and cannot solely be the responsibility of philanthropists, philanthropy is a major force in the battle against widespread poverty. As documented in this book, philanthropy is practiced in every nook and cranny of Indian society: from the big cities and corporations to grassroots organizations, and at every level of the socioeconomic pyramid.

The rising numbers of religious and social charitable trusts are testament to the growing number of institutions through which people are channeling their money. Especially promising is the increased participation of Indians in philanthropic endeavors that go beyond their own ethnic and family circles. This book examines the practice and viability of this promise and its implications for India's future.

Since the early decades following India's Independence, the state has stepped back from its commanding role in the economy and provision of public services and goods. In turn, civil society or social sector organizations, corporations, and philanthropy have taken on a larger role to fill the vacuum. While its nature is ever evolving, philanthropy—with its deep roots and ubiquitous nature, albeit not always formally recognized—is fundamental to India's identity. As philanthropy in the country is playing an increasingly important role, this book sets out to understand the evolution, current practices, and future promise of philanthropy in India.

This book is the result of a three-year study on the many aspects of philanthropy in India and a reflection of the interests of all three authors. Based on our experiences, each of us has a unique vantage point from which we offer insights. All of us have spent time in India—two of us were born there and spent many of our formative years in India. One of us practices philanthropy actively by running schools for marginalized children and strategically funding nongovernmental organizations (NGOs) in India; the other has spent time meeting with key actors in the Indian philanthropic space as well as working for Indian NGO organizations and in the corporate social responsibility (CSR) space; and the third one of us has spent much of her academic career writing on and researching various aspects of philanthropy, including being the coeditor of the book, *The Palgrave Handbook on Global Philanthropy* (Weipking and Handy 2015).

Despite differences in our backgrounds, we came together to write this book because we shared a mutual interest and an admiration for the practices of philanthropy in India. The deep history and roots of philanthropy that underpin what we see today give us much hope and optimism for the growth of philanthropy in India, and its promise in making sustainable social change.

Philanthropy is practiced in different ways for different reasons by individuals at all levels of the socioeconomic pyramid, and by institutions, both small and large. When we began our initial investigation into the many ways philanthropy is practiced in India, we saw immense richness in the details and wanted to capture the lives and stories of individual philanthropists in each of our chapters. No two stories are the same, and we hope that these stories give the reader a sense of the nuances and subtleties involved in the practice of philanthropy.

In no way is philanthropy new to this part of the world. Indeed, all religions in India have age-old traditions that embody the concept of philanthropy. Although the many forms of philanthropy practiced today trace their roots back to thousands of years, the philanthropic practice has been influenced by India's history of colonization starting from the Mughal period to the British Raj, with the introduction of Islam and Christianity. The key factors that influence current practices of philanthropy include government policies and changing technology.

In India, philanthropy is often seen as an answer to many of the country's widespread social ills such as hunger, disease, illiteracy, and unemployment. And as a result of this view, the number of NGOs (also referred to as nonprofits elsewhere), not-for-profit and for-profit microfinance institutions (MFIs), and charitable trusts have been on the rise. Further, the liberalization of the economy since the 1990s, the advent of technology, and a growing and affluent citizenry and diaspora are causing philanthropy to grow, change, and formalize in unprecedented ways. Still, a lot of philanthropic giving in India is done informally and thus remains below the radar. In this respect, the practice of philanthropy, as we currently understand it, is incomplete.

This book takes a wide-angle view of current religious and secular practices of philanthropy and its influences, including the range of public charitable organizations, both religious and secular, through which donations as well as volunteer efforts are channeled. Using case studies and rich narratives, we illustrate the many varied practices and the promises of philanthropy.

In Chapter 1, we ask the question: What shapes the practice of philanthropy in a country? We examine the role of religion, history, politics, cultural elements, and government regulations—which in the Indian context includes Hindu and Islamic (among other) religious underpinnings, colonization and industrialization, the Independence movement and teachings of Mahatma Gandhi, and post-Independence economic trends. While philanthropy in India comes from a deep-rooted background of religion and tradition, it has also been subject to modern and foreign influences at various periods of time that have impacted perspectives on philanthropy, introduced new methods of institutionalized giving, and enlarged the scale on which philanthropy is practiced. These elements continue to shape social norms and the practice of philanthropy in India today.

We continue in Chapter 2 with a historical overview of legislation that governs charitable trusts in India and then proceed to examine proposed legislations that could impact charitable trusts. Using a series of case studies, this chapter highlights the role and importance of a variety of public, private, religious, and secular trusts in India. Aseema is a fine example of a public charitable trust that has governmental permission to accept foreign contributions tax-free. To add, donors are allowed to deduct the amount that they have donated from their taxable income. These funds have allowed Aseema to operate municipal schools through a partnership with the government and consequently offer quality education to hundreds of street children. In the narrative of Sri Kshetra Dharmasthala Rural Development Project (SKDRDP), a religious charitable organization, we find a very different set of core values and missions. It is no surprise that SKDRDP has leveraged its funds to create a place of worship, but it also channels resources to help the local community. It has helped farmers enhance their skills and acquire loans to buy better machinery, thereby lifting an economically depressed area out of poverty.

In Chapter 3, we turn our focus to philanthropic actions at the individual level. We look not only at the HNWIs at the top of the pyramid and India's middle class, but also at those at the bottom of the pyramid. The challenge of individual giving is that much of it is done informally—particularly at the bottom of the pyramid—thus not publicly known or accounted for. This chapter attempts to shed light on the practices of individual giving through four case studies, ranging from a high-net-worth couple, insights from professional middle-class Rotary Club members, the generosity of a low-net-worth individual, and lastly, five short examples of giving at the bottom of the pyramid. While the challenges and scale of philanthropy practiced by the wealthy differ from those of the poor, individuals across all levels demonstrate an inclination to give strategically and make an impact.

In Chapter 4, we shift gears from individual giving to corporate giving. Corporate India, which is still largely family-owned and family-managed, is very active in philanthropy. This chapter examines the practices of family-owned companies whose traditional practices of meeting employees' needs have shifted away to contemporary forms of philanthropy. This shift was first initiated by government-owned public sector enterprises that sought to provide its employees (and the community in which they were located) benefits and programs hitherto unavailable. It changed how business saw their role in society, and these practices soon spread to businesses. It is now labeled as CSR, and was largely motivated by expectations of the public and government. Our narratives include that of Sir Jejeebhoy, one of the earlier well-known philanthropists, who was influenced by British modes of secular philanthropy. He won British favor through his donations to hospitals as well as educational institutions in both India and Britain. We also present a narrative of the Tata Group, one of the most enduring and famous industrial groups known for its wide-ranging efforts at large-scale philanthropy.

Most emigrants maintain some ties with their countries of origin, and in Chapter 5, we examine philanthropic giving as a way Indian emigrants maintain these ties. The Indian diaspora is significant and relatively prosperous and many diaspora members have a desire to help those back in India. In this chapter, we examine the breadth and depth of such philanthropic behavior and the factors that are likely to motivate and facilitate giving. This giving is undertaken through associations formed by Indians living abroad, or done directly through individual gifts. We also discuss the recent efforts of the Indian government to engage the diaspora in India's socioeconomic development agenda. Since 2003, the government hosted an annual diaspora conference, the Pravasi Bharatiya Divas (PBD), that facilitates interaction between Indian diaspora, the Indian government, and cultural and charity organizations. The Ministry of Overseas Indian Affairs (MOIA) also coordinates activities aimed at reaching out to the diaspora. Some of the trends explored in the chapter are illustrated through three narratives of diaspora Indians engaged in philanthropy.

Chapter 6 examines how traditional charitable practices have given way to various new philanthropic practices. We give a brief snapshot of emerging trends, though we are aware that newer trends have emerged while this book was being written and continue to develop as this book goes to print. Today, boundaries and limits in philanthropy are being tested, as creative minds combine information technology (IT) to expand the reach of philanthropy worldwide. Evidence of this can be seen in the case study on GiveIndia, which uses the Internet to connect donors to recipients. GiveIndia is only one of many organizations that use modern IT to change the face of philanthropy. Another case looks at Dasra's successful venture philanthropy model of Giving Circles to connect donors to NGOs. The third case study reflects how India's successful female business leaders chart their own model of philanthropy.

In general, this book has been a joyful journey. Learning about the depth and breadth of philanthropic practice in its many forms has been a humbling experience. We were reminded of humanity's essence as we saw how people cared for one another, from the top of the pyramid to the bottom and everywhere in between. The stories and narratives of philanthropy in action are not only mentioned in the pages of this book but are also etched deeply in our hearts. We are so grateful to all of the individuals who are mentioned here—and the countless others who are not mentioned, but whose practices of philanthropy make this world a better place for all of us.

1

The Practice of Philanthropy

Introduction

What shapes the practice of philanthropy in a country? On an individual level, philanthropy is driven by social, cultural, and historical structures as well as lifestyles, values, attitudes, and orientations (Schervish et al. 1986: 11–12). The same could be said about philanthropy in a country. Some of these elements, particularly within structure, hold greater weight than others, while habits can be manifested at both the conscious and unconscious levels. Further, philanthropy itself evolves throughout time, mixing modern and traditional practices of a country (Copeman 2011: 1052). In this chapter, we provide some background on the various elements that shape the norms and practices of Indian philanthropy today.

The chapter begins by going back in time to examine how philanthropy first evolved and was codified in India within ancient communities. Religious underpinnings are explored, with particular attention paid to Hinduism and Islam, the two main religions in the country. The chapter then turns its focus on the development of philanthropy over the past two centuries with the advent of colonization and industrialization, and later the Independence movement and the teachings of Mahatma Gandhi. Post-Independence philanthropic trends are also observed. Finally, the chapter reviews the current government policies that incentivize philanthropic giving and the regulations that govern charitable trusts, as well as the importance of corporate and individual philanthropy in India. Given the complexity and many levels of philanthropy, this chapter does not attempt to provide a complete and detailed history of Indian giving. Rather, it offers an overview that is useful in understanding the promise of philanthropy outlined in subsequent chapters.

Religious Underpinnings

For thousands of years in India, religions of all backgrounds have played an invaluable role in driving charitable acts. Census data shows around 80.5 percent of Indians are Hindu, 13.4 percent Muslim, 2.3 percent Christian, 1.9 percent Sikh, 0.8 percent Buddhist, and 0.4 percent Jain.[1] Hence in India, traditions of giving from all of these religions intermingle and build upon each other. There are concepts of *daan* (giving) and *dakshina* (alms) from Hinduism, *bhiksha* (alms) from Buddhism, and *zakat* (prescribed offerings) and *sadaqa* (voluntary offerings) from Islam, among others (Viswanath and Dadrawala 2004: 263). Though selfless giving is promoted, some lines of influential Indian philosophy claim that destiny shapes individuals and that destiny cannot be altered. This notion seems to imply that philanthropy is not performed necessarily to change the course of an unfortunate recipient's life, but rather as the giver's way of adding onto his/her own life-after-death balance sheet. Overall, most people in India today give charitably on account of a compulsion or feel-good impulse, without extensively verifying the details of what their religion stipulates. Philanthropy, therefore, draws on a wide range of motivations stemming from not only religious values but also other traditions, sense of duty, and habit.

Hinduism

The Upanishads, a 4,000-year-old collection of philosophical texts, form the theoretical basis for the Hindu religion and dictate the practices of religious gift-giving in India. Hindu daan[2] has numerous forms, and is not the only form of gift-giving. Traditionally, it is one of four ways to deal with conflict: *saam* (conciliation, true or false praise), daan (placating with gifts), *dand* (use of force), and *bhaid* (sowing dissension) (Agarwal 2010: 22). Daan is also not

---

[1] Table 21: "Distribution of Population by Religion," Census of India 2001. Latest available data. http://censusindia.gov.in/Census_And_You/religion.aspx (accessed June 9, 2013).

[2] Also commonly spelled *dan* or *dana*.

restricted to India, as an array of Jain and Buddhist forms of daan does exist across South and Southeast Asia (Copeman 2011: 1052). While etymologically daan holds a common Indo-European root *do-*,[3] it does not directly translate to the English *donation*, as over time the attached connotations in each society have differed. For one, daan is closer in meaning to gift or gifting. Another difference is that in the West, charity (an act of immediate relief for the poor) and philanthropy (an act for serving broader public purposes) are distinguished. In contrast, the Indian concept of daan includes elements of both charity and philanthropy (Sundar 2000: 30). Further, daan lies within the duty of the individual rather than institutions, and should only be made from surplus money after household needs are met, so as not to cause hardship on the donor's family and dependents (Agarwal 2010: 43; Bornstein 2009: 627). Daan should also not be made from stolen or unjustly earned money, for the giving of such funds will not result in purification. Rather, this money will be returned to the rightful owner to whom the money belonged in the first place (Agarwal and AccountAid 2005a). Nonetheless, a large percentage of donations made to temples in India each year probably consists of black money.

In early Indian history, purely religious gifts (*ishta*) comprised only one small part of daan, which also included general charitable acts (*pushta*) for the community at large (Kasturi 2010: 110). In Hinduism, to achieve *moksh*—release from the painful cycle of life and death—one must gradually detach oneself from the material world by giving (Agarwal and AccountAid 2005a). Hindu philosophy is therefore filled with concepts of nonpossession (*aparigraha*) and equalism (*samabhavana*) (Meera 2007: 22–23). While scriptures outline proportions of income that should be given as daan, these proportions are no longer followed in practice (Agarwal and AccountAid 2005a). For example, *Skand Puran*, the largest of 18 *Mahapurans*, suggests that 10 percent of one's income should be given away (Agarwal 2010: 43; Agarwal and AccountAid 2005a). Yet few Indians today are aware of the many different forms of daan and their purposes, as they have become disconnected from the literary heritage on the topic (Agarwal 2010: 35).

Great importance is attached to the performance of duties and obligations as part of Hinduism's acceptance of one's place in the social hierarchy. Dharma is linked to karma in that good performance

---

[3] Latin work *donum* and Sanskrit work *danum*.

and fulfillment of the dharma role, such as giving alms to the poor or the poor accepting alms, guarantee the individual a higher position in the next life (Pappu 2004: 165; Rolnick 1962: 441–442). Donations are made at any time the individual finds the right combination of recipient and place, with some occasions such as the solar or lunar eclipses being particularly auspicious (Agarwal 2010: 60). In today's society, however, attitudes are rapidly changing, and many are becoming critical of how

> Hinduism teaches the poor to endure everything quietly, to be 'content' with their poverty, for the fruits of their contentment will be gained in the next birth or in paradise. But it does not teach the rich to be content; it condones their pursuit of wealth, as long as a part of it is given to charity. (Rolnick 1962: 445)

Further, daan is used today in political and cultural realms to express power, status, and symbolic capital (Kasturi 2010: 110). Daan is therefore vulnerable to certain misuse, appropriated to justify the existing social structure.

Many forms of daan exist—by one estimate at least 130 specific forms—each with its unique set of rituals and ceremonies, making traditional daan "more of an event rather than a simple transfer of resources" (Agarwal 2010: 41). There are many traditions, laws, and customs that explain why one should give, what to give, when to give, to whom to give, and how much to give. The many forms of daan were often built into life-cycle rituals and rites of passage, giving cause for celebration and giving at every vital event (Raja 2012). According to ancient texts, the most valuable gifts were those which enhanced spiritual knowledge, followed by gifts that offered secular knowledge, and, finally, gifts that satisfied physical needs (Sundar 1996: 414). Giving can also be seen in the forms of *shram daan*, volunteering your time or working with your own hands; *anna daan*, free food offering, either from excess or specially prepared for giving away; *vastra daan*, giving of clothes; and the ultimate form of giving, *gyaan daan*, the giving of knowledge to the world before you pass away. Two highly valued forms include: gifts given on impulse, such as giving to a beggar without stopping to think, and a gift given in secret (*gupt daan*), as it removes any reward related to the giver's status and thus contributes to merit and good karma (Bornstein 2009: 626; Laidlaw 1995). *Tamasik daan* is daan given to an unsuitable person, without consideration of appropriate time or place, without showing proper respect, or given in an insulting manner (Agarwal and AccountAid 2005a). *Rajasik daan* is based on whatever benefits are sought by the giver, whether the benefit is direct or indirect, material or spiritual (Agarwal and AccountAid 2005a). *Utsarg* or "letting go" is when an item or property is given up for general public use; for example, providing water for travelers through *jalaashay* (wells, ponds, or reservoirs) (Agarwal 2010: 54). Other forms of daan include *ashraya* and *pratishraya*, building rest houses and shelters for travelers, orphans, homeless, or other destitute persons; *arogya daan*, taking care of the sick; and *devalaya*, constructing and dedicating temples for public use (Agarwal 2010: 59–60). *Nitya daan* emerges from a sense of duty, with no sought return or merit, and the benefits therefore "are never exhausted—they flow eternally" (Agarwal and AccountAid 2005a).

An important element in understanding daan is the relationship the act holds with the individual giver. While in the West, individuals remain attached to their donations in terms of keeping interest in the outcome and deriving satisfaction in knowing how the money has been used, Hindu givers are required to cut off all emotional and legal ties to the gift and any expectation of return—thus often daan is deemed a 'disinterested' gift (Bornstein 2009: 264–265). Nonetheless, responsibility for ensuring the accountability and proper use of the daan lies with the giver; one must select the recipient prudently to ensure the daan will be effectively used once it becomes the recipient's property and detached from the giver (Agarwal and AccountAid 2005a). Conversely, recipients of daan have no right to demand the gift or make claims on the giver, which differs from humanitarianism and other forms of giving in which recipients have rights (Bornstein 2009: 642). Daan brings merit or virtue (*punya*) to the giver, which can be accumulated and earned as good deeds (*achche karam*). Thus, daan is primarily an act for one's own benefit, while any benefit the recipient may derive is secondary (Agarwal 2010: 30; Bornstein 2009: 632; Sharma 2001: 180). Refusal to help the needy during a calamity, however, is supposed to bring dire afterlife consequences for all those in a position to help (Sharma 2001: 180). In Hindu tradition, every transaction of giving results in the formation of a relationship, thus "giving is to be approached with caution and care" on account of the donor–recipient relationship that results from an exchange (Anderson 1997: 200; 1998: 58). While traditionally the relationship was personal and intimate, such a relationship is more difficult to establish today. Nonetheless, "Hinduism is clear that it is the duty of those with wealth, not their option, to give" (Anderson 1997: 185, 199). Giving is therefore a balance—even a tension—between the givers and recipients of daan.

Islam

Compared to Hinduism, Islam has a broader notion of institutional charity, including compulsory zakat and voluntary sadaqa, as well as *khums* (mandated for Shia) and *awqaf* (endowment). During the indigenization of Islam in North India, Muslim rulers and Islamic gentry assumed a role as gift-givers who contributed to all of civil society—supporting even secular public projects such as bridges or aqueducts—as it was deemed part of the religious life and health of the community (Sharma 2001: 179). Today, an estimated INR 14 billion (US$236.3 million) is transferred annually from wealthier Muslim individuals and institutions to the rest of Indian society—this amount constitutes on average about 10 percent of the annual income of a poor Muslim household, therefore playing a crucial role in their lives (Shariff 2010: 261, 267).[4]

Zakat is an alms-giving obligation in the form of tax required of all Muslims who are financially sufficient. As it is one of the five pillars of Islam, it is strongly enforced by the community and offers social, religious, and moral benefits as it purifies wealth from sin. Refusal to pay roughly 2.5 percent of income can lead to severe condemnation and retribution. The nature of the consequence that follows is supposedly linked to the item on which the zakat was payable; for example, if zakat was evaded on camels, the individual may be trampled and bit by fat camels (Agarwal 2010: 68). Zakat is implemented and imposed not by the State but rather by religious institutions and networks, and can be paid in cash or kind to a small or large number of eligible individuals who are followers of the Islamic faith and not zakat givers themselves (Shariff 2010: 258–259).

Zakat does not outline how the recipient should spend the money, although the understanding is that it should be used for areas of

[4] Estimate by Abusaleh Shariff "Economics of Religion: Spiritual Capital and Philanthropy amongst Muslims in India."

need such as family's education or health. A 2005 study by The Confederation of Voluntary Associations (COVA) surveyed 4,450 households in Uttar Pradesh, West Bengal, and Gujarat, and found that the vast majority of zakat givers saw it as a religious duty. Further, 60 percent of respondents also saw it as a way of promoting a just society, and about 50 percent considered zakat an ancestral practice that should be continued as a sign of respect (Shariff 2010: 262). Many Muslims are inclined to undertake additional charitable acts beyond zakat and at various times of the year.

Sadaqa is personal, voluntary charity that comes with no set of guiding rules or limits in terms of how much or to whom one should give. The sadaqa must be money earned honestly, and acts to protect the poor from impoverishment and ensures they do not turn to unlawful means to feed themselves (Agarwal 2010: 64–65). Theologically, "*sadaqa* is considered a loan to Allah. This loan will eventually be multiplied many times and returned to the giver" (Agarwal and AccountAid 2005b). Only among some Shia, there are khums mandated for the benefit of orphans, the poor, travelers, and imams (Agarwal 2010: 66; Agarwal and AccountAid 2005b). Awqaf (the plural of waqf/wakf or endowment) is a voluntary donation of an object or property toward some charitable end (Shariff 2010: 255). The festival of Eid also witnesses high levels of charity, in which families give one and three-quarters of common measure of food[5] to the poor (Shariff 2010: 262).

Other Religions

As Hinduism did not have a system of institutional giving, Buddhism, through the order of monks (sanghas), and later Christianity played an important role in organizing charity and institutionalizing philanthropy in India through the construction of schools, hospitals, homes for the elderly, and so forth (Jha 2012: 255; Viswanath and Dadrawala 2004: 263). In Christianity, *tithing* is the mandated form of giving collected for the maintenance of the church, salary payment of the clergy, and mission work around the world (Agarwal and AccountAid 2005c).The Eastern Orthodox Church never accepted

---

[5] For example, if using the common measure of 1 kg, a family of six would give away 10.5 kg of food, such as rice.

tithes, and the practice was abolished in France with the revolution (1789), as well as in Italy, Ireland, Scotland, and England, throughout the 19th and 20th centuries; but in some parts of southern India, some church members still pay *tithes* regularly (Agarwal and AccountAid 2005c). Most Christian giving, however, is voluntary and done directly or indirectly through intermediaries and institutions. Like other forms of religious-inspired giving, Christian giving promises no worldly returns but great rewards in heaven.

Sikhs also follow a mandated practice giving, *dawsandh*, in which every Sikh donates one-tenth of one's earning to the gurdwara. In addition, all Sikhs engage in *seva*, or direct service, often through the construction, cleaning, and maintenance of gurdwaras. Every gurdwara has *langar*, a kitchen, where all people can eat.

Jains engage in the giving of daan to spiritual guides, the unfortunate, and the helpless, in order to cleanse one's wealth and reduce excessive disparity between the rich and the poor (Agarwal 2010: 97). A Jain is expected to give daan every day, regardless of how little the amount is. The merit and social importance of Jain daan lies in it being a "pure" or "free" gift, without the creation of any obligations or personal connections (Bornstein 2009: 626).

There are a small number of Parsis in India—only 69,901 according to the 2001 census, mostly in and around Mumbai—but their "philanthropy is legendary in India" and their establishment of institutions is "highly regarded for its modern approach and munificence" (Agarwal 2010: 102). Parsis draw on their Zoroastrian faith, and their important contribution will be touched upon again later.

Social and Cultural Underpinnings of Philanthropy

While religion continues to play an important role in the lives of Indians, there are also certain secular, cultural traditions that shape philanthropy. For one, India's deeply rooted social structure has had a great impact on community relations and gifting. Traditional Indian society is built and maintained by a "superstructure of attitudes, values, and behavior patterns" and "a web of reciprocal relationships" (Rolnick 1962: 440). While sociological studies paint India as a communal society, one in which "Indians were warm, gregarious and seldom alone," being closely connected with their extended family and caste group, interactions outside one's caste were traditionally limited and formal (Das 2002: 17). French sociologist Marcel Mauss in 1966 noted that when a gift is exchanged, "the recipient is in a state of dependence upon the donor." For this reason, the [high priestly caste] Brahmin could not accept gifts even from the king—as "divinity among divinities, he [the Brahmin] is superior to the king and would lose his superiority if he did other than simply take from him" (Mauss 1966: 58). Mauss further explained that "the gift is thus something that must be given, that must be received and that is, at the same time, dangerous to accept," and as "the gift itself constitutes an irrevocable link," it requires various precautions (Mauss 1966: 58–59). For example, an organization may be successful in working with a certain caste or village community group, but may find its actions divisive when trying to incorporate the entire village (Das 2002: 18). Yet much has changed in the Indian caste structure since the 1960s, and behaviors and beliefs are evolving.

At the family level, there are constant demands and responsibilities and built-in inequalities, alongside varying degrees of rights and entitlements between members; strangers do not have any rights as it is impractical to open oneself up to unlimited demands (Bornstein 2012: 150). Obligations and responsibilities toward kin and friends are not deemed humanitarian or part of charitable work because they are simply one's duty (Bornstein 2012: 150). Therefore, acts of liberal humanitarianism as practiced in the West—toward others one has no connection with—are considered problematic in the Indian context. These acts may even arouse suspicion over whether the individual is neglecting duties toward his/her own family and raise questions to why the individual is looking to engage with strangers (Bornstein 2012: 151). This particular perspective gives insight to why generosity can be deemed dangerous in Indian tradition, and "giving is to be approached with caution and care and with a clear understanding of the relationship between donor and recipient that results from this exchange" (Anderson 1998: 58). In India, on account of caste dynamics, family demands, and the potential risks associated with either giving or receiving a gift, philanthropy is socially and culturally constructed as a deliberate activity.

Early Traditions

Vertical (rich to poor) philanthropy and horizontal (poor to poor) philanthropy are part of India's culture, but how these inclinations are carried out varies across time. Most societies since ancient times have followed an implicit social contract that puts charitable acts under the duty of local elites and nobles. This was most evident during times of scarcity and crop failure, when states and local elites would distribute grain and open free kitchens (langars, *bhandaras*) serving cooked food (Sharma 2001: 182). As a result, rulers in India were perceived as providers of food (*annadata*). Another form of elite gifting was granting land as daan to allies and religious institutions, or building infrastructure such as bridges or aqueducts (Kasturi 2010: 111). Gifting played a valuable role in connecting donors with their economic functions within society and in building social bonds between merchants and rulers (Haynes 1987: 346; Kasturi 2010: 111). Consequently, gifts were used to claim authority and status. In addition to obtaining symbolic and economic capital, gifts also provided a certain stabilization to the political order (Haynes 1987: 346; Kasturi 2010: 111). Colonial observers noted that rural elite saw charity as related to their concerns over the preservation of the workforce and social cohesion (Sharma 2001: 173). This desire to maintain peace with the masses through acts of generosity is echoed by some philanthropists today.

The inverse side of charity by elites are the daily acts undertaken by the community. Precolonial charitable traditions reinforced ethical and social codes, cultural values, religious merit, and "the maintenance of individual and family reputation within the community" (Palsetia 2005: 202). Before the British broke up self-sufficient villages communes, the family and village community provided welfare, but over time, the state came to play an increasingly dominant role (Sundar 1996: 412). Nonetheless, the welfare of the less privileged was largely dependent on private charity, and social organizations funded themselves through community support (Sundar 1996: 412; 2010: 32). It was only over time that such organizations became more formally organized.

According to ancient texts, the most valued gifts were those that enhanced spiritual knowledge, followed by gifts that enhanced secular knowledge, and, lastly, gifts that satisfied physical needs (Sundar

1996: 414). Therefore, many gifts were directed toward improving educational opportunities and structures—including the provision of free food for students, construction of buildings, and endowment of chairs (Sundar 2000: 87–88). Other popular gifts were land, housing, or money to build or maintain temples, food and drink for pilgrims, endowments for the maintenance of monasteries and educational institutions, and assistance to the sick (Sundar 1996: 414). The causes supported today are in some respects not so different from those supported in precolonial times.

Precolonial philanthropy also held an important business function. Long before the emergence of the term CSR—as far back as the ancient guilds in the early and later Vedic periods (around 1500–500 BC)—businesses undertook various forms of charity, which played a role in developmental efforts (Meera 2007: 13, 20, 22–23; Sood and Arora 2006: 6). By engaging in charity, often in the form of patronage of traditional Indian causes, such as temples and rites, donors gained reputation (or *abru*), legitimacy within local society, and commercial advantages (Palsetia 2005: 197). In fact, since the 11th century, temples functioned as institutions of capital investment, accumulation, and distribution—with many similar functions that commercial banks perform today—drawing on the major endowments from local nobles and trading guilds to cover capital, operating expenses, and loan money (Rudner 1987: 362). For example, the *Nakarattars*, a caste of salt-traders in the Tamil-speaking part of South India, 'invested' profits from their salt trade into religious gifts which were then transformed and redistributed as honors—the currency of trust (Rudner 1987: 377). Trustworthiness gave the Nakarattars further access to the market for salt. And so through money, gifts, and honors, they established themselves as the chief merchant-banking caste in South Asia by the 19th century (Rudner 1987: 377). Strategic and purposeful charity, whether in secular or religious forms, brought mutual benefits to both givers and receivers.

Although the above text only begins to deconstruct the many social and cultural layers of Indian philanthropy, it is evident that both religious and secular charitable inclinations were present in India long before outside influences arrived. Continuing along those traditions, variations of familial responsibilities, elite charity, and business strategic giving contribute to the practice of philanthropy in India today.

Philanthropy during India's Colonial Period

Colonial rule brought new attitudes and approaches to philanthropy, which, over time, were integrated into the Indian context and merged with indigenous traditions. From the expansion of East India Company rule (1773–1858) to the period of direct rule under the British Raj (1858–1947), the British utilized charity as a tool—first to gain a foothold in the Indian subcontinent (present-day Bangladesh, India, and Pakistan) and later to engage local Indian elites. As the East India Company grew in power throughout the 18th century in Surat, it used gifts and loans to forge relationships (Haynes 1987: 348). By the 1820s–1830s, when the East India Company tightened its control over western India, colonial officials began to shake off earlier traditions of building ties and relationships through personal tributes, and instead gave gifts motivated by a sense of mission and cultural superiority (Haynes 1987: 349). Such gifts came to be viewed as bribes and thus unacceptable in public (Haynes 1987: 349). As the colonial state began to perceive itself as the ultimate source of philanthropy within a framework of 'useful' public works, it criticized and dismissed indigenous forms of charity (Sharma 2001: 136, 182). While "new imperial idioms" were introduced and the forms of giving shifted between precolonial and colonial times, charity still maintained a significant role in forming individual reputation, authority, and definition of community (Palsetia 2005: 197–198). Even daan did not remain fixed in a precolonial form, but acquired new meanings, goals, and forms as it expanded in scale, and provided a cultural and political space for elites and reformers to express their status and concerns over community and rights (Kourula and Halme 2008: 132). In this way, philanthropy was constantly evolving to meet changing times.

British Attitudes

The British brought with them ideas of charity, drawing on the contemporary debates occurring in Britain, and consequently impacted philanthropy in India. Victorian-era values placed great emphasis on private efforts to improve the human condition (Haynes 1987: 350).

According to historian David Owen, "for most Englishmen, the hundreds of charitable institutions [in Britain itself] represented one of the glories of the British tradition and stood as a monument to the superiority of voluntary action over state intervention" (Haynes 1987: 350). While Victorians viewed philanthropy as a space in which Protestantism tested itself against Catholicism, philanthropy was spun as a test and point of national pride against other religions in the colonial context (Harrison 1966: 357 in Caplan 1998: 413). The New Poor Law of 1834 reformed England's poverty relief system, led by the belief that private charity was less inclined to abuse than public relief, thus placing emphasis on the provision of work for the able-bodied and return to independence of the poor (Sharma 2001: 191). Victorian notions distinguished between the deserving and undeserving poor, and work was seen to carry valuable disciplinary and moral effects that could reduce the dangers of an unoccupied laboring class (Sharma 2001: 140). As the British began to play a greater role in cultural production around the 1860s, colonial officials began to encourage wealthy Indians to donate, hoping to redirect some of the money spent on religious festivals, deities, and marriage ceremonies to more "productive" channels (Haynes 1987: 350; Palsetia 2005: 198). Yet the British failed to recognize the importance of traditional giving forms. Overall, private forms of indigenous charity did not disappear, but public forms became more structured and institutionalized under the colonial state.

Early Colonial Period: Gaining a Foothold

British expansion in India was interlinked with missionaries and famine—creating a context in which humanitarianism was considered a way to earn the goodwill of the people. Consequently, cultural colonization complemented political conquest. This was particularly true during crises, when British colonials felt they could demonstrate "paternal patronization" and gain some friendliness in return (Nag 2008: 151). Missionaries also at times appropriated "a natural disaster to enhance their proselytization projects." For instance, missionaries set up schools and health-care facilities during the famine of 1911–1912 and 1929 in Lushai Hills, aware that their success depended on their popularity with the people (Nag 2008:

172, 203–204). During the 1837–1838 famine, the ideas behind the 1834 New Poor Law influenced colonial reactions, as the British saw the famine as primarily a shortage of purchasing power rather than an actual shortage of food (Sharma 2001: 182). Skeptical that some Indians would abuse or take advantage of charity, famine relief was offered in the form of 'works of public utility' for the able-bodied, and the needs of the remaining affected population were left to private charity. Though Indian rulers and regimes also provided some relief during natural disasters, the colonials differentiated themselves through their central response and 'secular' or impersonal manner (Sharma 2001: 169). In this way, the colonial state spread horizontally and vertically, centralizing power and disseminating structures of authority. Still, the state's actions are not to be mistaken for welfare; though it assumed some responsibility for mitigating the most disruptive elements of famine, the state did not seek to address structural mass poverty (Sharma 2001: 169, 231). By displacing older forms of charity, the colonial state legitimized itself but also had to bear the burden of its own legacy of famine relief, as people shifted their expectations from the indigenous elite to the state during the famines of the 1860s and onward (Sharma 2001: 233). Thus, charity was blurred with undertones and expectations of state welfare.

Wanting to establish themselves as the ultimate source of benevolence, British colonials strongly criticized indigenous forms of charity as ostentatious, wasteful, superstitious, or irrational (Kasturi 2010: 116; Sharma 2001: 176). By contrasting modes of charity, the British painted their charity as more humane, rational, utilitarian, and effective, and only recognized and supported indigenous charitable efforts that conformed to the dominant ideas of Christian charity, namely shifting away from personalized or ritualistic acts to public forms (Sharma 2001: 187, 191). Charles Lushington's 1824 review of charitable institutions in Calcutta reflected this view that British activities existed "to benefit their fellow creatures, more especially the Natives of the regions, by the creation of Charitable Institutions, by the establishment of Hospitals, the formation of benevolent Societies, the encouragement of moral and literary Instruction, and by the circulation of the Holy Scriptures" (Lushington 1824: 5). In 1837, George Pollack, president of the committee of the Kanpur Relief Society, commented that "private charity may do much to alleviate individual suffering, but the relief of hundreds for an indefinite period, comes only within the means of Governments"

(Sharma 2001: 170–171).The English press reinforced these ideas that only Christian charity and the government were concerned about the plight of the Indians, offering scare recognition—or debunked accounts—of indigenous charity, juxtaposed with great praise for Christian charity (Sharma 2001: 184–185). This fit into a wider trend in the late 1800s, when social reform movements criticized certain Hindu practices, such as polytheism, idolatry, child marriage, and taboos associated with widow remarriage (Bornstein 2009: 627).

While indigenous charity was not entirely indifferent to the distinctions between the 'deserving' and 'undeserving' poor, benevolent acts were not denied to someone who did not work, including holy men, the sick, the disabled, widows, orphans, and others (Sharma 2001: 181). Yet, given the context of the New Poor Laws in England, colonials strongly pushed for the distinction between the deserving and undeserving poor, claiming that the able-bodied poor were willfully idle and unworthy of charity (Sharma 2001: 181). Over time, English notions of the poor gained some acceptance among middle-class Indians, leading to the stigmatization of many previous recipients of charity.

In 1860, the Societies Registration Act was enacted to provide a legal context in which the growing number of voluntary organizations could be registered. Between 1863 and 1920, the Hindu Religious and Charitable Endowments Acts were passed, introducing a new legal paradigm that separated sacred and secular forms of gifting, based on the assumption that socioreligious giving lacked useful goals as it was predominantly occupied with religious worship and education (Kasturi 2010: 115). As a result of these Acts, endowments could become self-regulating trusts, and the funds controlled by committees, protected by colonial law and courts. In 1920, the Charitable and Religious Trusts Act was enacted to give individuals the right to demand information from public trusts on goals and public accounts of income (Kasturi 2010: 116). As a result, trustees were held more financially accountable for the funds they spent in public endowments (Kasturi 2010: 128). In 1927, the colonial state established the Hindu Religious Endowments Committee to draft a bill that would provide better governance, administration, and supervision of Hindu religious and charitable endowments (Kasturi 2010: 129). In the process, the committee also recommended broadening the definition of religious endowments, pointing out religious charities that previously were categorized as secular (Kasturi 2010: 129). Throughout the colonial period and in the early 20th century, socioreligious giving was dynamic, evolving alongside shifts in power, politics, and public life.

Practice of Philanthropy during Colonialism

Under colonial influence, charity diversified from providing religious and communal services to spearheading public projects and initiatives. Education in particular became the favored focus of philanthropy during the colonial period, and the British encouraged giving toward modern secular schools and British institutions that taught 'moral and material progress' (Sundar 1996: 414). Education was an arena where the interests of both the colonial elite and the high-caste residents merged (Haynes 1987: 353). In addition to education, charity was also organized around helping orphans, widows, and victims of accidents, led by committees with formal rules regarding membership, functions, and collection of donations (Caplan 1998: 412; Sharma 2001: 192). These voluntary associations, by existing in the public sphere, allowed a wider range of individuals—not just the rich and powerful—to participate (Sharma 2001: 192).

While on some levels the rise of voluntary associations democratized charity, the Indian mercantile elite continued to use philanthropy to gain channels of access to the British, influence the development of civic society, and forge new types of public roles for themselves as urban leaders throughout the 18th and 19th centuries (Haynes 1987: 350; Palsetia 2005: 198). As Indians adjusted their charitable activities to match "Western-style philanthropy," the British encouraged Indian elite philanthropy as it provided funds for civic programs with minimal political payment, and simultaneously 'socialized' Indian elites to imperial control (Palsetia 2005: 198, 211–213; Sharma 2001: 192). Philanthropy was a forum through which one could demonstrate leadership, good governance, loyalty, honesty, gallantry, and trustworthiness. As the traditional power base of many Indian elites declined during colonialism, charity became the elites' new avenue for promoting a new kind of identity and increasing moral authority as intermediaries between the British and Indians (Palsetia 2005: 206). Thus, Indian elites compensated for their declining power through greater participation in religious and socioreligious charity (Kasturi 2010: 111). Particularly in Bombay and western India, Indians appropriated "imperial norms in the interests of Indians" while undertaking schemes that balanced Indian interests, local institutional interests, and colonial government interests through charitable engagement (Palsetia 2005: 198, 205). Philanthropy therefore was not only used to alleviate distress but also used to display wealth and gain public recognition (Caplan 1998: 410).

The new middle class—consisting of upwardly mobile castes, professional groups, and merchants—also engaged in "ostentatious displays" of charitable giving to express their rising status (Kasturi 2010: 111). It was a smaller set of Hindu, Jain, and Parsi elite businessmen, however, who gained the most recognition as community leaders devoted to the development of their city and as loyal members of the empire (Haynes 1987: 354). One example is Jamsetjee Jejeebhoy (1783–1859), an influential and successful Parsi merchant, citizen, and philanthropist in Mumbai, and the first Indian knight in 1857. Driven by a desire to promote his position in British colonial society and to enhance sociopolitical British–Indian interaction to benefit Indian welfare, Jejeebhoy established the Jamsetjee Jejeebhoy Hospital (Palsetia 2005: 203) (see case study on Jamsetjee Jejeebhoy in Chapter 4). At the same time, adjustment to Western philanthropic notions "was always tempered by notions of personal dignity and status long embedded in local culture" (Haynes 1987: 354). Parsi charity was central to the preservation of Parsi identity as a minority community within the broader social environment of Mumbai, and its practices were preserved through building physical infrastructure such as rest houses, water tanks, and wells, and through charitable relief during famine (Palsetia 2005: 202). Motivations for philanthropy were suited to shifting contexts and audiences.

Early 20th Century: Industrialization

The period from the 1880s to the 1950s saw the emergence of notable indigenous wealth through industrialization and the growth of indigenous industry in India. Shifting away from classic philanthropic outlets such as Hindu temples or Muslim zakat, many of the emerging secular philanthropists in India—based in the urban manufacturing and financial houses of Mumbai—began to support higher education institutions, NGOs, and corporate philanthropy (Sidel 2000: 2).

A number of them were Parsis, who built roads, hospitals, parks, schools, and colleges for fellow citizens, whether Hindu, Muslim, or Parsi (Guha 2012). The early 20th century also "witnessed important debates regarding the need to reform existing practices of charity and philanthropy," reflected in a shift away from personal and religious giving toward secularized and organized initiatives that could benefit a larger community (Sundar 2010: 32). The turn of the century also saw the rise of new ideas in India, in particular socialism, with notions of 'class struggle' and 'social revolution' (Rolnick 1962: 445)—mirrored in the democratization of philanthropy, increasingly led by ordinary individuals and built upon contributions from a wider segment of society, not just the wealthy (Sundar 2010: 32). The onset of World War I further impacted the nature of philanthropy in India as the government, desperate for sources of revenue, imposed new duties and income taxes (Haynes 1987: 355). As a consequence of an impersonal tax schedule, businessmen were no longer able to develop close relations with the imperial elite and "Hindu and Jain traders lost confidence in their ability to attain protection through gifting activities" (Haynes 1987: 355).

The wealth from India's corporate gains played a role in developing modern, institutionalized philanthropy in the country. Some of the early industrial houses are still well-known today, including the Tatas, Birlas, Godrejs, and Mahindras. Arguably the most famous is the legacy of the Tatas initiated by Jamsetji Tata, who set up an endowment for the higher education of deserving Indians in 1892—long before Rockefeller or Ford set up their philanthropic foundations (Lala 1998). Sir Ratan Tata, the youngest son of Sir Jamsetji Tata, left behind a corpus that established the Sir Ratan Tata Trust (SRTT) in 1919 (see case study on the Tata Group in Chapter 4). Sir Dorabji Tata, Sir Jamsetji Tata's oldest son, donated all his wealth and substantial shareholdings to the Sir Dorabji Tata Trust he founded in 1932—on par with his contemporaries Joseph Rowntree and Andrew Carnegie in the US. The Tata business house pioneered, organized, and 'Westernized' secular philanthropic investment in India, and remains important in the philanthropic sector today (Viswanath and Dadrawala 2004: 269). Businessmen were also involved in contributing to the Indian nationalist cause, with the intent of both enhancing their reputation and strengthening relations with the Indian National Congress (INC), an important emerging force at the national level (Haynes

1987: 356). The Tatas and other corporate houses are covered in greater detail in Chapter 4.

Philanthropy Through the Independence Movement and Mahatma Gandhi

Indigenous industrialization in India coincided with the growing momentum of the nationalist and Independence movement, which was formalized when the INC held its first meeting in 1885. Yet the period of 1914–1960 was the real "golden era of capitalism and business philanthropy"—influenced by Mahatma Gandhi's ideas—toward national, social, and cultural causes (Sundar 2000, 10–13). Gandhi was a devout Hindu who took inspiration from Hindu teachings, but was still critical of certain Hindu customs. He was open-minded about what other religions had to offer, and often drew from other religious traditions, such as the Christian traditions of charity and social justice (Dasgupta 1996: 4–5; Guha 2012; Handy et al. 2011: 6). Gandhi played an important role in reinterpreting religion's terms and bringing many of India's traditional concepts around giving and service into a modern social context (Juergensmeyer et al. 1998: 268). Gandhi's legacy in the nongovernmental sector looms large, as his vision of self-rule (swaraj), nonviolence (ahimsa), and service (*seva*) lives on today. Not only that, he inspired individuals to establish village-oriented community organizations that became capable of delivering social services over time (Jha 2012: 256–257). He was also a strong advocate for women adopting an active role in social and political life through equal but separate duties from men (Sundar 1996: 419). Arguably, Gandhi was more concerned about inequality in gender or caste than economic inequality (Dasgupta 1996: 88). Gandhi held a more individualist rather than collectivist view of society's welfare, with a central focus on the individual over caste, class, tribe, race, or state lines (Dasgupta 1996: 13). He did not view charity as a virtue in itself, but rather as an action that should be judged based on the expected impact on recipients, donors, and society at large (Dasgupta 1996: 32). Further, Gandhi did not agree with the Hindu custom of feeding the poor (*sadarvarta*), with exceptions made for individuals who were crippled, disabled, or otherwise unable to work, because he believed food without effort only added to poverty and reinforced idleness and laziness (Dasgupta 1996: 33–34). In this sense, Gandhi's views echoed British colonial notions that distinguished between the deserving and undeserving poor. On economic issues, however, Gandhi greatly differed from the mainstream with his emphasis on the ethical aspect of economic behavior. He claimed the two were inseparable, as one's behavior as an economic agent could not be disassociated from one's behavior as a moral agent, shaped by reflection, knowledge, experience, and ethical principles (Dasgupta 1996: 6, 13).

It was under this idea—that public and individual can 'point in the same direction'—that Gandhi developed his notion of 'trusteeship,' in which the wealthy hold their wealth in trusts and use it for the service of broader society. This would place responsibility on the wealthy to manage and grow their economic resources for public interests (Dasgupta 1996: 31, 118). Trusteeship was not the same as Rousseau's social contract or Hobbes' contract theory (Rothermund 1969: 314). Nor was it quite paternalism, philanthropy, or charity–but rather wealth that already 'belonged' to the public used for the benefit of others (Sundar 2000: 176). Gandhi appealed to the self-interest of businessmen first by highlighting how their contributions to areas such as urban transport or sanitation would also bring benefits to themselves and, second, by acknowledging that the wealthy were entitled to a reasonable standard of living as long as it corresponded to the nature and extent of social services they offered (Dasgupta 1996: 31, 118). Therefore, trusteeship held no specific guidelines, but was more of an idea that wealth did not hold a moral taint and could be well-used by trustees for the betterment of society.

While communism and socialism gained popularity in India following the 1917 Russian Revolution, Gandhi disagreed with the socialist doctrine because he saw it as unjustly confiscating the property of the wealthy; his idea of trusteeship was presented as an alternative (Dasgupta 1996: 118). Trusteeship was thus supported by the wealthy for precisely the reason that it offered an alternative to socialism. It also provided a bridge during India's Independence movement between the propertied class, who held a stake in Indian traditional social values, and those who demanded change, equality, and social revolution (Rolnick 1962: 446). Trusteeship was an appealing concept that was "amenable to a different interpretation," allowing for the support of the masses while keeping the allegiance of landlords and industrialists (Rolnick 1962: 448).

Though trusteeship was adopted and used by various groups, debate emerged around the concept. Critics of Gandhi's trusteeship, including his ally Jawaharlal Nehru, claimed that it offered nothing new as all religions already encouraged the upper classes to perform charity. Furthermore, trusteeship was criticized for having too high expectations of the rich (Rolnick 1962: 449). Some even argued that trusteeship endorsed the old order and worked to maintain a static hierarchical social structure (Rolnick 1962: 460, 449). Another critical view was that trusteeship defended—or almost glorified—poverty, reinforcing the traditional idea that there is no shame in being born poor, and the rich should not be hated (Rolnick 1962: 447). Thus to many, trusteeship seemed like a paradoxical concept, as it strove for an egalitarian society where wealth was voluntarily given up but continued to operate within traditional notions of charity (Rolnick 1962: 446, 448). Still, the Congress Party at the time acknowledged the usefulness of trusteeship in reconciling traditional values in contemporary India and its potential to address various social problems without encouraging class conflict (Rolnick 1962: 458–459). Trusteeship fit into the Congress Party's need for financial and administrative support of the propertied class, princes, and industrialists (Rolnick 1962: 458). Overall, it was difficult to know what Gandhi truly meant by trusteeship, as it remained an elastic ideology.

Following independence, Gandhi's ideas on economic policies for India—and in particular, his moral approach to economics—met their limitations as the INC government did not want to put his policies into practice (Dasgupta 1996: 173–175). Nonetheless, Gandhi's name remains large to this day, and it is politically wise to acknowledge and praise his ideas. Even the NGO sector in India feels closely connected to Gandhian principles, philosophy, and practices (Viswanath and Dadrawala 2004: 264). Though many Indians continue to claim inspiration from Gandhi's social ideas, his ideas of trusteeship remain closer to the realm of theory than practical reality, as individuals and groups continue their actions under their own liberal interpretations.

Philanthropy in Independent India

Early post-Independence (1947–1980s)

After gaining independence from the British in 1947, India's new state realized that economic and social development was necessary in order to complement and complete its new political freedom (Viswanath and Dadrawala 2004: 264–265). The new constitution incorporated values of social justice, and the state took control over many welfare and development activities. One example was the establishment of the Central Social Welfare Board in 1953, which held the dual responsibility of bringing welfare services to disadvantaged sections of society and developing a nationwide infrastructure of voluntary agencies through which these services could be made available. This reflected the ideology of the time and the influence of socialism, in which welfare and equality were humanitarian values—not just charity, but a human right (Unnikrishnan 2002: 153). It was widely accepted that in order to overcome poverty and backwardness, industrialization was needed (Sundar 2000: 155). And so the state, market, and voluntary or civil society sector were seen to jointly tackle nation-building, particularly in agriculture, health, and community development sectors (Jha 2012: 257). Even many voluntary sector leaders moved into government roles (Sundar 2010: 33). As India adopted a broadly socialist economy, emphasizing the protection of local industry and central planning, the state became more interventionist and increased control over the economy—leading to what became known as the Licence Raj or Permit Raj (which persisted up to 1990).

Since the First Five Year Plan in 1951, the government provided funding to NGOs, acknowledging the value of their voluntary action in supplementing government efforts (Sundar 2010: 66). In the early post-Independence period, voluntary organizations focused on rural transformation, enhancing agricultural practices or village crafts, while philanthropic investment capital went to education, health care, population and gender issues, natural resource management, energy, and enterprise development. Christian mission organizations emphasized education, public health, and rural development (Jha 2012: 258; Sundar 2010: 33). Within the context of economic modernization, organizations sought knowledge and technology transfers from the developed world, while the government sought foreign aid (Sundar 2010, 34). In the post-World War II era, the industrialized West was equally interested in initiating aid programs to develop and strengthen democratic societies around the world, and the 1950s saw the emergence of international aid agencies. Critics suggest that foreign aid may have "absolved local philanthropy from taking responsibility for local development," as foreign funds were easier to access (Sundar 2010: 265). Further, as the state increased its role in welfare and development activities, there was a decline in voluntary action and philanthropic giving. Inflation and high taxes reduced private wealth and donations, and many wealthy families reasoned that taxation was enough of a charitable contribution (Sundar 1996: 420). The early post-Independence era was also one in which organizations maintained a paternalistic attitude toward the poor as passive beneficiaries (Sundar 2010: 33).

By the late 1960s, India faced economic stagnation and political instability; the business community was constrained and mistrusted, and philanthropy had declined as a result of the state taking on social welfare (Sundar 2000: 10–13). Amid growing frustration over the government's inefficiencies and ineffectiveness and a shift toward more favorable tax policies, businesses and wealthy individuals returned to donating (Sundar 1996: 421). Meanwhile, the state and foreign agencies continued to partner in development initiatives. Within this new dynamic, the NGO and voluntary sector reasserted its role, but its link to business—forged during the Independence movement—was weakened, leaving the NGO sector to rely upon the government and foreign aid to fill funding gaps (Sundar 2010: 34–35).

The 1970s and 1980s saw renewed interest in the role of the private sector amid disillusionment with the government's ability to address poverty. Corporates began to realize the business benefits of corporate philanthropy—distinct from family business philanthropy—and were encouraged by the government through carrot-and-stick methods (Sundar 2000: 10–13). Businesses worked to become more ethical in their practices, and engaged in more diverse causes such as afforestation, science education, monument preservation, and women's rights (Sundar 2000: 10–13). During the Janata government (1977–1980), industries and businesses were granted special tax exemptions for charitable donations and involvement with NGOs in rural development works. However, in 1983, the incentive was removed amid debate over the role, funding, and impact of the scheme, resulting in a decline in donations (Jha 2012: 284; Sundar 2010: 37–38). Nonetheless, it renewed the discussion around government and voluntary sector relations.

Since the 1990s

By the second half of the 1980s, amid a balance of payment problem reaching a crisis point by 1991, India received a bailout from the International Monetary Fund (IMF) in exchange for agreeing to a number of economic measures. As a result, India's economy was opened up to trade and investments, barriers to private businesses were removed, taxes and tariffs were lowered, and competition was encouraged. With greater globalization, a shift from the government to the private sector and unequal distribution of growth, the period since the 1990s saw the emergence of coalition governments, greater representation of backward castes, ethnic policies, and a rise in Hindu and Muslim fundamentalism (Sundar 2010: 42–43). Subsequently, social tensions rose and the government proved weak at delivery and governance amid corruption (Sundar 2010: 43). Without modern social security or market-based products to insure vulnerable Indians against transitory shocks, many were left "to find recourse in traditional social system and networks that are known to have high degree of volatility" (Shariff 2010: 254). In this new environment in which the importance of strengthening market institutions was understood and promoted, Indians began to relook at the role of voluntary, philanthropic organizations and NGOs, and how they fit between the market and state (Das 2002: 13–14).

With a growing economy, rise in business and personal fortunes, and a new generation of professionals in India, philanthropy came to be seen as an instrument for long-term economic development and social change (Das 2002: 166). Using an econometric model, economist Veena Jha reveals that higher rates of economic growth can indeed be correlated to higher rates of philanthropy, and higher levels of philanthropy to higher trickle-down (Jha 2012: 285). During the 1980s and 1990s, the first professional agencies emerged—including Centre for Advancement of Philanthropy (CAP), Sampradaan Indian Centre for Philanthropy, National Foundation for India, ActionAid, Partners in Change, and Society for Service to Voluntary Agencies (SOSVA), to name a few—

to professionalize the philanthropic sector by undertaking capacity building, feasibility studies, pilot projects, monitoring and assessing field activities, and so on. NGOs in the 1990s gave some of their best contributions to the areas of education and health, working with great amounts of funding from the World Bank and other international agencies for primary education through the District Primary Education Programme (Das 2002: 14). While this should have encouraged new partnerships between the government and NGOs, this did not always occur for various reasons—one being the emergence of some dubious NGOs that gave the sector a bad name (Das 2002: 15).

There has been a real boom in the registration of NGO organizations since the 1990s; out of a total of 3.17 million registered societies or nonprofit institutions (NPIs) in India, only 875,000 NPIs had registered up to the year 1990, while 2.25 million NPIs have registered since 1991 (Government of India 2012a: 94). Of course, the numbers can be somewhat deceiving, considering there is no procedure for de-registering a society and a notable percentage of the 3.17 million are likely defunct (Government of India 2012a: 94). Further, most NGOs are small—almost 75 percent have only volunteers or one paid staff, and only 8.5 percent employs more than 10 paid staff (Jha 2012: 261). Nonetheless, the growing trend in the NGO sector is clear.

In the 1990s, Indian foundations began trying to emulate foreign donor practices and enter mainstream development (Sundar 2010: 265). Just as philanthropy in the US came to be seen as more modern, institutionalized, and rationalized than charity—often described as impulsive and with short-term effects—in India, national identity was also built up around similar notions of civility, progress, and the ability to aid others in need (Bornstein 2009: 628–629). After the 2004 tsunami, India refused to accept global aid, positioning itself as a benefactor and a nation that was now developed and no longer a needy recipient (Bornstein 2009: 629). The remainder of this book looks at the present period, in which Indian philanthropy is seen to be reaching new levels of maturity.

Government Policies and Regulations

The practice of philanthropy is shaped by policies and regulations (Table 1.1). A number of the regulations still in use today date back

Table 1.1:
Overview of laws related to philanthropy in India
A select summary of laws affecting charitable activity in India; state-level laws are not covered.

Law	Year	Summary
Societies Registration Act	1860	One of three ways to register NGOs in India (alongside Trusts and Section 8 companies). At national level; modified versions operate at state level
Indian Trusts Act	1882	One of three ways to register NGOs in India (alongside Section 8 companies and societies). Regulates the functioning of private trusts and trustees, and specifies the manner in which any surplus funds may be invested for future use of the trust Some states have their own Public Trusts Act; while states without their own legislation rely on the national-level Act
Charitable and Religious Trusts Act	1920	Provides control over the administration of Charitable and Religious Trusts, expedites obtaining of information regarding trusts created for public purposes, and enables the trustees of trusts to obtain the directions of a court on certain matters
Income Tax Act	1961	All trusts, societies, and companies are treated the same by the Income Tax Act with regard to tax exemptions. Donations across India are encouraged through either: (a) organization registration under Section 80G, which provides donors with 50% tax exemption; or (b) project registration under Section 35AC, under which donors receive 100% tax exemption
Foreign Contributions (Regulation) Act (FCRA)	2010	Indian NGOs receiving foreign funding must be registered under FCRA. FCRA regulates which causes and persons may receive foreign funding
Multistate Societies Registration (MSSR) Bill	2012	Not yet passed—but proposes to centralize legislation, recognizing the need for a single regulatory body that governs all charitable and religious societies across the country. Complicated logistics means the Bill may take some time to pass

Law	Year	Summary
Indian Companies Act	2013	One of three ways to register NGOs in India (alongside Trusts and Societies). Companies formed under Section 8 of the Act receive NGO status for "promoting commerce, art, science, religion, charity or any other useful object," and have limited liability. They require a minimum of two members if private, and seven members if public, and must meet stringent disclosure requirements Private corporations above a certain size must spend at least 2% of their average net profit on CSR activities

Source: Prepared by the authors.

to India's colonial period. The government has swung between encouraging philanthropy and civil society to clamping down on NGOs in fear of dissent, foreign meddling, or terrorism at different periods of time. These tensions reflect a country in transition, seeking to find a new balance in its social contract. One expert pointed out that India had achieved political and economic independence in 1947, but still needed a social revolution against inequalities, poverty, the caste system, and ethnic divides. India's constitution was thus rather revolutionary, with a prescription of how to change society, placing social reforms as a central objective through a welfare state.

In many developed countries, central governments adequately provide key social services such as education and health care. In India, however, the scenario is different. Some argue that as India is such a large and complex country, it is too easy to blame everything on the shortcomings of the government; others argue that as NGOs and foundations substitute or make up for government lapses, there is less pressure on the government to deliver these services. Nevertheless, the Indian government remains the largest source of funding to NGOs. According to a 2006 study by Copal Partners, the government annually gave an estimated US$3 billion (INR 131 billion), compared to India diaspora giving of about US$1.2 billion (INR 55 billion), and corporate and private giving of about US$447 million (INR 20 billion) (Jha 2012: 260). In the 2010–2011 fiscal year, India's public expenditure on education *alone* was US$11.6 billion—many times more than the contributions made by Indian individuals (Reddy et al. 2012: 9). As the Indian government has shifted away from welfare to a more regulatory state and international funding has declined, there is growing pressure on domestic private actors to step up. The growth of public–private partnerships (PPPs) stands as one example. Another is the US$1 billion India Inclusive Innovation Fund, a private fund backed by the government that provides seed capital to social investment aimed at the bottom of the pyramid.[6]

What is the role of Indian public policy in shaping private philanthropy? In 2007, the Indian government launched the National Policy on Voluntary Sector, a framework between the government and voluntary sector established through a consultative process over a number of years. Incentivizing domestic philanthropy is part of the Policy, stating that "there is considerable untapped potential to channelize private wealth for public service. The Government will support and encourage existing, as well new, independent philanthropic institutions and private foundations...."[7] Yet different Indian government ministries and departments appear to be doing contradictory things, as there have been no moves toward greater tax incentives for donations, organizations have experienced greater scrutiny by tax authorities and the Foreign Contributions (Regulation) Act (FCRA), 2010, has increased regulation on obtaining foreign funds. In some ways, the Policy was always more of an external-led endeavor approved by Cabinet but never debated in Parliament, and reflects a political class that is not fully behind it—and a divided third sector that lacks a strong, unified voice.

Registration of Organizations

India's system of legislation is extremely decentralized, and has nine laws that regulate giving practices for the different classes of nonprofit organizations (Bornstein 2009: 641). These nine laws are (a) Public Trusts Acts; (b) Societies Registration Act, 1860; (c) Indian Companies Act, 1956; (d) Income Tax Act, 1961; (e) Cooperative Societies Act, 1904; (f) Trade Union Act, 1926; (g) Indian Trusts Act, 1882; (h) Charitable and Religious Trusts Act, 1920; and (i) FCRA, 2010. Adding to this complexity are multitiered pieces of legislation,

---

[6] See http://www.innovationcouncil.gov.in/index.php?option=com_content&view=article&id=52&Itemid=34

[7] Section 6.1 in National Policy on the Voluntary Sector (2007: 10).

some at the national and some at the state level. For example, the states of Maharashtra, Gujarat, Rajasthan, and Madhya Pradesh have their own Public Trusts Acts (Bombay Public Trusts Act of 1959, Madhya Pradesh Act 1951, Rajasthan Trusts Act of 1959); Andhra Pradesh and other southern states have their own Endowment Acts; and states without their own legislation rely on the national-level Indian Trusts Act (1882) and registration categories (Jha 2012: 283). NGOs can register as a public (charitable) trust, a society, a company, a cooperative, or a trade union. Registration of societies, trusts, and companies is reviewed in the following paragraphs and in greater depth in Chapter 2.

A society is "an association of persons united together to achieve some common purpose," and is structurally similar to a company but restricted to charitable, literary, scientific objects, and so forth (Agarwal and AccountAid 1999). The Registration of Societies Act (1860) is at the national level, although modified versions operate at the state level (Jha 2012: 283). Trusts, on the other hand, are primarily made up of the donor(s), the trustees, and the beneficiaries, and are "generally created by annexing an obligation to some property. This obligation, when accepted by the owner/trustee, results in the creation of a trust" (Agarwal and AccountAid 1999). Accountant and author Sanjay Agarwal argues that public trusts are the least suitable choice for registering an NGO, as trust registration inhibits the ability of trusts to modify activities if the original settlers are unavailable or unwilling. In addition, in many parts of the world, Indian trusts are not recognized, lack adequate legal protection, and run a greater risk of being mismanaged and governed in an undemocratic style.

A Section 8 company falls under the India Companies Act (2013), a uniform law across India, which is protected by powerful commercial interests—and therefore Section 8 companies are robust in terms of difficulty for takeover (Agarwal and AccountAid 1999). Nonprofit organizations require a minimum of two members if private, and seven members if public. While a Section 8 company can be formed for any not-for-profit activity, it does require more paperwork and the founders must hold regular board meetings and an annual general meeting (for members or 'shareholders'), must provide audited accounts to members, and file the audited accounts, annual report, and an annual return with Registrar of Companies (ROC). The result of these more stringent disclosure requirements is that Section

8 companies are more transparent, which boosts public confidence in them (Agarwal and AccountAid 1999).

Income Tax Act

Donations in India, across all states, are governed by the Income Tax Act (1961), and are encouraged through two main regulations: (a) organization registration under Section 80G, which provides donors with 50 percent tax exemption, and (b) project registration under Section 35AC, which is more difficult to obtain, but under which donors receive 100 percent tax exemption. Any income of a nonprofit organization must be spent or accumulated in India in order to maintain tax exemption status (Sidel and Dadrawala 2008: 33). The government also steers contributions using different levels of tax deductions; for example, contributions to government funds receive 100 percent tax deduction, to rural development programs 100 percent, to the scientific sector 175 percent, and to the statistical research sectors at 175 percent (UBS-INSEAD 2011: 75). While this tax slant toward rural development is mirrored in its popularity among Indian philanthropists, it would be too simplistic to assume that individuals donate simply based on levels of tax returns. The scientific sector, for example, receives a high tax deduction rate, but does not receive as much philanthropic funding as other favored areas of focus.

In India, religious institutions are not required to report the donations they have received, and individuals do not get any tax reduction for religious giving. Therefore, there is minimal motivation to record religious giving. While anonymous donations to registered charitable organizations are not exempted from taxes (under Income Tax Act, section 11), anonymous donations to religious and religious charitable organizations are exempted on account of prevailing practices of gupt daan or confidential donation, where donors try to conceal their identity in order to gain spiritual merit (Sidel and Dadrawala 2008: 30).

For a not-for-profit or foundation to be eligible for tax exemption, it must be organized for religious or charitable purposes, which include relief of the poor, education, medical relief, and the advancement of any other object of general public utility.[8] Clearly,

[8] Section 2 (Point 15) in Government of India (1961).

philanthropy toward health, education, or humanitarian relief is 'safe' in regulatory and political terms—reflected in the popularity of these sectors among foundations. The last category may result in more discretionary power for the tax authorities, leaving organizations to convince authorities how their think tank or social enterprise education model is charitable—which may be a disincentive for some philanthropists. Arguably, these regulations and categories are outdated and caught in a charity mode, and do not lend themselves to today's needs and emerging sectors.

Tax exemption status has a direct impact on NGOs, and may be an incentive for middle-class givers. Not surprisingly, when taxes were high during the 1950s and 1960s in socialist India, private philanthropy suffered amid the general feeling that so much already went to the government. Yet even today, with a significantly lower tax rate, the tax deductions for charitable donations are viewed by some business leaders as "hardly attractive" (Dadrawala 2003: 67). For example, donations in the form of material goods receive no tax benefits. Generally, total deductions for donations may not exceed 10 percent of the donor's total gross income, impacting large-scale giving.[9] As believers in the private sector, numerous business philanthropists feel they can make a larger social impact with their money on their own than could the government with their money. The government, on the other hand, is inclined to suspect tax evasion as a motive behind individuals establishing trusts. The reality is most likely somewhere between—primarily motivated by other factors, Indian HNWIs also welcome any tax benefits that come from establishing a foundation.

Foreign Contribution Regulation Act

Foreign funding to Indian organizations has stirred controversy for many years. Even "several Indian leaders, including Sardar Patel and Mahatma Gandhi, had been critical of activities of foreigners" (Agarwal and AccountAid 2005d). The debate became especially heated on March 20, 1967, when questions were raised in Lok Sabha as to whether the US Central Intelligence Agency (CIA)

---

[9] Point 4 in Section 80G: "Deduction in respect of donations to certain funds, charitable institutions, etc." of Government of India (1961).

had contributed funds to donor agencies in the US, which in turn had passed the funds on to Indian organizations (Agarwal and AccountAid 2005d). The issue of foreign funding and the financing of Indian academic and research institutions by foreign intelligence agencies was crucial in the 1967 general elections in India (Agarwal and AccountAid 2005d). While the idea of FCRA was conceived in 1969, it took several years to be drafted and finalized as a bill, coming into law in 1976 under the guide of the Ministry of Home Affairs. Amid the atmosphere of large protest movements leading to the Emergency of 1975–1977, and in an attempt to prevent money from going to Jayaprakash Narayan's movement against Indira Gandhi, the government used the FCRA to control—and arguably weaken— the voluntary sector (Bornstein 2009: 628; Das 2002: 166). The FCRA was amended in 1985, stipulating that Indian organizations cannot receive foreign funds unless registered with FCRA; it also claimed that even if foreign funds pass through several Indian hands, they are still deemed foreign. The FCRA was revised once again in 2010, making access to foreign funds even more difficult for NGOs. In 2010–2011, total foreign contributions received by 22,735 associations were INR 10,334.11 crore (Government of India 2012b: 288–289). This comes to an average of INR 4,545,462 (US$72,775) per association, lower than in previous years.[10] From 1960 to 1990, when foreign funds were relatively easy to access, foreign aid in part "absolved local philanthropy from taking responsibility for local development." Now with FCRA 2010, Indian NGOs are pushing to access more domestic resources (Sundar 2010: 265). Yet, an insufficient amount of Indian philanthropists support domestic professionally run NGOs, leaving them still dependent on foreign funding—and the bureaucratic process of obtaining clearance from FCRA. Indian author and commentator Gurcharan Das chides that "today, the FCRA is mainly used by bureaucrats to extract bribes. It has not stopped a single terrorist from getting foreign funds, which was its purpose" (Das 2002: 166). Foreign actors have a long history

[10] During 2009–2010, 21,508 associations received INR 10,337.59 crore of foreign funding (average of INR 4,806,392 per association). In 2008–2009, 20,088 associations received INR 10,802.67 crore of funding (average of INR 5,377,673 per association). In 2007–2008, 18,796 associations received INR 9,663.46 crore (average of INR 5,141,232 per association). Annual reports available on the Ministry of Home Affairs website (http://www.mha.nic.in/AnnualReports). These figures do not include inflation, which averaged 7.71 percent from 1969 until 2013, as per the Ministry of Commerce and Industry, India.

in playing a role in Indian philanthropy, and while the amount of funding fluctuates, it is clear the engagement continues to shape the sector.

Companies Act 2013

Indian businesses have a tradition of undertaking socially responsible acts, but their approaches have typically been informal, charity based or strategically self-serving. The Indian government is now encouraging a more structured channeling of corporate energy and enterprise toward responsible distribution of wealth in the communities in which they operate. In 2011, the Ministry of Corporate Affairs released National Voluntary Guidelines on Social, Environmental, and Economic Responsibility of Business, a more detailed version of the 2009 CSR Corporate Guidelines. The recently passed Companies Act 2013 prescribes that private corporations of a certain size spend at least 2 percent of their average net profit on CSR activities (Government of India 2013). This reflects the existing mandatory CSR spending for Central Public Sector Enterprises (CPSEs), which once was 0.5 percent but was increased to 1 percent in 2012 and now to 2 percent to align with the new Companies Act (indiacsr 2013). The Act, alongside broader global trends, has awakened India Inc. to pay more attention to CSR, although has also stirred some concern that mandating CSR will result in funds being put to political or business promotion use, increased corruption and wastage, and an inclination toward tangible, short-term 'band-aid' issues that are easy to capture and report. The government, in turn, has set up structures to address these issues (for further information, see Chapter 4).

Discussion

The most common criticism of the legal structure regulating philanthropy in India is that it is "archaic" and excessively regulatory. For example, the Societies Registration Act (1860) was conceptualized as a membership for professional and fraternal societies oriented around literature, sciences, and so forth—thus is arguably not suited for modern-day development organizations (Jha 2012: 290). NGO registration and reporting is also complicated to navigate, as they have to submit separate return files to authorities at the state level with the Office of the Charity Commissioner, the Registrar of Societies, or the ROC; at the federal level with income tax authorities; and with the Home Ministry if foreign funds are received (Jha 2012: 290–291). To add, the categories in which organizations become eligible for tax exemption—poverty relief, education, medical relief, and the advancement of any other object of general public utility—do not cover a wide enough range as today's development organizations are also engaging in activities such as research and training. While organizations have been shifting away from charity to strategic philanthropy since the 19th century, the government regulations seem to be stuck in the charity mode. Some have argued that a reduction in government controls would allow philanthropy to flourish in India (Das 2002: 166). Because the social sector in India is as susceptible to corruption as any other sector, many believe that proper implementation and regulation of laws are also desperately needed. In sum, regulatory reform has the potential to build greater trust and cooperation between the government and third sector.

Conclusion

Without a doubt, India has come a long way in the philanthropic realm, from being one of the largest recipients of foreign aid in history to setting up its own aid-giving agencies today.[11] The tradition of philanthropy is not in any sense 'new' in India, but rather one that draws on a rich history that stretches back millennia. Hinduism, among the other religions in India, has a 5,000-year-old tradition of giving outlined in sacred texts, which leads some Indians to feel that they do not need Western culture to teach them about philanthropy. Still, outside forces—the colonial powers and other religions—have influenced the philanthropic space in India by contributing different ways of thinking about philanthropy, introducing methods of institutionalizing philanthropy, and enlarging the scale on which

[11] Between 1951 and 1992, India received about US$55 billion in foreign aid ("New Sources of Aid: Charity Begins Abroad" 2011).

philanthropy is practiced. Thus, when looking at India's approach to philanthropy, one must be mindful that it comes from a deep-rooted background of Indian religion and tradition, but has been also subject to modern and foreign influences and continues to evolve.

This chapter has analyzed the various historical, religious, social, political, and cultural elements that have come to shape Indian philanthropy as we know it today. In addition to religious roots, the caste system, community and family networks, and princely rulers each played a role in shaping social relations through gifting acts. The British, in their early engagement, used charity as a tool to help build relations with locals; as Charles Lushington—who, in 1824, wrote about British benevolent and charitable institutions in Calcutta—stated, "what is benevolent is not always charitable, though what is charitable, is, on the face of it, always benevolent" (Lushington 1824: 9). As the British solidified their control over the region and heavily promoted their Christian-based approaches to charity, indigenous leaders turned to secular public philanthropy to shape a new role for themselves and strengthen their ties with the colonials. The emphasis on the secularization and institutionalization of charitable acts in some ways democratized voluntary organizations by bringing them into the public sphere. Amid the rise of the nationalist and Independence movement, indigenous industrialization, and Mahatma Gandhi's idea of 'trusteeship,' early forms of CSR also emerged. As a newly independent country, India sought to develop a robust welfare state, drawing on philanthropy as an economic tool to address poverty. Today, views on the impact of government policies that regulate the philanthropic sector vary almost as much as the regulations themselves.

The question of distribution and utilization of wealth is age-old, with ideologies and models ranging from complete state control (such as communism) to voluntary transfer of wealth rooted in social and moral obligations. In India, as in most countries today, state transfers are complemented by voluntary charity and philanthropy. While philanthropy and socioeconomic development share similar roots and principles, development truly emerged post-World War II and is relatively new compared to philanthropy (Robinson 1997: 295). Philanthropy must be acknowledged as an evolving approach that adapts to contemporary circumstances. "By itself, philanthropy lacks the scale to solve India's social problems. However, philanthropy can catalyse social change" (Reddy et al. 2012: 9). In the subsequent chapters, we will continue to explore philanthropy's promising role in bringing impactful change to India.

2

Charitable Trusts in India*

Introduction

India has a long history of civil society involvement that dates back to the Vedic period, as evidenced by historical laws of community participation and decisions (Mishra 2002). Unlike in Western nations where state and civil society developed simultaneously and eventually grew independent of each other, the state and civil society in India were built on existing religious and traditional power structures (Kaviraj and Khilani 2001).

This chapter begins with a historical overview of legislation that governs charitable trusts in India, and then covers discussions of proposed legislations, such as the MSSR Bill that aims to centralize the many state laws. The majority of the chapter is structured around a series of case studies that present the role and importance of a variety of public, private, religious, and secular trusts in India—including the public and secular Bala Mandir Trust, Bollywood's Salman Khan's trust 'Being Human,' and Shabana Azmi's Mijwan Charitable Trust; the private and religious Sri Sathya Sai Central Trust and Tirumala Tirupathi Devasthanams (TTD) Trust; and finally, the public and religious charitable Mar Thomas Religious Trust, Iman Foundation Religious Trust, Alimaan Charitable Trust, and Dawoodi Bohra Religious Trust.

Historical Overview

In India, a more secular civil society began to emerge only toward the end of the 19th century when the pre-Independence Indian business

*We thank Noshir Dadrawala and the Centre of Philanthropy for their help with information for this chapter.

community started organizing corporate trusts to extend a helping hand to the less fortunate, and the British government, in turn, enacted several acts to recognize these corporate efforts: the Societies Registration Act as well as the Income Tax Act of 1860—the latter act allowed for a 50 percent tax exemption on individual charitable donations—followed by the India Trusts Act of 1882 and the Charitable Endowment Act of 1890. The British government also added the Charitable and Religious Trusts Act in 1920, and allowed tax exemptions through the Income Tax Act of 1922. After India's Independence, the Income Tax Act of 1961 extended these tax concessions to companies that contributed charitable donations. Public charitable trusts were also established, and received tax exemptions so long as they served a 'charitable purpose' that served the fluctuating public at large. Moreover, the definition of 'charitable purpose' was broadened. Charitable trusts could be established for a wide range of causes such as education development, poverty or medical relief, and provision of recreation facilities for public use. Charitable organizations could now also include NGOs, societies, or trusts (Adukia 2005).

Types of Charitable Trusts

As charitable trusts have proliferated and grown in importance over time, it is important to distinguish among the many types and subtypes of these trusts. A simple way to differentiate between a public and a private trust is to examine the beneficiaries of the trust. If the beneficiaries make up a substantial body of the public, then the trust in question is public (USIG 2013). A public trust exists "for the purpose of its objects, the members of an uncertain and fluctuating body," and is managed by a board of trustees (Dadrawala 2013). If, however, the beneficiaries are a narrow and specific group such as the employees of a company, then the trust is private.

Public charitable trusts must register with the office of the relevant Charity Commissioner, which not only holds jurisdiction over the trust and administers tax exemptions, but also ensures that the public trust fulfills the charitable purpose for which it is registered. Usually, three trustees are required for a public charitable trust to function and disperse funds for the public benefit. Indian public charitable trusts are generally irrevocable (USIG 2013).

The CAP's CEO Noshir Dadrawala (2013) emphasized that NGOs in India are formally established as trusts, societies, or companies, and share several characteristics:

1. Even if they receive financial support from the government, they are independent and autonomous in their management and governance.
2. They are self-governed by a board of trustees, managing committees, or governing councils made up of individuals who generally serve in a fiduciary capacity.
3. They produce benefits for others outside their organizations' membership.
4. They are subject to a nondistribution constraint and hence are prohibited from distributing monetary residuals to their membership.

Public Charitable Trusts

Public trusts are popular because it is relatively easy to register and manage them (Dadrawala 2013). All one needs to do is draft a trust deed stating the trustees, the objectives of the trust, and the intended beneficiaries who are a part of the general public. The trust is then registered under the State Trusts Act, or as a Society under the Societies Registration Act or as a Section 8 company under the Companies Act, thereby making the organization eligible for government tax rebates—namely the Income Tax Act that provides tax benefits to such trusts as well as tax deductions to persons donating to recognized trusts. The trust can focus its resources on a myriad of charitable causes, such as relief for the poor, education, health care, environmental preservation, and preservation of historic and artistic monuments. Generally, a public trust is of a more permanent nature than a private trust (Adukia 2005: 25).

Religious endowments and *wakfs* are variants of public trusts that come into being when an endowment, usually property, is dedicated for religious purposes. For centuries, Hindus have dedicated endowments for religious and charitable purposes. These dedications usually fall into the categories of *ishta* (in the realm of Vedic sacrifices, rites, and gifts) or *pushta* (all religious and charitable acts not associated with

Vedic sacrifices and rites). Wakfs are also dedications of property for religious or charitable purposes, but specifically within the Muslim sphere (Adukia 2005: 122). The wakf institutions deal with the religious, social, and economic aspects of Muslim life, and support mosques, *dargahs* (shrines built over the tombs of revered religious figures), schools, colleges, hospitals, and *'musafirkhanas'* (temporary abodes for travelers), thereby catering to the social welfare of Muslims in India. Philanthropic Muslims have donated many wakf properties in the past, amounting to more than INR 1,500 million today. Unfortunately, wakf properties are notoriously mismanaged and crippled by corrupt Muslim leaders, indifferent politicians, and others who have 'robbed' wakf properties of their potential to generate income (Ahmed and Khan 1998; Stibbard et al. 2012). The Government of India has stepped in to decrease the vulnerability of wakf property to corrupt purchases by putting all wakf property under wakf boards to facilitate administration.

Societies

Societies can sue and be sued. However, their liabilities are limited and, unlike trusts, their private assets cannot be sequestered to fulfill liabilities demanded by society. Moreover, societies are generally more democratic in their governance structure. Elections decide the governing council or managing committee, and founding members can be on the governing council so long as they have been elected. In a few cases, they can also be accepted as 'life members.' Members of the general body can vote and demand accountability and reports of the society's actions and impacts. Once the objectives have been achieved, the society can choose to fold its operations.

Companies

Companies formed under the Section 8 Act receive nonprofit status for "promoting commerce, art, science, religion, charity or any other useful object," and have limited liability. Such companies are allowed more operational freedom as opposed to public charitable trusts or societies.

Despite their differences, all trusts, societies, and companies are treated the same by the Income Tax Act with regard to tax exemptions (Dadrawala 2013). In most countries, national laws guarantee tax exemptions for charitable trusts. In India, however, no national law exists for tax exemptions. Each state has different legal requirements that make it hard for institutions to extend their activities into other states. The multiplicity of laws—which burdens volunteer organizations with enormous amounts of paperwork and needless requirements—has prevented the growth of a strong institutional framework. A more comprehensive legal framework would support the nonprofit sector and help its growth. Given that India is a federal union, implementing a centralized institutional structure similar to that of the US may be appropriate. Currently, a central law is being drafted and is expected to tighten financial scrutiny and regulate religious trusts and NGOs to "allay global concerns about money laundering and terrorist financing activities by such entities" (Ramakrishnan 2011). An earlier Government of India report[1] suggested that any new law would have to take the following three tasks into consideration:

1. Define clearly what is meant by 'charity' and 'charitable purpose.'
2. Spell out the institutional mechanism clearly.
3. Clarify the interface with the state government.

Currently, each state in India has its own laws with regard to charitable trusts. Recognizing the need for more centralized legislation, the government has been floating the 2012 MSSR Bill, which would require all societies to register themselves in accordance to the provisions of its laws. Several NGOs that we contacted for comments had not heard of the MSSR Bill. More importantly, those that did know about the Bill were skeptical about it being passed in the near future because of the complicated logistics of requiring all types of NGOs in India to complete the registration requirements. Though the MSSR Bill may remain just an idea for many years to come, there is a recognized need for a single regulatory body that governs all charitable and religious societies across the country, and the MSSR Bill offers insight to how this structure may look (Adukia 2005: 65–66).

[1] http://darpg.gov.in/darpgwebsite_cms/Document/file/Social_Capital9.pdf. Accessed on September 6, 2014.

Public Charitable Trusts

The NGOs presented in this section are all listed as charitable trusts—perhaps because it is easier to register as such and also easier to manage (Dadrawala 2013). We start by looking at the Bala Mandir Trust before moving on to look at some Bollywood public charitable trusts.

Bala Mandir (BM) is registered as a trust. Mr Kamaraj and Ms Manjubhashini established BM, an orphanage whose name means "Temple for children," in 1949. Mr Kamaraj was then the chief minister of Tamil Nadu, and Ms Manjubhashini, a freedom fighter. BM started with two children abandoned in the Congress Exhibition Grounds. Influenced by the sight of abandoned children and by Gandhi's ideals, the two teamed up to build BM and provide rudimentary school for the orphans and children from the nearby urban slum. Over time, both the orphanage and the school grew; today, the school provides education up to the high school level. The orphanage has sheltered thousands of children over the years.

In order to ensure that the home and schools were using the best educational methods, the BM Research Foundation (BMRF) was founded in 1983, and it has since conducted formal studies on holistic childcare and education. In their quest for better ways of learning, BMRF teamed up with the 'Learning through Play' program in Toronto. One of the team members who examined this program was impressed by the way children learned effortlessly when their learning was integrated into games and play. In 1997, BMRF partnered with the Hincks-Dellcrest Centre in Toronto to establish a 'Learning through Play' program. This program has since been integrated both into BM and into its Research Foundation with great success. BMRF also documents effective parenting and childcare practices, and disseminates this information through its resource center that was opened in 2005.

In 1996, when Mrs Manjubhashini passed away, Ms Maya Gaitonde took over as the General Secretary of BM. Her involvement had been as a volunteer and inspired by her husband, who had been a great supporter of BM and had spent much time volunteering and playing with the children from 1955, until July 2013, when he passed away. BM caters to the children in the orphanage as well as those from the slums who attend BM's schools. The BMRF is a special project, which endeavors to discover the latest and most successful techniques of imparting education and make this information available to other schools and foundations. BM is proud of the fact that funds from private donors, both Indian and foreign, as well as government grants for salaries are always streaming in. BM believes that those who visit and see the good work it is doing are compelled to contribute even without being asked.

An interesting story elucidates this point. A financial consultant had come to visit BM but was disappointed to find that his scheduled lunch sponsorship at BM had not been penciled in and the spot was given to someone else. The visitor had been given the opportunity to walk around the premises and take an informal look at the activities being conducted. Instead of being upset, and impressed with the quality of activities, he suggested that the scheduling mix-up would not have occurred if the organization had been computerized. The consultant, also an IT professional, therefore, took it upon himself to computerize the entire organization at a cost of INR 20–30 lakhs.

Bollywood and Public Charitable Trusts

Given the recent publicity around philanthropy, it is no surprise that Bollywood actors are also donating to NGOs and trusts, with some even starting their own charitable trusts—the most notable of these are Salman Khan's 'Being Human,' which helps underprivileged children get an education as well as health care, and Shabana Azmi's Mijwan, which helps in the development of a small village in northern India. Bollywood actor Vivek Oberoi also leverages his star power to give back through his foundation. The 38-year-old Oberoi—who made it onto *Forbes*' 'Heroes of Philanthropy' list—has donated $3 million to date, and has helped raise $25 million in support of education, health, and disaster relief.[2]

Salman Khan's Charitable Trust: Being Human

The 'Being Human' campaign fund-raises through a variety of activities, and donates proceeds to carefully selected causes to spread

[2] http://www.indiatribune.com/index.php? option=com_content&id=6402:four-indians-among-asian-heroes-of-philanthropy&Itemid=410. Accessed on August 19, 2014.

education and health-care services to the underprivileged. Salman Khan has made a clear commitment to his trust: "I'll do films *idhar udhar* (here and there) but charity will be my priority. I've got so much and I want to give back something." Salman claims that he is not so selective about the films he acts in, but he is very selective about the NGOs that he supports. Thus, he thoroughly researches the NGOs to make sure their stated purpose and actions match up. Like any good venture philanthropist, he directs his donations to NGOs that make a measurable difference.

The Trust's many initiatives include:

1. Being Human Art—an exhibition of Salman Khan's paintings; one such exhibition was a big success in Dubai.
2. Being Human merchandise—clothing with the brand logo as well as watches are on sale in various locations around the world, including France, Spain, Belgium, UAE, Egypt, Bahrain, Saudi Arabia, Oman, Kuwait, Jordan, Lebanon, Qatar, and India.
3. A more recent initiative of Being Human encourages fans to accept an INR 1 deduction from their salary every day so that at the end of the year, the many contributions of INR 365 add up to a sizeable sum.

Some ventures that the foundation has helped finance:

1. The Marrow Donor Registry—partnered in November 2010 to spread awareness about the benefits of marrow donations, generate donors, and create a robust donor registry in India.
2. Fortis hospitals—partnered with this medical establishment in 2013 to provide free treatment for children with congenital heart disease.
3. Aseema—provided funding to Aseema's secondary school for street children in Santacruz (West), Mumbai.
4. Akshara—supports 18 underprivileged children studying at the I.C.S.E. Mumbai-based Akshara School.
5. Eye camps—provides free eye checkups and procedures in various areas of Mumbai.[3]

---

[3] Being Human, http://www.beinghumanonline.com

Shabana Azmi's Charitable Trust: Mijwan

The famous Indian poet Kaifi Azmi believed that India's economic progress needed to extend to its more rural villages where 80 percent of India's population resides if progress was to be meaningful. Thus in 1992, Azmi created the Mijwan Charitable Trust, also known as Mijwan Welfare Society (MWS), in order to uplift and empower the small village of Azamgarh in Uttar Pradesh where he was born. Though Kaifi Azmi became renowned in the world of Bollywood for his Urdu poetry and lyrics, he never forgot his humble beginnings in the village of Azamgarh—a poor, small backwater area that did not even appear on the map. From a place so mired in poverty and illiteracy, Kaifi Azmi's MWS helped it grow into a model village replete with schools and colleges for both boys and girls, as well as a computer training center and a sewing center. After he passed away in 2002, his daughter Shabana Azmi—popular Bollywood star and social activist—took up the mantle of MWS.

Recently, the girls from the Kaifi Azmi Girls College won the prize for cultural activities in the National Youth Competition organized in Jaipur for writing and acting out a play against the dowry system in India. Despite a government ban against men demanding dowry money from their prospective brides, the oppressive custom still persists. At the award ceremony, one of the girls stated:

> This award empowers us to hold our head up high and stand up against years of tradition to tell our parents say No to Child Marriage. We will not get married before 18 years of age because it is illegal and because we have many other dreams.

Hearing those words would have been a dream come true for Kaifi Azmi, who had rooted for young women in the village to pursue better lives instead of marrying at a very young age. Azmi had seen how early marriage often forced young girls to drop out of school to undertake household duties. Thanks to Azmi's creation of schooling opportunities, health services, and microcredit loan programs, a progressive transformation has taken place, and the young women of the village have bold dreams for their futures: one wants to become an engineer, another wants to become a nurse, and one is a supermodel in the making. The project seems to have universal appeal as evidenced by the variety of people who have since jumped on to the bandwagon and identified with the project that had initially begun as an individual effort.

> *Main akela hi chala tha jaanibe manzil magar*
> *Log saath aate gaye*
> *Aur karvaan banta gaya*
> (I had set off alone toward my goal
> And people kept joining me
> And the caravan grew)

People from all walks of life support Shabana Azmi and her ventures today. For example, when her young godchild Nimrata visited the village, she was inspired to contribute toward the village's welfare. Nimrata became the youth president of MWS and encouraged other young people to join, thus bringing in a fresh energy. Together, they arranged an intercollegiate contest among the top fashion design schools, and brought in top Indian designers such as Manish Malhotra and Anita Dongre to mentor the finalists. The contest culminated in a fashion show fund-raiser called 'Sonnets in Fabric,' where some of Bollywood's top actors took to the catwalk to model the fashion creations produced in Mijwan (Dastur 2009). The proceeds went to the construction of a district learning center in the village and other projects. "I have always believed in the power of youth to act as catalysts for change. Fifty percent of India is under 25 years, they can change the world if they are motivated to get involved and tap into their own reserves of strength," Shabana said.

The fashion contest and show have become an annual feature, and serve as a platform for design students to showcase their talent. In 2012, students from five fashion and design institutes took part in the intercollegiate contest, where short-listed students had their creations modeled by top stars and models. "These stars are youth icons and it will be a huge boost for these students to have their creations showcased by them," Shabana said, adding that she is grateful to all the stars and designers for being a part of this venture absolutely free of cost. The venue was swarmed with corporate icons such as billionaire Mukesh Ambani, whose wife Neeta Ambani opened the show by walking down the ramp sporting the latest Mijwan embroidered creation. Bollywood celebrities such as Priyanka Chopra and Diya Mirza followed, leading a retinue of colleagues down the ramp wearing exquisite Mijwan embroidery.

The surprise guest of the evening was Olympic winner Mary Kom, who walked down the ramp wearing a pink embroidered dress designed by Manish Malhotra.

Because villagers are able to secure livelihoods by selling their crafts to the fashion show, they can continue to live and work in the village instead of migrating to the cities in search of work. The city is notoriously inhospitable to rural villagers, who are forced to live in demeaning and overcrowded slums. These fashion shows have now become a regular feature of MWS and are supported by both the fashion and Bollywood fraternity. In fact, Manish Malhotra has decided to adopt the village and support projects for a one-year period—no small undertaking—as a venture that could lead to all kinds of future collaborative possibilities.[4]

Events such as the much-publicized fashion show have caught the attention of donors searching for a worthy cause. A case in point is Mark Ellis, an English gentleman living in Cambodia, who decided to cycle 20,000 km around India and give back the funds he would raise to the many poor communities he would cycle through. After careful consideration of projects worth supporting, he decided to raise funds for the Mijwan Welfare Trust. In January 2012, he cycled from the Gateway of India, Maharashtra in central India, through Goa, Karnataka, and Kerala and then made his way to Kanyakumari, India's southernmost tip. Then, Ellis turned to tackle the north, cycling through challenging mountainous regions and the world's highest motor pass at Khardung La at 5,359 m. He then tackled Punjab, Rajasthan, and Gujarat before he cycled back to Maharashtra. He donated all of the funds he raised to MWS.[5]

Public charitable trusts such as Mijwan, Being Human, and BM successfully raise funds for good causes, and are major players in India's thriving NGO realm. A study commissioned by the government in 2009 estimates that there are about 3.3 million NGOs in India. That translates into one NGO for almost every 400 Indians (Shukla 2010). There is no doubt that these numbers have increased since that study. NGOs have long attempted to alleviate poverty in India in numerous ways. Initially, these organizations were instrumental in times of crisis, providing urgent relief. Over time, however, the organizations have shifted to create long-term developmental strategies for causes such as education, technical

---

[4] MWS 'Manish Malhotra,' www.mijwan.org
[5] 'Cycling around India,' January 2012, http://www.cycle-india.com

and vocational assistance, advocacy, and women's empowerment, to name just a few. They are now considered important players in the field of development, and one of the key catalysts of progress in India.

Religious Trusts

Philanthropy in India has been and continues to be driven largely by religious considerations, hence the domination of charitable trusts for religious purposes (Dongre and Gopalan 2008). In order to understand the difference between public charitable trusts and religious trusts, it is important to return to the definition of a public trust as one that benefits a segment of the public at large. This definition suggests that a public trust can be either secular or religious. When a trust is created for religious purposes—for the advancement, support, or propagation of a religion and its tenets—it is a public religious trust. A religious trust can be public or private depending on which segment of the population it supports. If the purpose of a religious trust is narrow and private, it must register as a private religious trust and is not eligible for tax exemptions. However, when religious organizations create a trust to fund a wider range of religious and social services, it can qualify as a state-established public charitable trust.

Religion and religious titans are mighty forces in India. For example, spiritual guru Sri Sathya Sai Baba established the Sri Sathya Sai Central Trust in 1972 to run several ashrams and provide education, health care, poverty relief, and utility services to society (Sri Sathya Sai Baba Trust 2003); his trust is said to be worth more than US$9 billion (India Knowledge@Wharton 2011). When he passed away on April 24, 2011, nearly half a million people—including the then prime minister of India, Manmohan Singh, the Congress Party president, Sonia Gandhi, as well as several luminaries from the worlds of cricket and Bollywood—attended his funeral, a testament to his impact on society (BBC 2011). His trust included a donation of US$108 million from Isaac Tigrett, the founder of Hard Rock Café, and a donation from Sarah Ferguson, the Duchess of York. Many speculate that Sathya Sai Baba may have been the richest man in India, overtaking Mukesh Ambani who is now on the top of the list at US$27 billion (Kroll 2011).

Surprisingly, the Sathya Sai Central Trust is not the wealthiest trust in India—the wealthiest trust is the TTD Trust, which oversees the Tirupati temple in Andhra Pradesh, India. The members of the trust were appointed by the State when it took over the operations of the temple in 1987, away from priests who had previously run it. According to a tongue-in-cheek article in the *Times of India*:

> The Lord is weighed down not only by the prayers and requests of lakhs of pilgrims, but also by more than 12,000 kg of gold, ornaments and other precious jewels and 11,000 kg of silver worth over Rs 50,000 crore. The 8-feet black-colored main idol is loaded up with at least 65–70 kg of gold ornaments every day and it is estimated that in a single day offerings to the Lord range between Rs. 80 lakh and Rs. 1.5 crores. One donation was a single crown studded with diamonds and rubies weighing about 30 kg and worth lakhs. (Kumar 2012)

While the exact wealth of the trust is unknown, one can derive an approximation from the knowledge that 3,000 kg of gold were deposited in April 2010 and 1,175 kg of gold were deposited in February 2011. The general manager of the State Bank of India, Hyderabad, stated that TTD is the highest depositor on gold among all the religious institutes in the country (*Times of India* 2011).

Facilitated by religious trusts, more people visit Tirupati than any other religious site in the world. The number can swell to as many as 500,000 pilgrims on special religious days. Yet the crowds are manageable and orderly, thanks to the religious organizations that facilitate these numbers (India Knowledge@Wharton 2011).

Shinde (2011) examines the role of religious institutions and charitable trusts in India's religious tourism industry, and asserts that the millions of pilgrimage trips to holy sites each year are sustained largely by charitable trusts that administer temples and facilitate the necessary tourism infrastructure such as accommodation, food and transportation, and the organizational processes that usually involve 'religious giving.' Given that much philanthropy in India is religiously driven (Dongre and Gopalan 2008), it is important to understand the mechanisms that enable this giving (Warrier 2004). The pilgrimage economy is a well-known facilitator of religious giving; a survey conducted in 2002 about the tourism industry suggested that more than 100 million traveled for 'religious reasons and purposes,' and that eight of the top 10 domestic tourist destinations were pilgrimage sites (NCAER 2003). A pilgrimage differs from other tourism in that it is far more intricate and includes praying, performing rituals, attending communal celebrations and talks, and visiting several places of specialized worship—all of these activities are interwoven into an elaborately structured enactment.

Vrindavan, a temple town in northern India, is sustained by religious and pilgrimage tourism. There exists 5,500 temples around the small town, and though the native population of the town is only 65,000, the annual population of religious tourists exceeds 6 million. The pilgrims are guided through chanting, dramas enacting the life of Lord Krishna, and worship that involves visiting various temples with specialized rituals. This process can span several days, and pilgrims often donate at each temple for the privilege of partaking in the temple's specialized rituals. Dedicated gurus who are experts in their own narrow field are usually paid for the rituals they conduct, and the devotees also donate to the coffers of each temple.

Traditionally, religious priests or aristocratic families owned temples, and sometimes the two were locked in a reciprocal relationship. Over time, the colonial administration and Western influence broadened the scope of religious philanthropy beyond temple and religious welfare, and began including social welfare and education (Joshi 1968). As the realm of commerce expanded post colonialism, commercial institutions began taking over philanthropy and social welfare from old defunct aristocratic families, and set up trusts to oversee the management of the holy places (Waghorne 2004). Today, a web of public and private charitable trusts oversees Vrindavan. Private trusts are in the domain of religious gurus who have received or inherited donations and endowments from families who want to contribute to temple building and the maintenance of ashrams that house and feed pilgrims. Motivated by an age-old religious impulse, these families seek out gurus who guide them through elaborate prayers and rituals in accordance to the protocol laid out in different sectarian rules. Wealthy business families have also established religious private trusts that are entrusted with the task of building and maintaining temples, ashrams, and the infrastructure of priests and other necessary personnel. Some of these temples and ashrams date back to over a century, and the families continue to act as guardians of the temples over several generations (Goswami and Madhur 1995). As we can see, many of the religious trusts help facilitate pilgrimages and the performance of rituals and prayers. Sadly, these religious trusts often overlook the public realm

(Shinde 2002), which leads to the degradation of the environment, a consequence of the constant influx of visitors.

Public trusts do not cater directly to religious prayers and performances, but provide auxiliary needs such as housing for the needy, food for the hungry, and education and health care to the public. These large-scale 'social development' services are costly, thus public trusts solicit donations from the public in order to garner the necessary resources. The members of these trusts are usually urban middle-class benefactors from various cities in India. Shinde (2004) studies religious institutions as members of civil society, and explores the role of Hindu religious institutions in India such as the Sathya Sai Central Trust that is involved in development activities ranging from agriculture, health, education, and social welfare, and also includes the building and maintenance of orphanages and homes for the elderly and the destitute. In general, these religious institutions are immersed in social welfare activities and environmental concerns and initiatives alongside their religious functions. For example, TTD, situated in the environs of the Tirupati temple, is engaged in afforestation and has encouraged green vegetation by planting more than 4.4 million trees, which helps bring down the overall temperature of the place. It also mobilizes resources for afforestation and distributes plants to institutions. The trust is involved in water resource management and pollution monitoring; the billboards that it sponsors around the town increase environmental awareness.

Other religious trusts that are similarly involved in matters of civil society are the Jaipuria Bhawan—a public charitable trust that was created by the House of Jaipurias, a business family well known in the Indian textile industrial arena. The Jaipurias run schools, colleges, public guesthouses, temples, charitable public guesthouses, temples, and charitable hospitals as part of their CSR efforts.[6] The Sri Ranchhod Education Trust also focuses on schools and colleges such as the Vrindavan BCA College and the Vrindavan. The trust started a college that offers a bachelor's degree in education in the temple town of Vrindavan.[7] This amalgam of religious and charitable activities suggests that many religious organizations cater to both the fulfillment of religious needs and the overall well-being of the people they serve. Not only do they facilitate the performance of religious rites and maintain the places of worship, but also assist with the

[6] 'Overview,' jaipuriabhawan.com
[7] 'Knowledge Center,' www.jayranchhodetrust

organization of religious visits and the smooth transfer and well-being of pilgrims, resulting in a well-rounded set of services. In addition, these organizations cater to the health and welfare of people living in the area where the places of worship are housed.

Public Religious Trusts and Public Charitable Trusts

As suggested earlier, trusts that are set up in India for social causes (and approved by the Income Tax Department) are exempt from tax payments, and donors can deduct their donated amount from their taxable income. Thus, public charitable trusts are set up for charitable or religious purposes so long as they benefit the public at large. It is fairly common for religious communities to have a public religious trust for the advancement of religion as well as public charitable trust for social causes.

St. Thomas Marthoma Religious Trust

The Church of St. Thomas Marthoma, located in a Mumbai suburb, established its religious trust in 1960 to cover the costs of the church's upkeep and affairs that members' tithe did not cover. Mr Thomas, one of the church's administrative heads, explained the hierarchy of the church and its funding mechanism. There is a central governing body that oversees the 20 churches across Mumbai, and while the central body provides interchurch assistance in special cases, every church is expected to look after its own finances. Thanks to the trust, the church is able to host and finance conventions, youth leagues, Sunday school, and counseling groups for senior citizens and married couples. The religious trust also finances other spiritual growth and Christian living initiatives.

The St. Thomas Marthoma Public Charitable Trust

The St. Thomas Marthoma Public Charitable Trust was founded back in 1986 when a senior bishop at the St. Thomas Marthoma

Church decided to put the small piece of land donated by a member of the church to good use. He was aware that many young children whiled away their time in the streets while their parents worked in construction or other similar jobs. The bishop therefore decided to build a small shed on the donated land, and then invited the young children to get a basic education there. He also added a midday meal to make the invitation more appealing. To collect donations in order to run the school, he created the St. Thomas Marthoma Charitable Trust. After 10 years, many children of all ages were attending the school. Using funds from the charitable trust, the bishop built one more shed to house the growing number of students, and switched the language of instruction from Hindi to English. By 1999, the donations to the trust had increased as people were impressed with the education efforts, and the church launched an ambitious project to build a two-level structure with the idea of launching a formal school. However, they fell short of funds as the cost of construction material increased. An urgent appeal for more funds was sent out, and the brother of a board member who lived in America sent the funds necessary to complete the building. By this time, the trust had also received FCRA certification to receive funds from foreign countries. Over time, a second building was constructed from both national and international funding, and the school became more formalized and followed a national curriculum.

By 2013, the St. Thomas Marthoma School was a well-established English medium school with 1,370 students. The school building stands in the middle of a large slum, and the only entrance to the school is a narrow alleyway through the slum dwellings. A total of 30 teachers and 10 staff members help conduct the school in two shifts (from 7.00 a.m. to 12.30 p.m. and from 1.00 p.m. to 6.00 p.m.). The school has a good track record, and all of the students have managed to pass the final board exam. The graduating students are offered counseling and assistance to help them enter college. Thanks to the funding received by the St. Thomas Marthoma Charitable Trust, the St. Thomas Marthoma School is able to educate the poorest children from the city slums. The school fees fall into three tiers: low fees, subsidized fees, or fees waived completely. One of the authors met with the students and was impressed by their determination to succeed. The teachers were even more impressive in their dedication as they trudged through the slum areas for meager salaries. The St. Thomas Marthoma School reflects the commitment of the church clergy, church members, national and international donors, the teachers, and the students. More recently, at the request of some of the mothers of the school children, the St. Thomas Marthoma Charitable Trust has funded a basic literacy course for the mothers. Some of these mothers have been able to find jobs because of their newfound literacy skills, and the demand for these courses has grown. The trust hopes to make adult literacy a part of their education projects after acquiring consistent funding.

The Imaan Religious Trust

The Imaan Religious Trust was founded in 1981 in order to serve the religious needs of the Islamic community. The trust receives 'khums' and 'zakat,' which are Islamic taxes levied upon the Islamic community and must be used to address the religious and welfare needs of the community. 'Khums' is derived from receiving one-fifth of a person's annual savings after all expenses are paid. The 'khums' money must be used to support the ongoing religious needs of the community and must not be withheld for the purposes of corpus. Every Muslim is obligated to pay the 'zakat,' which is 2.5 percent of a person's total wealth or one-fourth of surplus wealth, which must be used for public purposes of community development and helping those in need. With these funds, the trust ensures that there are enough mosques to accommodate the number of religious followers in villages and cities. During the month of Ramadan, it provides the poorest families with food for 'iftar' or breaking of the fast. The trust is also responsible for paying the salaries of teachers who teach in religious schools. Thus, the Imaan Foundation Religious Trust lives up to its name, and caters to the religious needs of the Islamic community.

Alimaan Charitable Trust: The Public Arm of Imaan Foundation Religious Trust

Created in 1987, this charitable trust has spread and now claims branches in all parts of India. The trust provides a range of benefits from higher education and low-income housing to support for orphans and widows. Moreover, the trust helps girls with marriage funds. The trust has also ventured into health care, constructing many hospitals and dispensaries and subsidizing medical aid to those who cannot afford it. The trust has received FCRA approval so it can receive foreign donations. The organization prides itself in being transparent and not taking money for administration fees, as all administration is voluntary. Given the fact that there are many slums and homeless people in Mumbai, one of the most important contributions of the trust has been the construction of 700 self-contained homes on the outskirts of Mumbai. This is an ongoing project, and the trust hopes to build several more homes to look after the homeless.

Dawoodi Bohra Religious Trust

A more recent development is the gentrification project by the Dawoodi Bohra Religious Trust through its social development trust, Saifee Burhani Upliftment Trust in Bhendi Bazaar—a crowded, messy hub of commerce in central Mumbai. Many of the people who have offices in the area or are visiting the area to conduct business activities are Bohras (Bohras are a business community of Muslims, and the Dawoodi Bohras are the wealthiest segment of this community). During the day, the streets are crowded with cars that drive past carts loaded with goods and crowds of people pressing to get by. The buildings are old and dilapidated with peeling paint. Goods are often stacked on the street waiting to be transported. This dilapidated environment will soon be transformed, thanks to the Saifee Burhani Upliftment Trust. The dense marketplace is to be replaced with tall, neat towers and high-rise buildings with gardens, recreational facilities, malls, and parking spaces, making this 'congested Bhendi Bazaar' into a 'modern haven with ample amenities.' The trust has managed to purchase 85 percent of the properties in the area, but chose to ignore the landlords who held out with 'unreasonable demands.' Given the importance of the project, the government has agreed that the project should start with the property that it has now. All tenants who were living in the slums prior to the project and those who had larger tenements will be given residence in the philanthropic venture. Any extra properties will be sold off. The trust emphasizes that this project is not simply about demolishing the old buildings and constructing the new buildings. It involves the establishment of modern and convenient infrastructure that will introduce clean spaces, green spaces, water harvesting, and recycling. The project was conceived in 2009, but was halted due to permit complications. Years later, all of the bureaucratic hurdles were overcome and the construction began sometime early in 2014 (Bundhan 2013). Although the trust has managed to demolish 50 buildings to date and has resettled 1,500 families, the project is moving slower than expected. Some residents still refuse to leave the premises, and the relevant government clearances are taking long (Editor 2014). Though the progress is slow, the projected plans will eventually beautify an area that used to be an eyesore and will become a part of the more modern and environmentally friendly Mumbai.

Conclusion

Public charitable trusts and religious trusts contribute immensely to India's progress and development. Although the Indian government was initially suspicious of the activities of these trusts and encumbered them with legislation that discouraged their growth, over time, the government has recognized these organizations are only trying to fill in the gaps of the welfare system to help the most marginalized members of society. This has led the government to offer tax credits to organizations involved in specified public charitable works. Despite these new government-initiated incentives, many of the NGOs we contacted said that the government could do more in facilitating funding, especially international funding, which remains tied in bureaucratic legislation. Despite these hindrances, the staff and the volunteers of charitable trusts are enthusiastic about the successes they have been able to achieve. For example, the staff and volunteers at BM were able to help scores of orphans and poor young children with their cutting-edge methods of teaching and research in education. Moreover, BM was able to attract funding effortlessly from those who witnessed its good works. Bollywood actors Salman Khan, Shabana Azmi, and Vivek Oberoi are also examples, as they were able to leverage their star influence to raise funds to finance their development efforts.

We find that religious trusts often play a dual function: they not only finance the upkeep of religious institutions but also extend a public charitable arm. In his book *Development, Divinity and Dharma*, Malcolm Harper examines the potential and power of partnerships between God, religion, and development (Harper et al. 2008). And our chapter validates that faith-based institutions are successfully getting involved with economic development in India. Moreover, many foreign donors opt to channel their funding through religious organizations. In a study of Indians in four US cities, Agarwala (2014) finds that the largest category of Indian transnational organizations for channeling diaspora funding were 'religious.' More importantly, members of the Indian diaspora view these organizations as trusted channels for their donations. Thus, religious trusts are able to attract funds and contribute to India's social and economic development. A good example of such a public charitable trust is the Chinmaya Organization for Rural Development (CORD). CORD in both Canada and the US channel their funds to CORD in India, which is making a difference in the downtrodden rural areas of Himachal Pradesh. The trust has received many awards, both nationally and internationally, for its development work. Similarly, the TTD Trust, The Sri Satya Sai Central Trust, the Thomas Marthoma Charitable Trust, and Alimaan Charitable Trust work to better the lives of the marginalized by providing free education, skills development, affordable housing, and food. Despite the good work that charitable trusts are doing, India remains largely afflicted by poverty, malnutrition, and illiteracy, to name just a few of the social issues.

India has about 3.3 million NGOs—possibly the largest number of active NGOs in the world, and they are registered under various acts and have diverse mandates. Moreover, more donors are giving to NGOs than ever before, and at higher levels. In 2010, it was estimated that NGOs raised anywhere between INR 40,000 crore and INR 80,000 crore in funding. The Government of India was the largest donor with INR 18,000 crore, and foreign contributors followed with INR 9,700 crore. About INR 2,000 crore was channeled through religious establishments (Shukla 2010). To add, an increasing number of corporates have begun partnering with NGOs as part of their CSR initiatives. Given the growing number of donors and NGOs, one can assume that great strides will be made in the resolution of social issues and sustainable development. However, in order to assure this, NGOs need to become more efficient, and must increase the scale of development. Training programs at colleges can offer prospective entrepreneurs as well current NGO managers some successful models of governance and management to increase both the transparency and the measurable impact of NGOs.

Case Studies

Case Study 1. Philanthropic Behavior in Action at Aseema: A Public Charitable Trust

The idea for Aseema was hatched in 1995 when three friends—Dilbur, a human rights lawyer, Neela, a documentary filmmaker, and Snehal, an advocate at the High Court—met and shared their concerns about the disturbing sight of street children. Theoretically, the state guarantees all children basic education, but the reality on the ground was dismally different. Children ranging from toddlers to young adults could be seen on the streets of Mumbai idling their time, begging at traffic lights, picking rags, or working in street stalls. The friends knew that these children needed an education in order to hope for a better future. Thus in 1997, they found a room at St. Stanislaus High School and started offering classes to a small group of 18 children ages ranging from 3 to 15. Initially, they set themselves the task of familiarizing the children to a school environment. This was no small feat, as the children, who had never been in a school setting before, enjoyed jumping on desks, throwing things around, and creating lots of noise. With time and patience, however, the children began practicing the expected school decorum. They learned to be quiet, sit still, and listen to the three friends as teachers and authority figures who they were beginning to recognize and trust. Eventually, a two-hour study period became the routine—the learning had begun.[8]

Today, Aseema is a Mumbai-based NGO and public charitable foundation that provides a caring and stimulating educational

[8] 'History,' www.aseema.org

environment where street children are encouraged to reach their potential. The social workers at Aseema reach out to the families of children who live on the streets and encourage the children to attend school. The advantages of schooling are spelled out: free meals, a good education with the promise of a substantially improved and secure future, and a support system that helps bridge the gap in learning.

Aseema officially got into the business of education by partnering with the Municipal Corporation of Greater Mumbai (MCGM) to support three of their schools. Municipal schools are typically scattered across the state and are supposed to provide schooling to the most underprivileged members of society. They are notoriously inadequate in the provision of staff and staff attendance and punctuality. The municipal schools that are partnered with Aseema have unique advantages such as a support center for children to strengthen their academics after school hours as well as an exceptional school program with caring staff. A set of trustees and a board of advisors lead Aseema and its 170 staff consisting of teachers, social workers, counselors, administrators, helpers, and volunteers.[9]

The Aseema donors are a motley group. Some are committed long-term donors, while others are transient. Support comes from large corporate houses, trusts, and individuals. Many donors say that "it is a privilege to assist Aseema" because of the commendable work it does: taking children from the most downtrodden strata of society and turning them into successful adults ready to take their place as contributing members of society.[10] They have high-quality educational programs, and the fact that English is the medium of education makes Aseema schools akin to 'private schools' attended by the upper echelons of society. Such quality schooling usually comes at a high cost, but it is available for free to all students affiliated with Aseema.

Partnering with MCGM has presented advantages all around. The MCGM provides basic education to about 4.5 lakh (450,000) children through 1,180 schools and 49 secondary schools. Yet the government's attempt at providing education to large numbers of students on a shoestring budget in municipal schools has taken a toll on the quality of education. Municipal schools in Mumbai are notorious for their lackadaisical manner of education. The teacher–student ratio is abysmally low, and often one teacher will look after two grades of students with uneven educational achievements.

[9] 'Staff and Volunteers,' www.aseema.org
[10] 'Donors,' www.aseema.org

MCGM invites NGOs to work with them in order to augment their efforts at education, keeping in mind that municipal schools generally have minimal supervision and the emphasis is on the number of students who attend school and the provision of some modicum of education, rather than the quality of education or grade outcomes.[11] For the last nine years, Aseema has partnered with municipal schools and provided them with teachers trained in the unique Aseema child-friendly approach. Aseema has managed to attract an impressive range of high-caliber professionals who donate their time to work with their students. Now Aseema schools offer classes in art, music, judo, sports, dance, cinema, and theater—extracurricular activities that are generally in the domain of private schools that charge high fees.[12]

Aseema has partnered with three municipal schools starting with a preprimary Montessori center set up in the Mumbai suburb of Pali-Chimbai since 2000. It allowed students to build a strong basic educational foundation, and a primary section was added over time. Currently, 200 young students between the ages of 2.5 and 6 years thrive at the Montessori center, which runs two shifts. This center was created to instill the love of learning at an early age by making education both fun and stimulating.[13] Once students complete their primary education at the Pali-Chimbai school, they move to the Santa Cruz Municipal School that was created in 2007 to receive the advancing flow of students into secondary school. An English medium municipal secondary school is rare as it suggests that a student has not only advanced into the secondary school phase but is also capable of having English language as the medium of instruction. Most municipal schools teach in Marathi and some in Hindi. At present, 127 Aseema students are studying to complete their secondary school education in fully equipped science and computer laboratories. A few of the students who completed high school have won government scholarships and are attending universities of their choice.[14]

In 2010, Aseema partnered with the Kherwadi Municipal School as part of 'Plan India'—a collaboration of NGOs working to uplift the slum communities in the Mumbai suburb of Bandra East by contributing to the health, education, and livelihood of slum children. Aseema undertook the responsibility of the English medium section

[11] 'MCGM Partnership,' www.aseema.org

[12] www.aseema.org

[13] 'Pali-Chimbai Municipal School,' www.aseema.org

[14] 'Santacruz Municipal School,' www.aseema.org

of the school. In the short time, Aseema has reorganized the school and streamlined the classes to operate from preprimary to Grade 10. About 439 students are passing through its educational system, and Aseema plans to add one class every year. Overall, there has been a discernible improvement in the quality of education with attention being given to steady attendance, punctuality, and high grades.[15]

Aseema has adopted a multi-pronged approach to uplift underprivileged students and their communities. As a part of this effort, Aseema started a Life Skills Program for students who struggle to cope with the rigors of schooling—either because the student started school late and thus has a weak foundation, or simply because the student is more inclined toward the trades or is averse to more theoretical approaches. The Life Skills Program teaches such students functional literacy, and then refers them to vocational training institutions in order to further develop skills of their choice. At the same time, students who drop out of formal schooling are encouraged to take their exams at the National Institute of Open Schooling, for which entry leads to courses in vocational and life enrichment. Aseema helps students prepare for this more flexible approach to education.[16]

In order to understand the psychological and health milieus that influence the students, Aseema has set up community work cells that organize visits to the homes of the students. Parents are encouraged to visit their children's school and join the Parent–Teacher Associations that have begun functioning quite effectively ('Product Division'). A counseling center complements Aseema's efforts to uplift communities as well. Well-trained counselors help students deal with the many problems endemic to living in dire straits and slum conditions. Social workers are assigned to troubled students to help them work through their problems. Moreover, interactive public sessions are organized to discuss topics such as substance abuse and confidence building that is likely to affect the students ('Counseling Center').

More recently, Aseema has been involved in building an *anganwadi* (preprimary center) for tribal children in and around Igatpuri, which is a few hours' drive from Mumbai. The manner in which the project started was propitious. Aseema's staff were looking for land around Mumbai to build a residential center for students when they realized a grim reality: remote tribal areas had few and poor-quality educational

---

[15] 'Kherwadi Municipal School,' www.aseema.org
[16] 'Life Skills Programs,' www.aseema.org

facilities. The schools lacked basic amenities and were situated at inaccessible distances. Urgently wanting to provide schooling to the tribal areas that were overlooked by government officials, Aseema began looking for a bit of land to start an education center. Luckily, a tribal woman came forward and offered her land to build a school so that the tribal people could get an education. Today, Aseema runs an education center on the donated land and two anganwadis (childcare centers). Additionally, construction for another center of education for older children is almost complete. Four local women were trained to be the first teachers, and they receive regular help from experts in Aseema Mumbai ('Education Center for Tribal Children'). It is a wonderful sight to see happy young faces walking to school toting bags in a place where no such opportunity existed a few years ago. Without a doubt, Aseema is making its mark—doing what it does best—by imparting holistic and child-friendly stimulating education. Hopefully, Aseema's reach will continue to grow!

In order to empirically assess the results of Aseema's efforts, we requested to meet with an Aseema graduate. One of the authors met with a young boy named Ashish who had graduated from Aseema recently. Dilbur, one of the three founders of Aseema, had recruited Ashish in 1997 when she persuaded his mother to let him attend school. He was one of the first students to attend Aseema. Ashish fared brilliantly in the initial test and was put into Grade 1. Aseema funded him from the start, and he was tutored at the support center every evening, as he could not get help with his homework at home. When Ashish entered Grade 9, he took advantage of weekend workshops offered by a well-known film director, Subhash Ghai. Ashish participated in this workshop for six years. After three years, he was ready to make his own film. At this time, he was completing his Grades 11 and 12 at a local college. He completed the film and gave it to the director on his birthday as a form of *gurudakshina* (offering to one's guru). Subhash Ghai, who had set up a famous film institute in India, saw the film and loved it. He offered Ashish a full scholarship worth INR 15 lakh ($25,000) to study at the institute specializing in editing and direction. Ashish hopes to make his future in the film industry, and will continue to work hard to achieve his dream. He ended the interview by stating that his mother often remarks that though she gave birth to Ashish, it was Aseema that shaped him into who he is today (Personal Conversations: Dilbur Parakh, Founder, Aseema, August 1, 2013).

Case Study 2. *Philanthropic Behavior in Action at Shri Kshetra Dharmasthala Rural Development Project (SKDRDP): A Religious Public Charitable Trust*

Located in the central hilly belt of Dakshina Kannada, the Dharmasthala Temple—currently under the leadership of Veerendra Heggade—has served its surrounding communities for almost six centuries. According to legend, the Dharmasthala Temple was established in the 15th century when Heggade's ancestor had a dream in which two strangers he had hosted the day before revealed themselves as angels and asked him to build a temple where he could provide hospitality to others in need. A year after the senior Heggade built the temple, strangers sent by the angels installed a sacred *lingam* (stone idol) there, converting it into a place of worship for the Hindu God Shiva. Although Heggade was a practicing follower of Jainism, another Dharmaic religion in India, he still managed this Hindu temple. Twenty generations of the Heggade family have since followed the example of the founder, managing the Dharmasthala Temple and providing food, health care, education, and economic opportunities to the community.

In 1974, Veerendra Heggade's leadership was needed more than ever, as the installation of the Karnataka Land Reform Act altered the system of land ownership in the community. The act imposed strict limits on the amount of land that could be owned by a single proprietor, consequently turning many laboring farmers—who the original proprietors had hired to work the land—into landowners overnight. Many of these new laborers-turned-landowners lacked the capital, know-how, and skills to efficiently cultivate and benefit from their land, which prompted Heggade to start a program that offered funds to the farmers. Despite good intentions, this program failed because the farmers simply spent the given funds to sustain their old drinking habits.

Young Heggade, while considering alternative courses of action and completing a statue of Bahubali (a Jain leader who symbolizes self-control and subjugation of the ego), developed an idea for a project called Shri Kshetra Dharmasthala Rural Development Project (SKDRDP) that would help the farmers gain their own livelihoods. SKDRDP focused on helping nascent farmers develop their land by equipping them with capital and expertise. The project hired expert field-workers called *sevanirathas* to help cultivate the land—from distributing seeds, tools, and fertilizers to the small marginalized farmers, to teaching them how to work their lands and plant tree crops. At the start, the sevanirathas worked for low salaries despite the taxing and demanding nature of their tasks, as they believed they were working for a larger cause related to the temple. As time progressed, however, the ventures grew and required more people to work the land. As a result, a collective method of working evolved organically, and groups of farmers gathered to complete the work on one plot together before moving on to work on another plot that required many hands. Two interventions were identified to encourage land cultivation: the food-for-work program and labor sharing. Though these initial projects did get a measure of success, it was found that profits were dissipated on alcohol consumption.

It was at this time the organization realized that two crucial elements were missing in the scheme: involvement of women to stabilize the program, and funds to make the program self-sustaining. A scheme was initiated to encourage women to get involved and become equal stakeholders. At the same time, the microfinance movement was gaining ground in India and the results were reassuring. The farmers' groups as well as the women's groups were encouraged to save, while internal lending and microfinance was also encouraged. Over time, the groups' efforts at microfinance became a successful practice, and were linked to banks as the amount of funds involved grew. The program formalized in 1996 into a program called Pragathinidhi when the Syndicate Bank began providing loans. More importantly, the provisions of adequate funds were easily accessible for a convenient tenure and involved weekly repayment installments that were not hampered by administrative functions. Pragathinidhi eventually increased in scale and implemented a more systematic approach. The success of the microfinance program can be attributed to SKDRDP motivating the formation of self-help groups (SHGs) and then providing training to these groups to manage their books and accounts while inculcating habits of savings and thrift. Further, the SHGs were taught skills to achieve their goals. The support that SKDRDP provided was the building block that lent long-term stability to the SHGs and encouraged the microfinance program to spread successfully (Eswar and Raghavendran 2014).

Labor sharing and microfinance have become an intrinsic part of the program. Every week, neighboring farmers meet at a chosen house and help work the land. The farmer whose house is chosen feeds all the workers for free. The business of microfinance is looked into as weekly savings are collected, loan requests are decided on, and payments made. The field operations have been organized into circles of 8–10 villages, and each village is assisted by its own sevaniratha. Each circle has its own project office with technical specialists who can be called upon by sevanirathas for assistance. Other specialized departments were initiated as the need arose in the community. A director heads each project that includes seven departments: microfinance, health insurance, SIRI (various production units), livelihood promotion, rural development, community development, and SHGs. These programs were built around a value system that ensured stability.

SKDRDP has grown into one of India's largest NGO-based MFI and rural development institution, reaching about 400,000 clients. Its success can be attributed to the fact that "it breaks many of the accepted rules of microfinance and development" (Harper et al. 2008: 117). To cite two examples of its unconventionality, SKDRDP lends equally to men and women, and mixes welfare with development by giving money to those desperately in need of immediate assistance and credit to those who have promising ventures.

The combination of spiritual leadership and good management practices can be accredited to the influences of Hinduism and Jainism. Though SKDRDP functions separately from the Dharmasthala Temple, there is an unmistakable spiritual inspiration from the temple that guides the organization. Many consider the 'divinity factor' to be the foundation and fuel for accelerated development. SKDRDP's methods and successes are now the subject of much research all around the world. Recently, SKDRDP was awarded the International Award for Financial Innovation and the overall Ashden 2012 Gold Award for Microfinance in London. The judges who selected SKDRDP stated:

> We were bowled over by the scale SKDRDP has achieved so far, along with the responsibility it takes for lending to the poor, nurturing users to take out effective loans. SKDRDP has huge potential to expand its work even further, and to inspire many others to follow its lead. (http://indiamicrofinance.com/skdrdp-energy-award.html#)

This case study was based on a personal visit of one of the authors as well as Harper et al. (2008) and Belli and Raghavendran (2014).

3

Individual Giving

Introduction

Charitable giving exists at every level of the socioeconomic stratum, with some individuals giving in a manner considered traditional or age-old while others are embracing new modes of giving in India's evolving philanthropic context. In this chapter, we explore individual giving at various levels, starting with a closer look at the wealthy—their motivations, areas of focus, the way they structure their foundations, and their partnerships with the government and other NGOs. We then turn to middle-class giving, with perspectives from the urban middle class, innovations to fund-raise by national-level social welfare organizations, and an example of how one NGO founded by middle-class youth has made steps to engage the middle class. The chapter then observes giving behavior and patterns at the lowest strata with a case study on philanthropic behavior among the urban poor, based on 10 interviews and a focus group discussion. We conclude the chapter with four case studies: the high-net-worth Sunil and Liz Mehta and their work with Dasra; insights from Rotary Club members, reflecting professional middle-class views and the pursuit of community through philanthropy; the generous low-net-worth Sitabai; and lastly, five short examples from giving at the bottom of the pyramid.

It is clear that the charitable giving behavior of the wealthy differs from that of the middle class, both of which in turn differs from that of the poor. The wealthy in India are eagerly setting up their own foundations as vehicles for their philanthropic activities. The emerging middle class is looking to make a greater impact by turning to trustworthy organizations to guide their donations, and demanding accountability from recipients. Not equipped with the same amount of resources as the wealthy, the middle-class donors know they need the accumulated support of many individuals to make any impact (Schervish 2003: 15), and act accordingly. At the bottom of the pyramid, giving remains largely informal with acts of generosity expressed in smaller, daily forms that are often nonmonetary and along community lines. While in broad strokes, the forms of giving may vary across income level, it would be a mistake to attribute new forms of Indian philanthropy solely to the work of certain individuals, companies, or organizations (Sidel 2000: 5)—as it would miss the complexity of giving at each level, and the numerous emerging forms of giving.

A wide number of factors influence the inclination to give and the amount someone chooses to give, including demographic factors (such as age, income, occupational status, number of children, social class, and education level), personality traits, perceptions of a charity or recipient, and the individual's membership in a network, society, social movement, religious, or other community group (Bennett 2003: 13). In addition, families with a relatively stable income are more likely to donate routinely than families with a highly variable or unstable income (Hughes and Luksetich 2007: 278). The external image an individual wishes to project also affects giving behavior; the desire to improve one's standing within his/her social group by giving conspicuously to visible causes is a strong incentive to give (Bennett 2003: 14). Between social priorities, personal capabilities, and choice of intervention, it is clear that charitable giving is a calculated rather than a spontaneous act, and thus differs from acts undertaken in an emergency (Radley and Kennedy 1995: 688).

Looking at the lowest socioeconomic strata, many argue that the poor are more likely to give directly to the needy around them because they can better empathize with other needy people's circumstances. On the other hand, the wealthy—especially those from a professional background—are more willing to donate to a wider variety of causes, such as the environment or arts (Radley and Kennedy 1995). The better-off may be inclined to give to educational or cultural organizations, as they are "deeply connected to certain conceptions of how society should be organised" (Ostrower 1997: 132). Thus, giving may be used by the wealthy to represent a "mark of class status," and offers the opportunity to "carve out a separate and exclusive arena for themselves" distinct from the philanthropic space of the less wealthy (Ostrower 1997: 133). Most studies regarding elite philanthropy have been conducted in the UK or US, and while there are some parallels with

India, such distinct areas of interest between the rich and the poor are not as well defined in the Indian context.

It was estimated that in 2011, Indian philanthropic donations neared $5–6 billion or between 0.3 percent and 0.4 percent of gross domestic product (GDP), making India a leader in private charitable giving compared to other emerging economies such as China (0.2%) and Brazil (0.3%) (Sheth and Singhal 2011). As a percentage of GDP, the estimate is an increase of 50 percent since 2006 (Sheth and Singhal 2011). Among the wealthy, the average contribution to charitable causes in 2011 was 3.1 percent of total income, an increase from 2.3 percent in the previous year (Sheth 2012). Further, the top 10 philanthropists in India donated over $2 billion in 2012, mainly by transferring business shares to set up foundations (Cantegreil et al. 2013). Still, considering that India's 100 richest people alone have a combined fortune of $276 billion or almost one-fourth of India's GDP as of 2009, the amount donated represents a small fraction of the upper class' prosperity (Jha 2012: 278).

Nonetheless, India's overall philanthropic contributions are impressive considering that in a typical month, 165 million Indian individuals donate money to some charitable cause—more than any other country in the world (CAF 2012: 22). This support is essential for NGOs, as according to one study by the Indian government, NGOs derive as much as 70 percent of their funding from private sources (Cantegreil et al. 2013: 22).[1] To add, 87 million Indian individuals volunteer their time each month, ahead of the Brazil, Russia, India, China, and South Africa (BRICS) and second only to the US with 105 million volunteering individuals (CAF 2012: 24). Further, India comes in third place, after China and the US, for the number of individuals who have helped a stranger in a typical month (at 165 million) (CAF 2012: 28). Yet, once India's billion-plus population is taken into account, the numbers become relatively less dramatic, and India ranks last in the South Asian region based on average participation (CAF 2012: 47). While numbers are difficult to capture, one report claims that 19 percent of Indians are donating money, 10 percent are volunteering time, and 19 percent are helping a stranger (CAF 2012: 66). Overall, Charities Aid Foundation's

[1] Other studies, however, provide a different view; one study cites that NGOs derive about 75 percent of their funding from the government (Jha 2012: 278), while business and individual philanthropy only account for 10 percent of total charitable giving in India (Sheth 2010: 3).

(CAF) World Giving Index (which ranks 153 nations according to charitable-giving behavior) placed India in 133rd place in 2012, a slide from 91st place in 2011, and not much higher than its 134th place in 2010 (CAF 2011, 2012). Individual and corporate giving tend to be higher in response to natural calamities (Jha 2012: 260), so when India experienced flooding among other emergencies in 2010, more people gave and at higher amounts. While individuals' monetary and volunteer hour numbers are dramatic in India, there remains great potential for growth.

As outlined in Chapter 1, a culture of scrutinizing the motivations and expectations of one's donation and recipient prevails in India. In Hindu traditions of daan, giving out of pity or contempt is considered "not the proper moral state," and a selfish motive leads to a 'less good' gift. Also, tradition cites that giving must go to a 'worthy vessel' in order to ensure that the giver him/herself is not 'scandalized' by the misuse of the gift (Bornstein 2009: 629). This shapes *how* individuals give: "the significance of giving to worthy recipients structures the gift, and enters into the equation of whether one gives with immediacy, impulsively, or through more regulated forms" (Bornstein 2009: 630). The emphasis on finding a worthy recipient is tied to daan notions of detachment from the gift once it has been given. Accountant Sanjay Agarwal found that in India, individuals are comparatively less concerned with what happens to their money once they give it away. This finding prompted him to write the *AccountAid* newsletter series, which educates and offers advice to middle-class donors (Agarwal 2010: 14). A study by the Delhi-based Sampradaan Indian Centre for Philanthropy in 2001 found that most giving was ad hoc and informal, with 77 percent of donations given "to individuals in distress, known to oneself, and to beggars," while only 21 percent given to organized, secular charity (Bornstein 2009: 640). This is in part tied to individual suspicion toward NGOs in India, and the conflicting tension between giving away without expectation and finding a suitable recipient for a donation (Bornstein 2009: 643). More recently, however, there have been signs that individual donors are looking to be more engaged. The 2012 India Giving report found that over a third (38%) who had donated money to organizations claimed to have researched the recipient organizations before donating, and 65 percent of donors said they would 'want to know where/how the funds are spent' (Maple and Harrison 2012: 6). This draws a picture of a large proportion of the population engaging in ad hoc and informal charity, with only a small but emerging group—clustered in the middle and upper socioeconomic classes—pushing for new modes of giving that promise longer-term change and development. The findings of this research also suggest that those at the bottom of the pyramid can be just as strategic in their philanthropic behaviors in their own way.

At the Top of the Pyramid

India is home to about 50 billionaires (4 percent of the world's total), 1,500 individuals with over $50 million in assets, and 700 individuals with more than $100 million.[2] Such large-scale donors form a particular kind of group and need their own theory of giving, as they are producers of a social agenda. With concentrated wealth, they are capable of creating entire institutions, movements or areas of charity, and can respond to unmet social needs neglected by the market and state. Further, their larger contributions shape the direction of beneficiaries by influencing the priorities, activities, and character of NGOs (Schervish et al. 1986). In India, individual philanthropy at the top of the pyramid is defined by the preference for establishing operational foundations and the active involvement of the founder, with some continuing the traditions of India's early indigenous wealthy, while others are establishing new patterns of giving. While in absolute terms, the non-wealthy give more of their time and money to philanthropic causes, making an impact requires a collaborative effort on the part of many individuals—which the wealthy can be less concerned about.

The research in this section draws from over 45 semi-structured in-person interviews, in addition to numerous, less formal exchanges with philanthropists, heads of foundations, philanthropic organizations, academics and experts, media, government, and industry bodies in Bangalore, Delhi, Mumbai, and Pune in 2012. Insights from interviewees have been included without attribution, but occasionally their own words are used. As a starting point, we consulted the *Forbes'* List of Billionaires in India (*Forbes* 2012); as information on billionaires as a separate group is somewhat limited,

[2] According to *Forbes*, India had 48 billionaires in 2012 and 55 in 2013. India currently has 158,000 millionaires (O'Sullivan and Kersley 2012: 49).

the study was expanded to include the activities of ultra-HNWIs and HNWIs who are multimillionaires.

HNWI philanthropists are distinguishable in that they are "uniquely endowed with material resources and cognitive dispositions that enable them, both as a group and as individuals, to fashion outcomes they desire to effect. Wealth grants a special capacity for *empowerment*" (Schervish 2003: 9). HNWIs do not only support causes or contribute to existing organizations, but also produce their own philanthropic projects (Schervish 2003: 13). They broadly tend to contribute in three main roles: (a) a managerial role, providing organizational expertise; (b) an entrepreneurial role, combining both human and financial capital to launch a new charitable enterprise or component within an existing unit; or (c) a venture role, combining managerial and entrepreneurial elements of finance and advice (Schervish 2003: 17–18).

Since India's economic liberalization in 1991, there has been significant growth in the high-tech IT and biotechnology industries, among others, which led to the emergence of a new wave of wealthy entrepreneurs. While these high-tech philanthropists share some traits with the wealthy who earned their money before the 1990s, they are in many ways fundamentally different from the inherited wealthy because of their formative experience, typically younger age and quick ascent to wealth (Schervish 2003: 23). Their way of giving integrates aspects of entrepreneurship—such as identifying creative spaces, commanding production, and thus the rate of return on their investment (Schervish 2003: 13). Another factor that distinguishes the newer generation of Indian philanthropists from previous generations of donors is the changed context in which they operate—the newer generation is part of a much more globalized and capitalist India.

While increased private donations from India's new generation of wealthy philanthropists are welcome, their philanthropic acts are not exempt from challenges and criticism. For example, while new philanthropy is broadly moving from traditional charity to a sustainable developmental focus, that developmental focus is not without conflict between perceptions of what is needed and actual areas of action (Sidel 2000: 14). The new philanthropists also find it more difficult to be as innovative in the social sector as they are in the business and technology sectors (Jha 2012: 281; Sidel 2000: 4). Further, while their approach and keen interest in engaging in philanthropy bring benefits, they can be perceived as heavy-handed intrusion—"an overbearing assertion of domination" (Schervish 2003). Their "self-assurance, can-do attitude, and relative inexperience can lead them at times to be arrogant and presumptuous" (Schervish 2003: 23). Still, it is important to remember that for all the media hype around dramatic donations, "the wealthy are by dint of personality no more egoistically myopic or socially responsible than anyone else" (Schervish 2003: 12)—and so expectations need to be held with caution. It is for these reasons that George Bundy (head of the Ford Foundation) used to say to Henry Ford II: "Henry, your job is easier; it is only to make money. My job is tougher—it is to give your money away, wisely" (Das 2002: 167). Without a doubt, his words ring true in India today.

Motivations

There are a myriad of reasons why individuals choose to engage in philanthropy, and some reasons are made more public than others. While many Indians are motivated to give for religious purposes, HNWIs are motivated to act philanthropically by a combination of personal compassion, guilt, forward-thinking, and risk management. Almost all individuals have some emotional, personal motivation for giving, whether triggered by an event, having a heart 'in the right place,' or being in touch with the myriad of need—as one philanthropist put it, "you would have to be blind not to see the various problems India is facing." One study found that perceptions of inequity were a key motivator, as 60 percent of Indians cite "giving back to society" as their main motivation, compared to about 25 percent who cite "affecting meaningful and measurable social change" as their top motivation (Reddy et al. 2012: 4). Many engage in philanthropy simply because they derive joy and energy from it. For others, particularly older adults, there is an element of moral responsibility and social obligation: "We are not doing anyone a favour.... We are simply giving back to society what we gained from them." In that sense, giving is simultaneously free and obligatory, altruistic and self-oriented.

Another common source of motivation for philanthropy—especially for setting up a foundation—is the desire to pass on family values, create meaningful roles for family members, and leave a positive legacy (UBS-INSEAD 2011: 16). Political motivations are less openly admitted, as are financial motivations such as tax benefits. Patriotic or nation-building motivations have declined from their height in the pre-Independence and early post-Independence era. Ultimately, giving is the result of a combination of—often rather personal—factors.

Since the 1990s, a generation of well-educated and globally connected entrepreneurs—often from more modest, upper-middle-class backgrounds—has become wealthy. These first-generation wealthy tend to approach their money differently than individuals of inherited wealth, whose families expect most of it to be passed on to their children. Many of these new generation philanthropists explain their motivations in terms of having earned enough wealth and feeling it is time to 'give back.' Reaching this point, however, may take some time. While there is a trend of younger-generation HNWIs becoming more engaged in philanthropy, the largest and most renowned Indian charitable foundations still operate under the leadership of ultra-HNWIs who are in their fifties, sixties, and seventies. Indeed, the simple explanation for this may be that many of the younger HNWIs are still busy building and leading their companies and making their money.

Alongside a horizontal type of pressure—with HNWIs noting who in their peer group is engaging in philanthropy (Andreoni and Scholz 1998)—there is a pronounced vertical pressure. The Indian public, increasingly educated, skilled, and with rising aspirations, has growing expectations that HNWIs and their companies will contribute to social development. In India, the wealthiest 5 percent of the population controls 40 percent of the country's wealth (Sheth 2010), and the wealth gap is only growing. Through some combination of fear and enlightened thinking, HNWIs are increasingly aware of the risks that inequality poses. India's wealthiest man, Mukesh Ambani, has built the world's largest house in Mumbai, a 27-story skyscraper that occupies 400,000 square feet—1,300 times bigger than the average shack in the surrounding slums (*The Economist* 2012: 3). Yet Ambani also believes that "an island of prosperity is unsustainable in an ocean of poverty" (Dadrawala 2003: 97). Another billionaire agrees: "With so much poverty, how long will people keep quiet? I wouldn't keep quiet if I were them; I would resent it like mad." For Anand Mahindra, creating opportunities in education is a way to avoid rebellion, anarchy, and violence in India from unequal wealth distribution (Dadrawala 2003: 34). There is a general consensus that something needs to be done to avoid social unrest and to prevent India from looking like Brazil or South Africa, where high security is needed around homes and businesses. Interestingly, this sentiment is not new. During the 1837–1838 famine when there was a breakdown of law and order, it was no coincidence that the British started relief operations; in other words, "life and property" were threatened by the "distressed state of the country" (Sharma 2001: 135–137). Fear of uprising by the poor, hungry for equal opportunity and social mobility, is age-old. In a society where dramatic wealth creation has occurred, the wealthy must make it known that their concentrated wealth will be used to help society in at least as efficient of a manner as the government would use it had it been taxed.

Areas of Focus

Among India's top business leaders, religious giving remains a private affair, while more secular giving through modern foundations is done with fanfare. While lower-income Indians may only have enough to donate to one cause—and almost always choose a religious cause—the HNWIs are able to diversify their giving portfolio and satisfy both their traditional and more modern giving inclinations.

Deciding which areas to direct one's giving is both personal and strategic, and may not always line up with the country's greatest areas of need. From an international perspective, the World Bank has outlined that India needs more public sector reform, transport infrastructure, removal of labor regulations, education, energy security, public health, and nutrition to achieve its economic potential. Certainly, some of these areas are best left to the government or PPPs, while others can be advanced through private philanthropic channels. It is widely acknowledged that it is the role of the government to set the broad vision or direction for national development; yet many Indian philanthropists follow their own objectives, out of personal preference or, at times, purposeful disagreement with government strategy.

Indian philanthropists, by and large, give the most to causes benefiting education, health care, and livelihoods. These giving preferences fit into a wider trend of Asians prioritizing educational causes, followed by poverty alleviation and development, then health and disaster relief (UBS-INSEAD 2011: 9). In contrast to Indian philanthropists, American HNWI donors from a high-tech background often seek out neglected social niches where there are the greatest needs and scarcest resources (Schervish 2003: 13). Younger generation Indian philanthropists, however, are more inclined to give to progressive causes such as the environment or civil rights, and are adopting more scientific, professional approaches to survey areas of need and solve problems. Nonetheless, many newer generation companies and foundations still tend to channel their innovation into classic sectors such as education, rather than move into sensitive or nontraditional areas such as mental health. Ultimately, determining where to give is both easy and difficult, as "you name any area in India...and it is a crying need."

The philanthropic focus on education as the panacea for India's problems goes back to the colonial period. While education has traditionally been a public sector service, the public system has struggled in reach and quality; and with an overall literacy rate in India of 74 percent (Census of India 2011), it has become clear more needs to be done. A number of foundations have opted to partner with the government to expand education services. For Indian HNWIs, education is an especially appealing cause as it is noncontroversial, supported by government policies, easily measurable in terms of outcomes (numbers of students enrolled or pass rates of exams, etc.), and is a pressure-release valve that reduces inequalities. Giving to education commonly entails building or operating schools rather than focusing on systemic change and quality standards. The majority of philanthropic attention is aimed at primary education, with secondary and higher education and special needs (learning or physical disabilities) receiving relatively less attention. Given the importance of education, it is not surprising that the countless for-profit models and ideas on how to better primary education often clash. As one expert quipped, "There isn't any more money that you can throw on children and education that is going to solve the problem" in India—suggesting the sector is already saturated and the problem is that of inefficiency, poor quality, and coordination. In some regions this may be true, but in other regions, education remains inaccessible. For the foreseeable future, education will likely continue to be the most sought-after and well-funded philanthropic sector.

Health- and livelihood-related initiatives are also popular among philanthropists seeking to undertake community-oriented endeavors. Vocational training programs (in areas ranging from computer literacy to carpentry) are generally more popular among corporate foundations than private philanthropic initiatives because they train future employees and are supported by the government.

In a country where many individuals can only think about day-to-day survival, issues that require a long-term focus—often lacking in notable government commitment or associated with a social taboo—receive less philanthropic attention. These issues include mental health, services for the disabled, sex education, sexual abuse, the arts, traditional crafts, water availability, environment and natural resource management, consumer rights, and legal aid, to name a few. Trends in India mirror those of family philanthropy in Asia as a whole, where there are relatively low levels of contribution to the arts and culture, civil rights, and the environment. Optimistically, there is growing attention in India to women's causes and the environment (UBS-INSEAD 2011: 9).

The preference for Indian philanthropists to experience tangible outputs means less funding for think tanks, research institutes, and knowledge space, as researchers are often viewed as an 'administrative' cost. Domestic think tanks are largely avoided by Indian donors for their perceived coziness with government and politics. Thus, evidence-based research with practical implications, and documentation and analysis of the successes and failures of foundations and philanthropic initiatives—which could greatly advance the field—are sorely missing. Most foundations undertake some kind of 'dipstick' survey to help design their programs, but do not position research as a central objective. Connecting research to policy change is a challenge in any context and may seem too distant of an objective particularly in India, where life-and-death matters are on the doorstep. There is also underinvestment in building philanthropic infrastructure, funds for institutional support, and organizational development.

Overall, there is a tendency for Indian individual philanthropists and foundations to operate in more than one area or very broadly defined areas, with rare examples of clearly defined and focused channeling of energy and funds. This is not to say that the dominant areas of education, health care and livelihoods are not important for India, or that all intangible activities are completely avoided; rather, that Indian HNWIs have the capacity to also direct their efforts toward underserved causes, and hopefully—by doing so in a more clear and targeted manner—over time, will do so to create notable long-term systemic change.

Foundation Structures (Models)

India's HNWIs demonstrate a clear preference for establishing foundations as vehicles for their philanthropic activities. In forming their foundations, Indian philanthropists seem open to learning from all experiences—from established models such as the Ford Foundation or Rockefeller Foundation, to the Bill & Melinda Gates Foundation's approach to clear-cut end goals and risk-taking, or Tata Trust's support for wide-ranging issues. Yet, even as ideas flow fluidly across borders today, philanthropy within each culture reflects "fundamental conceptions of how civic life should be structured," embedded in local experiences and values (Hammack and Heydemann 2009: 12). In India, for instance, the founders of philanthropic foundations take a more hands-on approach—applying their business operational skills to the social sector—and prefer to keep the money within their own foundations to feel more connected to the outcomes.

Private Indian foundations are shaped predominantly around the personal convictions, preferences, and strengths of the founder. For example, Shiv Nadar has a passion for education as he remembers how he once benefited from it, and thus directs his Shiv Nadar Foundation to undertake various types of education initiatives. Further, he has applied his expertise in institution building (of his company, HCL) to build a new university through his foundation. This demonstrates how the founder of a foundation can carry over expertise from his business area to enhance his private foundation. Another example is Kiran Mazumdar-Shaw, chairman and managing director of Biocon, a biopharmaceutical company. Mazumdar-Shaw carries over her expertise from the biopharmaceutical company to her position as a Managing Trustee of a foundation that operates mainly in the health-care sector and also works to enhance education and sanitation infrastructure (see case study in Chapter 6: Trends). In another case, Café Coffee Day's (a beverage chain) founder V.G. Siddhartha has a trust in his home village in a coffee-growing region, which undertakes service sector vocational training. Inevitably, the experiences, skills, connections, and reputations of HNWIs carry over from the business world to the philanthropic realm as they build foundations and pursue philanthropic activities.

The preferred model for Indian foundations is operational, combined with elements of grant-giving and, on occasion, partnership with other organizations or funders. The most commonly cited reason for choosing an operational (or hands-on) approach is the desire to be engaged and in control. This desire reflects the entrepreneurial spirit of the business leaders who not only want to develop a successful foundation but also want to take full credit for its success. To add, leaders hesitate to entrust their money with NGOs, which resonates with a broader Indian cultural trend of intergroup distrust.

Indian preferences correspond with a broader Asian preference for family-owned philanthropic initiatives maintaining operational control, rather than working collaboratively or as grant-making entities (UBS-INSEAD 2011: 42). One study found that in India, two-thirds of private foundations' funding went to their own operational activities and one-third as grants to other organizations.[3] One way in which this plays out is that foundations adopt a hybrid model with both operational and grant-giving arms. Take the Avantha Foundation, which operates as a funding agency with some direct implementation and occasional partnerships: under its governance program, the foundation provides direct funds to elected representatives, and works with NGOs to help elected representatives gain expertise. The Bharti Foundation started out granting initiatives in the area of education for underprivileged children before deciding to build schools themselves (the Satya Bharti schools, since 2006). The Narotam Sekhsaria Foundation stands as one of the rarer examples of a purely grant-giving foundation—although the family is also behind various other philanthropic foundations, which run on more operational- and partner-based models.[4]

Private philanthropic foundations in India are predominantly family managed or individually managed rather than professionally managed[5]; this trend is more pronounced among smaller foundations. Across Asia, many philanthropic organizations have a relatively low

---

[3] As a percentage of respondents (UBS-INSEAD 2011: 50).
[4] Salaam Bombay Foundation and Ambuja Cement Foundation.
[5] In 2010, 62 percent of respondents said family managed or individually managed and 38 percent said professionally managed (UBS-INSEAD 2011: 43).

administrative cost—yet considering the preference for operational models, this reflects underinvestment in professionalization and institutionalization rather than efficiency (UBS-INSEAD 2011: 45). Many Indian foundations, established with personal funds, are so closely integrated with the founders' companies that they share the same name, and have some of its back-office support work (such as finance or legal) done by departments within the companies. In many cases, the founder may discuss decisions with a board, but ultimately he/she has the freedom to run the foundation as desired.

The current model of Indian private foundations raises some questions of sustainability. One foundation based its sustainability on the fact that it is backed by one of the wealthiest individuals in India—if they need some extra funds, the HNWI can simply write out a personal check "without losing a minute's sleep over it." The foundation, however, also has a platform for other corporate partners and individual donors to contribute to its corpus. Often, Indian foundations start out with personal funds and an operational model, and then look for other funding sources and partnerships as they expand their work. Some HNWIs have already earmarked a percentage of their fortune to their foundation, so that family or others cannot claim it after their passing. Another measure that can be taken to ensure sustainability is to integrate social enterprise approaches, although in some sectors, there is a certain degree of social resistance to creating for-profit models, which makes philanthropists cautious. Given that the boom in philanthropic foundations in India is relatively recent, it may not seem surprising or urgent that a number of foundations struggle with models of sustainability. But, the issue of sustainability must be addressed, as the legacies of foundations depend on it.

Relations and Partnerships between Actors

Looking to expand their philanthropic reach, some HNWIs are inclined to collaborate with partners as long as they are transparent and like-minded, while other philanthropists make clear that they prefer to implement programs themselves. The problem is that given India's size, "all the money in the world can't solve problems without collaboration." Arguments used by foundations against partnering with NGOs include the view that Indian NGOs are unprofessional and are middlemen taking away a percentage of hard-earned money before it is passed on to the community.[6] Evidently, these foundations do not place high value on the local knowledge and community trust that NGOs possess. Further, as each actor has a different set of goals, engagement between sectors can mean compromise. Yet as projects geographically expand and become harder to monitor from the foundation's headquarters, local partners can fill the gap. Distrust between the private sector and NGOs is common worldwide and is especially embedded in India's history, but both sides must adjust in order to expand philanthropic reach. In addition to NGOs becoming more professional and accountable, private foundations should become more open—for example, about their internal dynamics—to build trust and partnerships, rather than paternalistic relationships.

Conclusions and Looking Ahead

In March 2011, Bill Gates, Warren Buffett, and India's 50 richest individuals gathered in New Delhi for 'The Giving Discussion,' which the media portrayed as a failure to convince Indian HNWIs to join the Giving Pledge. In June 2012, another meeting was held and led by Indian billionaire Azim Premji in Bangalore, and was lauded as a greater success in advancing a discussion on philanthropy among the country's wealthiest citizens. This difference is indicative of how India's HNWIs are becoming more open to participating in forums on giving and more self-assured as they chart their own philanthropic path—largely through operational foundations.

There is a rich history of high-status Indians engaging in philanthropy. In some ways, historical role models undertook philanthropic acts that even HNWIs today have not kept up with—such as the research center established in 1957 by Kasturbhai Lalbhai, one of the richest industrialists in Ahmedabad; or the other libraries founded with the support of rich Jain industrialists in Ahmedabad in the early and mid-20th century (Johnson 1996: 108–109). Today, society expects giving to be truly altruistic, strategic, sustainable, and not for personal means. The media plays an active role in following Indian HNWI donations, and there is

[6] Forbes Marshall (Dadrawala 2003: 67).

some debate over how generous Indians really are, although it is likely HNWIs give notably outside the public's knowledge. Arpan Sheth, author of Bain & Company's *India Philanthropy Report*, remarks that it is more important to ensure that individuals are 'giving right' rather than dwell on the exact amount being donated (India Knowledge@Wharton 2011). Ideally in the future, private foundations will invest more in innovative and risky projects, ensure these projects strengthen national systems, fund projects further away from home, and work more closely with local civil society organizations and other actors (Watson 2012).

Moving forward, religiously motivated giving in India will likely remain high, while in the secular space, HNWIs will continue to establish their own operational foundations and only cautiously expand partnerships. As the annual Dasra Indian Philanthropy Forums and Azim Premji's 2012 meeting in Bangalore suggests, the philanthropic infrastructure to support wealthy donors will grow. Still, the need for donor education is great, and it will take time to sensitize India's millionaires and billionaires to accept that they would greatly benefit from learning more about the challenges of the social sector and how to donate. On the bright side, wealthy philanthropists and their foundations are starting to move into neglected niche areas, as seen in the case of Rohini Nilekani setting up a foundation to focus on water (Arghyam Foundation), or the billionaire investor Rakesh Jhunjhunwala supporting the Mumbai-based think tank Gateway House. Nonetheless, certain tensions in the HNWI philanthropic space will continue, between religious and secular giving, earning wealth versus giving it away, supporting charitable causes addressing immediate relief needs versus creating systemic change, overseeing how every rupee is spent versus arm's-length giving, and between collaboration and intergroup distrust. It is clear that further research—by wealthy philanthropists on both the greatest areas of need and approaches to giving, and on HNWI philanthropy itself—is needed.

Indian HNWIs tend to take on an entrepreneurial role, in that they provide financial capital and stay actively involved in their philanthropic activities. They go beyond just acting as managers to provide organizational expertise, or standing back in a venture role (Schervish 2003: 17–18). Further, due to their business backgrounds, many of these individuals are spatially empowered to influence others—which they should leverage in the philanthropic sphere—

and are psychologically confident about their vision and abilities to implement it. Still, many challenges remain at present. Most private foundations are operational and invested in directing a certain socioeconomic outcome, which limits the potential of donations that could play a more catalytic role if private foundations gave in a hands-off manner. Collaboration exists amid distrust, as partnerships are inevitable in the Indian context. Wealthy philanthropists carry over their business tendencies but do not take enough risk with their donations. Thus amid certain contradictions and emerging achievements, giving at the top of the pyramid continues to rapidly expand and evolve.

In the Middle

There has been notable hype generated around the emerging middle class in India. Currently, there is no exact estimate of the number of middle-class Indians because there is no consensus on the definition of the new income-based middle class in middle-income countries such as India. Looking at those just above the poverty line can be deceiving—as 829 million Indians (or 68.8 percent of the population) live on less than $2/day, which means that 435 million Indians are *just* above the poverty line of $1.25/day (The World Bank Group 2010). While some studies place the number of middle-class Indians between 150 million and 300 million, Christian Meyer and Nancy Birdsall at the Center for Global Development estimate it is closer to 70 million or less than 10 percent of the country's population, using a $10 per capita per day (2005 PPP) measure (Meyer and Birdsall 2012). Understanding the philanthropic inclinations of individuals at the top and bottom end of the middle-class range, therefore, presents its own challenges as their modes of giving may vary greatly.

A 2012 CAF-commissioned report on India Giving—conducted in 20 cities with a sample size of 9,000 focusing on the 'general public'—confirmed the widespread nature of individual giving across the country. The report found that 84 percent of individuals interviewed gave money to a charitable cause at least once within the previous year; however, only 27 percent of donors gave directly to a charitable organization, while the most common and preferred form of giving (cited by 70 percent of donors) was directly to the beneficiary (Maple and Harrison 2012: 5). Further, for seven out of ten Indians, and across demographics, giving is linked to religious purposes (Maple and Harrison 2012: 5). Geographically, the report found that the north demonstrated a higher percentage of giving (100 percent compared to 73–85 percent elsewhere), due to religious drive, while those in the south were more likely to give to 'charitable' causes (61 percent). In the west, individuals could afford to give higher amounts, while those in the east were more inclined to give using nonmonetary means (Maple and Harrison 2012: 5). The report is also hopeful regarding India's future, as findings show that those who earn more also give more.

The India Giving report also revealed certain challenges in individual giving. Of the individuals surveyed who had given to charitable organizations (2,600), over 80 percent had given in cash, while only 5 percent online, by check, or through their salary (Maple and Harrison 2012: 6). Religious giving is particularly cash oriented. Further, almost one-quarter of donors believed that others were motivated by tax benefits, and another quarter believed others were motivated by money laundering. Four out of ten felt their donations 'may not make a difference in peoples' lives' and 52 percent felt that a lack of transparency hinders donations to NGOs (Maple and Harrison 2012: 5–6). Even more worrisome is that in urban areas, the report found the most common reason for not giving was 'not feeling responsible,' rather than an inability to give (as is the most common reason elsewhere) (Maple and Harrison 2012: 5–6). The report concludes that the dominance of cash giving, tendency to give to individuals, and low awareness of charities among donors present challenges for the future of individual giving.

The View of Urban Middle-class Donors

A focus group discussion[7] with individuals from India's emerging urban middle class found that their motivations for philanthropy are often religion based, whether to meet religious obligations (such as zakat for Muslims), or the promised return in the afterlife. Festivals are therefore a popular time for giving. As one individual expressed,

---

[7] Discussion held on the side of a COVA (www.covanetwork.org) meeting in Hyderabad in August 2013. Accessed on August 18, 2013.

givers leave it to the almighty to determine who is deserving or not; as the donor, their only concern is that they have given. Personal satisfaction derived from giving is another key motivator. Both the young and the old are philanthropic, but their level of generosity and expression of giving are linked to how they have been raised and their current circumstances.

The forms of giving vary, but an underlying notion of value for money exists. It was expressed, for example, that giving to organizations that work to empower individuals and improve their livelihoods is appropriate giving. If one gives to individuals, the giving should not be piecemeal, rather cases identified for substantial support, such as a business investment or marriage. Some philanthropists go to places such as government hospitals and seek out those most in need, particularly those requiring expensive treatments such as cancer patients, and arrange for their medicines to be paid. Generally, individuals prefer to give to individuals they know, such as family, relatives, and neighbors. Those who migrated to Hyderabad and have done well may support individuals or causes in their home village, which again is a known recipient. Nonetheless, many individuals—particularly the elderly—always have some small coins to give as alms in case someone comes asking at their door. It is also common to see drinking water pots outside of homes for public use in the old city. Some in the discussion said that giving time through volunteering in the community, raising awareness of rights, or working to make government schemes more accessible is more valuable than money.

The participants raised some concerns over conceptual challenges with philanthropy, namely the possible negative impact it can have. They were concerned that individuals become reliant on begging, rather than being motivated to work and live with dignity; and that some beggars are so successful that it becomes more lucrative to beg than work. Further, some beggars abuse children and exploit them to get more money. As donors, they are concerned with distinguishing who are the 'real' beggars in larger urban contexts. They also worry that 'professional' beggars spend the money on vices. The participants expressed they would judge the 'realness' of the beggars based on how much a beggar markets oneself, or if the beggar is physically able and appears capable of working. Because it is challenging to decide who is a 'worthy' recipient, individuals prefer to give to relatives, neighbors, and their kin network—as they know who has a real need.

The participants of the discussion were well aware of challenges related to philanthropy, as well as broader trends such as corporate giving. They observed that corporates tend to support larger, more high-tech NGOs (e.g., those that can deliver nice presentations and reports), and subsequently tend to overlook local, small-scale NGOs that are often the ones in need of more funding. In other words, corporates tend to invest in the same NGOs, projects, and initiatives in convenient locations, and do not get to the real grassroots level of philanthropy. Hence, local organizations that lack and need infrastructure and resources do not receive support from corporate donors. The other challenge is time. Corporates often do not work on Saturdays and Sundays, and can organize their staff to volunteer on these days, whereas individuals in other sectors work six-day workweeks. The undertone was that for a certain group of professionals, philanthropic acts may be prearranged and made easy for them to undertake, even if rather limited in terms of impact. This discussion clearly illustrated that middle-class donors are aware of and think critically about emerging philanthropic trends.

The individuals involved in this discussion were certainly well informed about the broader philanthropic context, quite critical of corporate donors, and concerned about making an impact for those most in need through grassroots or other personal channels. Middle-class donors more openly acknowledged religion as a key motivator for giving than did HNWIs; but just like for those at the top, working through some formal channels and ensuring they are effective are very important for the middle class.

Innovative Fund Mobilization by National-level Social Welfare Organizations

Indian NGOs have four main sources of funds: self-generation, loans, grants, and donations. The latter two, grants and donations together constitute two-fifths of total NGO receipts (Parthasarathy 2011). Over the last several decades, NGOs have become technologically more sophisticated and embraced the use of various technologies in their efforts to disseminate information and elicit funds. This was hastened in 2003 by the government of India's decision to restrict foreign funding flowing into the country. The traditional approaches to fund-raising such as direct mail appeals and door-to-door fund-raising are becoming less successful, while Internet-based giving such as internet appeals, crowdfunding and peer-to-peer fund-raising strategies are becoming more popular and widespread.

In the last few decades, several NGOs have launched innovative marketing strategies to fund-raise. Below are three examples of NGOs using innovative methods of fund-raising, among the many NGOs today that have fully embraced the Internet and its potential for reaching donors and volunteers.

SOS CHILDREN'S VILLAGES OF INDIA

This is an award-winning NGO and recognized by the Government of India in 2006 for its "best practices of impact, scalability and replicability, innovation and sustainability in their programmes, and in creative and successful resource mobilization." One of its fund-raising strategies is the 'Hand in Hand with SOS Children's Villages of India.' This appeal touches an emotional chord by suggesting that "your hands are only special when you do something for others." It is followed by practical suggestions for diverse mode of helping, such as 'Sponsor a child,' which requires a contribution of "as little as Rs. 800/- per month for a minimum of one year to sponsor a child's nutritional education, general development and health related needs." There are suggestions to start a fund-raiser as well as 'Talk about it' through Facebook and Twitter feeds. Overall, the appeal is forthright, and the 'hand in hand' campaign is likely to trigger the impulse to give while the suggested donation amounts are manageable and give an individual the satisfaction of contributing to the welfare of a child. Moreover, the donations can easily be made online, thus enabling donors to track their history of donations and how their money was used.

CRY (CHILD RIGHTS AND YOU)

CRY is an Indian NGO established in 1979 with the aim of restoring children's rights in India and by working across levels from direct action to advocacy, mobilizing public opinion, and policy change. CRY partners with many grassroots NGOs to help thousands of Indian children denied basic children's rights. In 2007, it started a new media blitz with "smiling kids," asking people to partner with them in projects rather than simply donate money. Turning to positive imagery was a critical departure from stereotypical advertising showing "crying children" who were destitute by Indian NGOs wishing to arouse sympathy among viewers. CRY encourages online donors to partner with them to support CRY's efforts in a variety of arenas; for example, their website suggests that:

1. INR 3,600—connecting five children to proper health care.
2. INR 12,000—ensuring that six children are removed from child labor and enrolled in schools.
3. INR 40,000—making a village child labor-free.
4. INR 120,000—ensuring 100 children are out of malnutrition with proper care.

The last line in this list is deliberately left blank, which allows the potential donor to enter any amount that they would like to contribute. By stressing the practical suggestions for partnering, CRY allows its donors to direct their money to the cause that best appeals to them and gives them ownership in the transaction.

HELPAGE INDIA

This is an NGO that provides support, advice, and medical assistance to disadvantaged elderly people in India. Established in 1978, it is dedicated to improving life for the elderly and working across India to provide medical services, poverty alleviation, and income generation schemes in urban and rural areas. Headquartered in New Delhi, it has 33 offices across India's major cities and more than 700 employees, including about 100 fund-raisers (Sawhney 2003). HelpAge India has attracted international attention and recognition with multiple awards that speak to its impact and innovativeness. One example is its method of mobilizing funds; HelpAge India has deployed Oracle CRM On Demand to provide fund-raisers with real-time access to donor information, which helps establish better relationships with the donors. This method allows instant access to detailed activity reports and does away with the onerous reliance on manual monthly reports. Now HelpAge's web portal can access all donor requests instantly while allowing donors access to up-to-date status on their requests (Berk 2011). HelpAge India has shared with other organizations innovative ways of harnessing technology to make a pitch for donations and provide quick and easy-to-use choices for the direction of funds and modes to elicit instant online donations. More important is the transparency that accompanies the donations that both garners trust and gives the donor and receiver access to information about each other, thereby making the entire process of donating trustworthy, personal, and gratifying.

A Middle-class Desire to Give: Creating an NGO

To better understand philanthropic giving behavior of middle-class Indians, we looked at the founding and fund-raising experiences of Dream a Dream, an NGO established by middle-class youth, which has successfully tapped into the middle-class group of donors. Dream a Dream was established in 1999 by a group of graduates with a mission to empower young people from vulnerable backgrounds by developing life skills and sensitizing communities to achieve a nondiscriminatory society where unique differences are appreciated. The fact that 12 young Indians from diverse backgrounds came together was remarkable in itself—from marketing officers, management graduates, software engineers, chartered accountants, to photographers and ad professionals—all bound by a single desire to give back to the community, acknowledging they were more powerful in a unit than acting alone. Initially, the NGO was operated using the founders' salaries, but after two years, they decided to take on the NGO work full-time and started to fund-raise more seriously. They decorated tables at a restaurant with artwork, and organized events at nightclubs on off-peak evenings, focusing on merging fun with a good cause and asking only for small donations from young and mobile audiences; many individuals were glad to give under these conditions. Over time, Dream a Dream set up corporate volunteering programs, and found that once it engaged employees as volunteers, their positive experiences made them advocates for the cause, and in turn drove forward corporate donations.

Still, Dream a Dream has faced a number of challenges in engaging individual donors. Generally, while employees are happy to be volunteers, they are less willing to give much money. India also lacks sufficient infrastructure to engage regular monthly donors. For instance, NGOs are not allowed to fund-raise on their own website, which forces them to go through umbrella organizations such as GiveIndia. For a small NGO, meeting the reporting requirements of these umbrella organizations can be expensive.

Nonetheless, Dream a Dream sees the potential in India's young donors, whose disposable incomes are growing. If younger, middle-class professionals became engaged as corporate volunteers early on, they are more likely to participate in giving as they move up in their careers and earn larger incomes. Twenty years ago, donors typically sought out needy NGOs that nobody else was supporting; today, donors are looking to support effective NGOs that show accountability and transparency. This welcome shift does bring certain challenges, as donors want their funds to go directly to programs and not to administrative, reporting, or other overhead costs. As a result, NGOs struggle to obtain unrestricted funding that would allow them to invest back into areas such as research and development. But, this shift shows that Indian donors are becoming more engaged and interested in making an impact with their donated time and money. For the younger generation of donors, Dream a Dream has found that it is important to initially not ask for too much money, but build up loyalty over time, and also to ensure that donors get something in return (such as a fun experience) for their contributions.

At the Bottom of the Pyramid

Often forgotten in discussions about philanthropy is that poor people are both givers and recipients of charity. Across India, two-fifths of all givers are from poor households, defined as those with an annual income of below INR 25,000 (or around $450) (Jha 2012: 263). To understand charity and philanthropic acts within the context of poverty, a wider range of behaviors need to be taken into consideration. Their charitable acts tend to be on a small scale, and often on a daily or weekly basis. With a lack of existing studies on philanthropy among the poor in India, it is useful to consider studies done in other nations to see whether there are commonalities.

Susan Wilkinson-Maposa et al., authors of *The Poor Philanthropist: How and Why the Poor Help Each Other*, focus on southern Africa and aptly summarize that:

> Help between poor people is widespread, deeply embedded, morally grounded and operates as a vital element for both survival and progress. Rather than random or disorganized, horizontal philanthropy is part and parcel of the social fabric. It follows proven, unwritten, acculturated rules with associated sanctions for non-compliance. (Wilkinson-Maposa et al. 2005: x)

They found that while material forms, such as food, money, or clothes, are prevalent in charitable giving, so are nonmaterial forms of assistance, such as knowledge, physical or manual support (such as time or skills), and moral and emotional support (Wilkinson-Maposa et al. 2005: x). Further, the most prominent actors in giving and receiving assistance are friends and neighbors, with local associations and formal organizations less present—although urbanization and economic modernization is somewhat increasing the involvement of formal agents. Who the poor go to for assistance also depends on the type of need, physical proximity, relationship, reputation, and socioeconomic similarity (Wilkinson-Maposa et al. 2005: x). Interestingly, poor people place value on the act of helping, and not necessarily on the quantum (Wilkinson-Maposa et al. 2005: x).

Considering the responsibility and obligation aspect of Hindu daan and other forms of religious giving, Wilkinson-Maposa et al. argue that it is misleading to view philanthropy as always voluntary: "Help is not always, nor necessarily, a 'free' choice. Such behavior can be driven by social duty as well as by a deep moral obligation" and that "principles of reciprocity and co-operation grounded in mutual support are a prevalent and defining feature of horizontal philanthropy" (Wilkinson-Maposa et al. 2005: xi). Therefore, while the "poor know something about getting resources to where they are most needed," poor-to-poor giving should not be romanticized as it does have its limitations (Wilkinson-Maposa et al. 2005: xii). In this section, we explore what are those limitations and opportunities within the Indian context.

Insight to Philanthropic Behavior Among the Urban Poor

One of the authors conducted ten individual interviews and one focus group discussion in October 2013 in Laxmi Narayana Colony, Hyderabad, and found that a number of the patterns explored by Wilkinson-Maposa et al. (2005) can largely be confirmed in the case of urban India. Of the individuals interviewed, seven were female and three were male; six were Hindu, two were Muslim, and two were Christian; their ages ranged from 23 to 70 with the average at 41.6 years. The average household size was 4.8 members, ranging from one to twelve members among individuals. The past or present livelihood activities among the women included turmeric reselling, sari business, embroidery work, laborer, dairy seller, chicken shop vendor, and fruit stall vendor. The men interviewed had positions ranging from a barbershop owner, to a worker at a chain milk vendor, to the owner of a disposable plates and cups business. The husbands of the women interviewed held these positions: owner of a printing press, lorry driver, private company worker, stonemason, chicken shop owner, mutton shop owner, and watchman. The livelihoods of these individuals represent livelihoods common to India's urban poor, and reflect how much time and energy an individual has to dedicate to subsistence outside of their philanthropic activities.

Aside from the 10 individual interviews, the focus group included nine women who are all involved in the SHG movement, which indicates their interest and willingness to collaborate with others and improve their socioeconomic conditions. It also reflects their inclination to undertake some philanthropic acts as a group rather than individuals. For these women, coming together was a way to open doors, gain security, and overcome big problems. Philanthropy is also a mode of relief from mental strain—the women talked about the happiness they got from helping each other. The women did, however, express frustration with others in the community who lacked or lost motivation to engage in philanthropic activity after a lack of immediate impact and results. Others in the community stated that giving brings too great of a financial burden on their own household; or they had a bad experience of helping others and not receiving any help in return. This reflects the reciprocal aspect of philanthropy and value placed on the gesture of giving, which, if broken, results in a decline in goodwill.

Motivations for philanthropic behaviors are manifold, but a common belief and source of motivation was the idea that philanthropy is a give-and-receive relationship; if one helps others, then one may also receive help in times of hardship. Another motivation is the ability to feel empathy and share an understanding of what it is like to be poor. Religious motivations, however, tend to be among the most deeply embedded—the belief that giving after praying will bring a good return in the afterlife. Christians expressed that they feel God sees everything, therefore everyone should follow moral values to help 'save everyone.' In turn, children should be inspired by good role models within the family and church. Elders, whether in the Muslim community or elsewhere, are also key motivators for philanthropic activities. Overall, people had different preferences and approaches to giving, with some individuals focused on aiding the elderly—as they cannot work or sustain their own living—while others preferred providing aid to children.

The poor help their family, neighbors, friends, and other community members in numerous material and nonmaterial ways. Assistance to relatives is the most common, often in the form of giving money as interest-free loans to support and pay for children's educational pursuits or weddings. Poor individuals also give clothes to their relatives' children and money to the grandparents, and may assist relatives by taking on a matchmaker role, providing for free a service that otherwise would be charged a fee.

In urban areas, it is common to assist fellow villagers settle in the city, provide skills, knowledge, advice and tips on city life, and help them find work opportunities and housing. In turn, the recipients of the help donate food or other material items to the poor in their home village. One individual recalled how he had a sort of sponsor who played an important role in helping him settle in Hyderabad, and upon his sponsor's death, he went back to the village to support his sponsor's family emotionally and financially.

Donating to and through religious houses is also very common among the urban poor. Aside from the funds donated during regular services or temple visits (from as little as a few rupees in the temple hundi box), Muslims put aside some rice to donate monthly to the Muslim community school. Christians often donate to causes such as orphans through the church, with the Father collecting the money on a weekly basis. During festivals, more people donate in the temple hundi box, and during Christmas, the church father may collect items such as clothes from members to hand out to the needy. Volunteering to religious causes is also common, such as giving time and knowledge as a church Sunday school teacher, or helping repair or paint a temple. This goes alongside donating funds for new religious building construction. In some cases, giving crosses religious lines, such as the giving of rice or money by non-Hindus during Hindu festivals.

Philanthropy also takes place among employee groups. One barber explained that within the colony, there is a barbers' association, which through a collection of INR100 per month from its 120 members, helps new barbers establish shops, works to resolve problems, and assists barbers and their families with financial or health problems they may have. The owner of a petty shop gives items on credit to the needy and views it as a donation rather than a loss if the money is never repaid. Donating labor is another form of philanthropy, particularly for those who work as construction laborers, or in more skilled trades such as masons or carpenters; they help build homes or shops without requesting a fee. While a livelihood activity may create a common support community, having a skill, time, or labor resource is an accessible form of philanthropy.

Out of the individual interviews and focus group discussion, there emerged a myriad of other philanthropic acts and behaviors occurring within the community. One lady helps the poor elderly and widows complete their paperwork to obtain government pensions. One individual collects funds for a funeral after someone in the community dies. Another lady brings community cases to politicians for causes such as requesting subsidized housing. Others have collected funds for a specific cause, such as flood relief or to pay for a needy student's school fees. Individuals generally expressed their willingness to help any individual with a problem. Providing guidance or advice to others on a regular basis is perhaps the most common form of helping.

When asked about the timing of their philanthropic behaviors, most replied that their giving is consistent throughout the year and is most often a response to a clear need or others' calls for help. Nonetheless, there is a slight increase in giving during festivals such as Ramzan or Christmas (and other times depending on the religion). The members of one household shared that they approach and help individuals or families in need after listening to the announcements made at the masjid regarding who needs assistance in the community. Some other households recalled being approached by a voluntary organization and giving them some funds; even though they held some reservations about the organization's reliability, they still felt the money somehow went to the needy. Therefore, while some individuals are more proactive and reach out to an individual in need, others are more passive and wait for someone to ask for assistance.

As both givers and recipients of philanthropy, poor individuals tend to give in the way that they themselves were helped. Many recalled receiving assistance from relatives, such as a loan to help start a business or financial support to pay medical bills, or from religious organizations for schooling. Many also shared stories of receiving help from friends when they moved from the village to Hyderabad. In a couple of cases, individuals claimed to not have received assistance from others, or even from their own families. One elderly lady (aged 70) shared that her children do not assist her when she is ill; she was among those who felt their financial situation was too constraining to engage in philanthropy. This reinforces the notion of mutual support as a key feature of horizontal philanthropy.

The way in which an individual engages in philanthropy—or at least their perceptions of it—evolves over time. Not surprisingly, households that express feeling more economically and socially stable now than they did five years ago also give more. Conversely, households that had better economic conditions in the past than they do now focus on their own responsibilities, and feel they have less money to give to others. The elderly who were interviewed recalled how prices in the past used to be lower, and how there was lots of house-to-house sharing of rice and curries for anyone who did not have any; today, prices are higher and nobody seems to share curries. The elderly are further disinclined to donate because they do not work and make money. One individual expressed that philanthropy, like one's feelings, is never consistent and changes depending on the circumstances.

The women in the SHG expressed feelings of increased awareness and empowerment as a result of their membership in a group. Before they were group members, they were dependent on their husbands or others; but now they are earning their own money, contributing to the family financially, and are in a better position to help others. Further, they are eager to share their acquired knowledge about things like certain government schemes, and exercise their independence to help other women. This example illustrates how improving one's own social awareness places individuals in a better position to help others.

Observations and perspectives on philanthropy within the broader community greatly varied—from some individuals feeling the wealthy (both those within the slum and outside) are selfish, to others believing that all people are generous. One woman estimated that around 20–30 percent of individuals think of others, while everyone else thinks only of themselves and their own families. Those with negative views felt that the rich do not have any interest or a mentality for giving, and are not contributing proportional to their wealth.

Within cities especially, people found it harder to trust others, and some feel that selfishness is on the rise. One young individual admitted that his friends are selfish and only think of themselves and their desires to make money, often taking money from others (including friends) and never repaying, or lying and slandering others for their own benefit. Self-interest therefore exists alongside philanthropy.

In exploring philanthropic inclinations and behaviors among the urban poor, it becomes clear that horizontal philanthropy relies on reciprocity, cooperation, and trust. Similar to those in other socioeconomic conditions, the poor are interested in making an impact. For example, one interviewee expressed the value of building a community hall so that many can benefit rather than just one person. The poor are also concerned about the proper utilization of the donation, in particular when it is given to a more formal agent, which reinforces a strong preference for philanthropy within the community to known individuals or through a trusted religious house (such as a church or mosque). Nonetheless, within a large urban context, the presence of formal philanthropic organizations is growing, and the organizations are offering new and alternative modes of giving, even if the majority of philanthropy is still done through informal channels. Philanthropy comes in many forms and behaviors, including offering advice, labor, loans, skills, and knowledge—some of which are easier to give than others. Whether a person is a member of an SHG also plays an important role in terms of awareness, empowerment, and ability to help others. At the bottom of the pyramid, many philanthropic activities are collective rather than simply individual. Nonetheless, there are limitations to the philanthropic activities of the poor—in particular the lack of time and funds each household has to spare, the younger generation's ambitions for wealth, and shifting levels of trust regarding reciprocity. The poor, out of both need and desire, have engaged in horizontal philanthropy for all of time, and it is only their behaviors that change depending on context.

Conclusion

The public sector, private sector, and civil society all play a role in poverty eradication, yet no single government or organization has the resources to address all of India's challenges on its own. In India, as in many developing countries, the government is unable to provide sufficient quality basic services, such as education or health care, necessitating action on part of the private sector and charity organizations. Fortunately, the number of actors in the aid universe has been growing since 2000, and different stakeholders are bringing different strengths to the table. The growth comes with a new set of challenges, however, such as the need for greater coordination among actors in order to avoid duplication of efforts (Watson 2012).

Individuals across all levels of the socioeconomic ladder contribute to helping others, although their approaches and results vary. HNWIs utilize their business background and financial capital to launch new foundations, and approach philanthropy in an entrepreneurial manner. These HNWIs are leading the charge to set trends and introduce groundbreaking initiatives in the philanthropic realm. India's growing middle class is difficult to define numerically, but it holds the potential for great impact. Like HNWIs, middle-class individuals are keen on knowing where their money is going and whether it is going to deserving recipients. They also seek value for their contributions and some type of return—whether it be a feel-good or an enjoyable experience. Among India's growing class of professionals, the earlier they become engaged in volunteer and charitable activities through their companies, the more likely they are to become donors in the future.

The poor are both givers and receivers of philanthropy; "Sometimes those who give the most are the ones with the least to spare" (McIntyre 1996). Studies in the US have produced inconsistent results regarding the relationship between income and probability of giving. Some studies in the 1980s indicated a U-shaped curve that suggests that both the rich and the poor are equally caring, countering images of the "stingy rich and generous poor" and leaving the middle class as the least generous (Schervish and Havens 1995). In the 1990s, however, studies showed that in the US, the poorest donated the largest proportion of their income to religious organizations and also to secular causes (Wiepking 2007). The story is further complicated in that many poor people may give nothing while almost all the wealthy give something, but the poor who do donate may give a greater share of their relatively low incomes (Schervish and Havens 1995). Further, while the poor may give in forms—such as advice or emotional support—that are spontaneous and difficult to measure, as wealth and income increase, charitable giving progressively becomes more formally planned giving (Schervish and Havens 2001).

Only a small percentage of India's donors are from households whose annual income is above income tax paying level (of INR 1 lakh/$2,000 per annum) (Jha 2012: 263). Religious motivations for giving exist across all levels, but were more openly acknowledged among the poor. The poor demonstrate a wide range of philanthropic behaviors beyond giving money by sharing their skills, time, advice, knowledge, emotional support, and labor with others in need. Group or community modes of giving are common, and individuals engaged in the self-help movement are more likely to be socially and financially empowered to help.

Across all levels of giving, there is clear interest in strategic giving—finding trustworthy and deserving recipients, and having some sense of control over the outcome of the gift. Both the HNWIs and upper-middle-class donors are concerned about accountability. The HNWIs can establish foundations with their wealth to address their concerns, and the middle class can seek reputable institutions to direct their giving. In their own ways, individuals seek to help their home villages; some set up trusts in the village, while others help fellow villagers find work when they migrate to the city. Generally, individuals at the top prefer to formalize their giving by establishing foundations, but even individuals at the bottom are inclined at times to give through organized channels such as volunteer organizations or SHGs.

The challenges related to individual philanthropy vary. HNWIs risk becoming too controlling of their foundations' work, being overconfident, not sufficiently partnering or venturing into more controversial areas of need, or having their motivations questioned. The middle-class donors are critical of existing philanthropic structures and trends, such as insufficient funds to the administration of NGOs, but do not feel they are in a position to change those structures. For the poor, their giving is largely based on their circumstances—the size of their households and their livelihoods—in terms of how much time and money they have to spare.

Due to the challenge of capturing numbers on individual giving, it is widely debated how generous Indians are. Sheth argues that "the 'unorganized giving' is not going to make that much of a difference because all the small giving—which happens elsewhere in the world as well—tends to be very small amounts. When you start adding it up, it won't be substantive" (India Knowledge@Wharton 2011). While the monetary amount may not appear substantive, the different forms of philanthropic behavior among the poor are important within kin and community networks. Further, the more important question is perhaps not how much is given, but whether it is the 'right' kind of giving. As Sheth elaborates, more discussion should emerge around the need for right vehicles to reach the intended recipients—those who really need help.

Philanthropy is both vertical, from the rich to the poor, and horizontal, among the poor. Both types of philanthropy are age-old. While religious giving and ad hoc acts of philanthropy are dominant, there is a range of approaches and philanthropic behaviors at every level, including underlying threads of carefully considered and planned acts. Philanthropy is universal, even if manifested by individuals in a myriad of forms.

Case Studies

Case Study 1. Sunil and Liz Mehta: A Giving High-net-worth Couple

Sunil, the heir of a long line of textile mill owners, was studying in England when he met his future wife Liz. Their story was not a simple one of meeting, falling in love, marrying, and living happily ever after. They were from different backgrounds, and their future paths initially seemed unlikely to converge. For one, Sunil knew that he had to go back to India because of his promise to look after his invalid sister, while Liz had never considered leaving England in her traditional plans for marriage and career. Nevertheless, Liz visited India with Sunil a year after they graduated, and decided to marry him and move to India. As she specialized in education, Liz soon began teaching at the Agha Khan School in India, and Sunil took over the family mill business.

Fast-forward 20 years later: with the advance of technology, the textile mills have closed down and Sunil rents out parts of the mills. Liz looks forward to retirement, but has one final dream project that Sunil promises to help bring into fruition. During her tenure at the school, Liz had been frustrated with the model of education she had to follow, and had long wanted to develop a model of better-quality education. As chance would have it, the Government of India publicly announced at the time that it would like to increase access to education for children, as well as improve the education quality to increase student retention. To add, Sunil visits former textile workers of his mills and asks them to make a wish list of the projects that they would like to see in their community. They unanimously asked for projects that would advance their children's education. Liz's dream would prove to be the project that would not only fulfill the wishes of Sunil's ex-employees but also align with the initiatives of the national government.

In 2004, Sunil and Liz officially launched Muktangan—meaning "freedom," both inner and outer—an education-focused NGO built on the three objectives of children's education, teachers' training, and outreach. First, to improve children's education, Muktangan has implemented an "active-constructive learning" education model in seven schools with 2,600 students. In short, this model puts in place a low student-to-teacher ratio that allows teachers to focus on students as individuals and to shape a curriculum that is relevant to students' lives. In addressing teachers' training, Muktangan has developed a three-year teacher training program, which draws prospects from low socioeconomic areas where the mill workers live. During the first year, the program extensively educates and trains young candidates from the community of workers. Then the newly trained teachers are integrated into a Muktangan school for an internship for the next two years. Here, they learn to apply their knowledge to practical teaching opportunities while being supervised by a full-time teacher. At the same time, they are encouraged to shadow the new recruits. Lastly, Muktangan's outreach program seeks to understand the communities it serves, and chooses to place teachers back in the communities from which they hail. This is incredibly effective, as these teachers are able to relate to the struggles of the low-income students they teach.

At the outset, the couple found five classrooms in a municipal school that were not being used because of roof leakages. In this unlikely place, a preschool program was initiated, children were educated in a manner altogether different from a traditional structure of schooling, and new teachers were trained. The hands-on format of education through play and interaction quickly brought about positive results. The children were curious, eager to learn, and more responsible. Pleased with the results of both the teacher training and children education project, Sunil and Liz requested the government to partner with them. The government provided a cascade of resources and benefits, such as a donation of 27 items for each student, including a school uniform, school bag, lunch box, pencil, pens, raincoat, umbrella, books, boots, socks, handkerchief, and hairband. With more resources, more grades were added, and eventually, they had a full-fledged school with 10 grades. Sunil and Liz were then approached by the MCGM to set up six more preschools that later expanded up to Grade 6. As more grades were added, teacher training became more pivotal than ever, but it was not possible to finance the training of new teachers to keep up with the growing schools given the set resources and funds. It was at this crucial time that Dasra came along.

Dasra describes itself as "India's leading strategic philanthropy foundation working with philanthropists and social entrepreneurs to create large scale social change" (see case study on Dasra in Chapter 6: Trends).[8] Dasra, looking to invest in the field of education, formulated a list of three NGOs that would best apply the investment; Muktangan made the shortlist. Each organization was asked to present on how they would use Dasra's funds, and Muktangan made the pitch that it would extend the training of teachers from one year to three years with a rigorous curriculum. The Giving Circle, a group of philanthropists who work with Dasra on particular development projects, awarded Muktangan enough funds to test its module. The Giving Circle also offered help in professional management. Over time, the Muktangan group developed modules for numerous departments including education, language, social studies, science, Hindi, English, Marathi, and mathematics.

While Muktangan was fortunate that Dasra came along at the right time to make the three-year teachers' training program possible, it faced new complications and challenges with the passage of the Right to Education Act of 2010—which requires that all the teachers in an institution must have a formal teacher's training certificate. For one, to earn an official teacher's training certificate, the prospective teacher must attend an institute that is recognized as wholly devoted to a training program for teachers. Unfortunately, Muktangan does not have such an institute, nor does it feel the need for one, as its training is embedded within the school. Aside from this, the local women who are trained at Muktangan do not have the means to attend a separate institution just to earn an official certificate.

At present, government schools provide the training for teachers, but Muktangan hopes to be involved in this process in the future. Muktangan is tweaking its own model of teachers' training to involve more active forms of learning. By measuring the impact of its active learning prototype on students, Muktangan hopes to produce a convincing argument for the prototype to be used in the future training of government teachers. Sunil has managed to convince members of Dasra to extend its support for five more years. Muktangan continues to look for new channels of funding so that it can help more children obtain a stimulating and meaningful education. In the meanwhile, the teachers at Muktangan remain officially uncertified despite the fact that their teaching transforms and educates hundreds of young minds and instills in them a love of learning. Sunil hopes that the day will soon come when the government recognizes the value of Muktangan's methods of teaching and not only grants the teachers official recognition but adopts Muktangan's teaching model.

Undoubtedly, Muktangan has already made tangible strides in progressing the education of underprivileged children while also empowering women from slum areas by training them and giving them a profession. To further testify to the progress of children's education, one of the authors of this book visited two schools of Muktangan, and was impressed by the way the children were being taught. She walked around the schools, watching the ways children interacted in activities, and asked pertinent questions in class. She then stopped by a teachers' training session. She witnessed how an experienced teacher explained to the trainees how to get students involved in discussions by connecting the concept that needed to be learned with issues relevant to the students' lives and by asking students how the concept related to them. The teacher managed to engage each trainee in a lively yet informative discussion. The trainer went on to differentiate between active and passive learning, emphasizing the importance of active student participation in eliciting curiosity and getting them to construct their own examples and stories to remember concepts.

The author also shared a long conversation with Sunil and Liz, who elaborated on their life story, passions, and day-to-day schedules. Though Sunil and Liz had originally planned to retire and live a leisurely life in their sunset years, they instead found meaning and purpose in fulfilling Liz's dream of establishing a model of quality education. Today, they are working harder than ever and start their days earlier than most people, with Sunil working in administration and Liz in the supervision of teacher training. Parts of the mills that could have been leased out are now used instead to hold classes where children from the community learn and where women from the community teach or learn to teach. Sunil and Liz have diverted their income and their leisure to give children a better education and to give women a fulfilling career. Sunil and Liz are indeed giving HNWIs!

Case Study 2. Rotary Club: A Vehicle for Professional Middle-class Giving

With 1.2 million members and more than 34,000 clubs worldwide, Rotary Clubs can be found in every corner of the world (Rotary International 2014). Originating in Chicago, US, in 1905 and spreading to Asia via Manila, Philippines, in 1919, a Rotary Club is "an organization of business and professional persons united worldwide who provide humanitarian service, encourage high ethical standards in all vocations, and help build goodwill and peace in the world" (Dochterman 2006: 1). Rotary Clubs are widely used by the upwardly mobile Indian professional classes to engage in philanthropy. Each Rotary Club is linked to a larger network at the district and international level, and its commitment to humanitarian service is reflected in programs such as the Rotary Community Corps (a Rotary Club-sponsored group of non-Rotarians who want to help their community through service projects); World Community Service (one club or district provides humanitarian assistance to a project of a club in another country); Literacy Projects; Rotary Volunteers (from the club up to international level); Matching Grants (in which the Rotary Foundation assists Rotary Clubs and districts conduct international service projects); to Health, Hunger, and Humanity Grants—and beyond (Dochterman 2006). It has been noted that Rotary Clubs outside India's largest urban centers are particularly active, with great member engagement through service.

According to a small survey conducted among 18 Rotary Club members in Hyderabad, India, the top two reasons for joining a Rotary Club are opportunities for friendship or fellowship, and trust that money channeled through Rotary is well spent. Individuals must be recruited to join Rotary—meaning they have a sponsor, without whom they would not have the chance to become a Rotarian—which builds the sense of fellowship (Dochterman 2006: 9). The weekly Rotary meetings offer a place for service-minded professionals to meet and build relations. Members feel that helping others brings personal satisfaction and joy, and that collectively as a Rotary Club, they can have a greater impact.

Each Rotary Club determines which projects to focus on. The activities of the surveyed Rotary Club members in Hyderabad included building homes for the homeless through the Housing for Humanity Project; promoting children's education through Interact Clubs; and conducting mega health camps and diabetic camps, led by one of the Rotarians and a team of doctors. Reflecting the giving preferences across India, the surveyed Rotarians expressed greatest interest in education and health (including hygiene, sanitation, and distribution of free medicine) followed by livelihoods, the environment, rural development, care for the elderly and other neglected persons, and slum development. The underlying reasons for these areas of interest vary, but are in part linked to Rotarian vocations—for example, Rotarians who are health-care professionals are interested in extending their expertise to help others, and are involved in the health camps. This relates to one of the four ideals of service outlined in the Object of Rotary, in which "the recognition of the worthiness of all useful occupations, and the dignifying of each Rotarian's occupation as an opportunity to serve society" (Dochterman 2006: 3). As Rotary Clubs are organizations for professionals, members are more likely to be doctors, bankers, or corporate managers than grassroots social welfare workers. Certainly, the members' vocations affect individual member and club interests. In addition to service through the club, a few of the surveyed Rotarians run their own small NGOs or trusts outside their regular work.

As middle- and upper-class professionals, Rotarians are well aware of the importance of accountability and how it can be difficult to achieve in India. Reflecting on the challenges to philanthropy in India, middle-class donors stated that it is difficult to assess the credibility of recipient NGOs, how those NGOs spend funds, and their ability to sufficiently monitor activities. Other challenges in philanthropy cited were the status of government laws and bureaucracy, the existing 'corporate system,' a sense that most individuals are only focused on making money, a growing gap between the rich and the poor, and the need to change attitudes in society (and the government). Others noted that many people fail to give in a constructive way, and struggle to find the right channels to give, which results in acts that do not maximize the benefits for the recipient.

Conversely, when asked about what factors could further enable giving in India, Rotarians responded that examples of good role models, greater transparency of NGOs, and improved collaboration and speed on part of the government would help. It was also noted that organizations such as Rotary Clubs are very important because they formalize giving through reliable and trusted channels. One respondent—certainly not alone— said that having more funds would enable greater donations by simultaneously touching upon the perceived bottleneck of individuals focusing too much on wealth creation, and the tension between when to earn and when to give.

Offering their insights on the status of philanthropy in India today, survey respondents were generally positive and said the status was improving, although responses were divided over whether the improvement was gradual or at a natural speed, or faster than expected. At the same time, some noted that current levels of philanthropy are inadequate and there is a long road ahead. While some Rotarians felt that individuals seek publicity more than real impact through their charitable acts, other Rotarians felt that there are many genuine, good-intentioned individuals who are giving. The survey respondents unanimously agreed that there is a need for more constructive approaches and institutions, support and effective legislation from the government, and increased emphasis on contributing time and talent, not just funds.

From this small survey of one Rotary Club, we can see that middle-class philanthropists mirror high-net-worth donors in their application of vocational skills and preference for education and health initiatives. They also face some of the same challenges that donors of any income level face, namely finding trustworthy and accountable partners to channel their funds. It is interesting that in this small, anonymous sample, there was no direct mention of tax benefits as an incentive for donating; clearly, motivation comes from other sources. It is evident that these middle-class philanthropists, by joining Rotary Club and attending its frequent activities, are looking to give not only their money but also their time and skills, and finding community and fellowship along the way.

Case Study 3. Sitabai: The "Giving" Low-net-worth Individual

In 2006, the local government authorities in Igatpuri—a small town a few hours' drive away from Mumbai, Maharashtra—issued a circular pushing for the establishment of an anganwadi (a preprimary center for children) in the village of Jambhwadi, Igatpuri. When representatives of Aseema, a well-known NGO in Maharashtra (featured as a case study in Chapter 2), heard that the village lacked a preprimary center and that the local government had recognized this need and was looking for assistance in setting one up, they stepped up to fill this gap. Aseema had started as a primary school for street children in Bandra, a suburb of Mumbai, and had grown into a full-fledged school after overcoming initial struggles. Dilbur, the founder of Aseema, visited the education office in Igatpuri and asked if the government was providing a room or any land to start the anganwadi. While the government authorities insisted that the village was in dire need of a learning center for the young, they were straightforward in their refusal to provide any facilities. After repeatedly being told "it should be done in a villager's home," Dilbur approached the villagers. The villagers acknowledged the need for an 'anganwadi' and offered to take turns and open their homes as a temporary 'anganwadi' during the day. This arrangement worked for a while, but the numbers of children who wanted to attend an anganwadi grew. The children were packed into the villagers' small homes in the sweltering heat, and were constantly distracted by the villagers' movements. Though Aseema did manage to run a modicum of an anganwadi for a while, it did not produce the desired results— the children were hardly learning.

Dilbur soon recognized that the existing facilities were inadequate to accommodate the increasing number of young children willing and ready to learn, and that the only way to run a successful anganwadi was to build new facilities in the village. Dilbur and her entourage of helpers scoped the village in order to gauge the availability of land as well as cost. To their dismay, they found that the acquisition of available land was not only costly but also bound by rules requiring tribal land to stay in tribal hands. Just as Dilbur began losing hope, an old tribal woman named Sitabai approached her. Dilbur immediately recognized her as one of the women who had been trailing her team when they made their rounds looking for land. She said to Dilbur: "I hear that you have come here to educate the children of our village and are looking for a place to do so." She then offered to give Aseema a portion of her land. "I grow my nachni (a local crop) here," she said. "But I don't need all this land; you can have a portion to build an anganwadi."

Dilbur was very touched, but being a former lawyer, she wanted to make sure that everything was legitimate and that Sitabai was indeed willing and able to make her offer. She discovered that Sitabai was a member of the Adivasi tribe, a group often lumped with 'schedule' classes that are the most downtrodden. Despite government calls for universal education, these groups have traditionally been neglected, and lack education as well as opportunities to better themselves (Arvind 2009). Sitabai—a widow who lived with her son and daughter-in-law and their children—had always been interested in education and believed that her grandchildren needed education in order to better their lot. More importantly, she believed that her tribe members would remain backward unless they received education. She had followed Dilbur's group around to ascertain how she felt about them and to make sure they would deliver on their promise of education. After listening to Dilbur voice her determination to bring an anganwadi to the village, Sitabai readily offered a large part of her land. She was especially excited for her four grandchildren, who were eager to attend the new anganwadi. Sitabai's son, who endorsed her beliefs, accepted her wishes to give up a part of the family land.

Sitabai, who was old and in poor health at the time, lived long enough to see the anganwadi be built, and was invited as the chief guest at the inauguration of the anganwadi that was named after her. She died soon afterwards, we are told, with a smile on her face. Her four grandchildren attend the Sitabai Anganwadi today.

Case Study 4. Short Stories and Insights from Giving at the Bottom of Pyramid

Philanthropy at the bottom of the pyramid is often unassuming, personal, community-oriented, and particularly moving given the circumstances. While there are many millions of such stories that could be told, this case study touches upon five short examples.

1. **Women-organized SHGs** in Narampet (in the Warangal district of Andhra Pradesh) contribute up to INR 5 per month (approx $0.08) toward providing rice and necessary groceries to a shelter where 10 children and eight elderly stay. The women also donate clothes. The town-level federation of SHGs manages the shelter and takes care to ensure the basic needs of the children are met. Further, the members of the federation want to use the income some members make from selling jute bags toward providing a home for the needy and those in vulnerable situations. These women, who have limited resources themselves, leverage their power as a group to assist those even less fortunate within their community. This is a prime example of horizontal philanthropy.

2. **R. Sekar** is a tea shop owner in Madurai, Tamil Nadu. In his quiet manner, Sekar helps struggling people afford the things they need whenever he can. Sekar gives tea and biscuits to Esaki, who is affected by leprosy, whenever he comes by the shop; sends milk and fruits to eight-year-old Sivatharini, who is diagnosed with blood cancer, when she is in the hospital or recovering at home; and provides stationery items, books, school uniforms, lunch boxes, and other school items to poor students (Basu 2013). He also sends five liter of milk along with buns and other savory foods to three homes for special and orphaned children every Friday. While every resident in the area knows of Sekar and his 35-year-old tea shop business, not many know of Sekar's charity work. Having experienced a difficult childhood where it was hard to get even one meal a day for the family, Sekar says he is inspired to do a bit of charity because it spreads happiness to others (Basu 2013). He feels no need to keep account of how much he gives to others. In his own words:

There are so many people with so much money but either do not have the time or the inclination to help. God gives us in his own way and we find our ways to help others... I am happy with what I have and can do with even less. I do not need more.

3. **Kanthimathi**, the 64-year-old wife of an ailing tailor, has been at the receiving end of charity most of her life, but gives back to the community with her time and effort (Basu 2014). Every day for the last 12 years, she has woken up early to cook a minimum of 10 kg of rice along with sambar, *poriyal*, and buttermilk—and an extra sweet dish on festive occasions. Outside the BSNL Exchange office in Madurai, Kanthimathi hands out the food to the hungry, the poor, and the diseased who show up. Her efforts continue the tradition begun by social worker Siva Anbanandan, whom Kanthimathi met 12 years ago at that very location. She instantly volunteered to help him cook and hand out food to those in need, and has done so ever since. Kanthimathi does not have the means to feed the poor, but receives help from the community to do so. One community member buys the vegetables, another donates the rice and oil, some nearby shopkeepers pool resources, and an auto driver and two young boys help her transport the food. It is an unusual sort of bonding, especially as Kanthimathi does not know anything about the people who turn up to eat the midday meal. For her it is simple: "Once you get a person to smile as they eat my homely cooked food," she says, "my day is fulfilled" (Basu 2014).

4. **Raghu Makwana** contracted polio at a young age and, not wanting to be a burden on his parents who were farm laborers, left home at age 20 for Ahmedabad (Chaudhari 2011; Sthalekar 2014). Living on the streets of Ahmedabad, Makwana was deeply moved by the hardships of others who had even less than he did, and resolved to one day help them (Agrawal 2011). He later did this by starting a tiffin service (called 'Tyaag Nu Tiffin' or Food of Sacrifice) for the people living in slums and on roads. Makwana rode around on his hand tricycle and delivered hand-cooked meals at 12:30 p.m. and 7:30 p.m. every day; he himself ate only once the deliveries were done (Agrawal 2011; Chaudhari 2011). One of his many kind endeavors was the tulsi project: whenever

he learned of a family in the nearby slums with some dispute or violent abuse, Makwana would visit them—even if they were complete strangers to him—to spread good cheer, share stories, talk about wise saints or recite a prayer, and then present them with a tulsi plant (Agrawal 2011). The hundreds of holy tulsi plants that he gave out are viewed as a blessing and a reminder of his spirit (Agrawal 2011; Sthalekar 2014). Raghu humbly noted, "I'm not doing anything great. I'm not on a mission to change the world. God has been very kind to me in my struggle to survive. Now it is my turn to repay the kindness by helping other needy human beings" (Chaudhari 2011). While Makwana tragically died in a road accident at age 29, his second nature for kindness earned him the nickname 'Love Warrior' (Sthalekar 2014), and he is fondly remembered by those he touched.

5. **Santosh Thorat** moved to Mumbai from a village about 300 miles away to find work, piecing together odd jobs in the building trades and as a temporary guard to support his family (Barnes 2010). A young father of five, Thorat picked up an extra day's work one day with a bulldozing crew as a temporary security guard to quell protesters in Mandala, a slum near his own home. The next day, he found out the assignment was to bulldoze his own neighborhood. He pleaded with his bosses to not flatten his house, and for two days, they knocked down other parts of the slum. On the third day, Thorat was told to take some time off, during which they demolished his house, leaving his family to live in a tent by the fourth day (Barnes 2010). This happened during the peak of Mumbai's demolition drive in December 2004, and Thorat decided to take action, asking "What if the funds used to bring down slums were put toward developing them instead?" He became a leader and caretaker of his 3,000-household slum (working alongside the organization 'Ghar Bachao Ghar Banao Andolan' or Save the House, Build the House Movement). The intensity of the housing protests has forced the state government to significantly subside the demolition drive. By January 2005, Thorat was helping reconstruct the homes in his own community and around the city. He also helped bring a computer center, sewing center, a new school, and 350 ration cards for subsidized food to his slum (Barnes

2010). As an insider, he became an effective leader, though he dismisses the idea that anybody is the leader. Even though Thorat says he cannot afford to be an activist every day, people keep asking him for assistance amid the threat of the return of the demolition crew—so he has continued to protest. His quiet form of leadership has helped save the homes of many.

Case Study Commentary

These narratives reflect different approaches and forms of individual philanthropy, and confirm the generosity of individuals at every level of the socioeconomic ladder. Many HNWIs prefer to establish and monitor their own organizations, and directly act upon their specific philanthropic visions. The Muktangan case illustrates this tendency, as Sunil and Liz pursued extensive philanthropic activities after generating substantial wealth, and chose to focus on education, which is a widely acknowledged area of need and of personal interest to many wealthy founders. On the other hand, middle-class professionals—who do not have the time or resources to pursue their own philanthropic initiatives, and place high value on fellowship and accountability—give through the Rotary Club or other groups to make a consolidated impact.

Philanthropy at the bottom of the pyramid occurs on a much smaller scale, often in response to a direct need. The acts are unassuming, and the individuals are good-hearted and expect nothing in return. Proportionally, they give a lot more than wealthier individuals in terms of time and resources. The case of Sitabai—who donated a portion of her land so that an anganwadi could be built—is a perfect example. The acts of charity are personal to these givers, who have experienced poverty firsthand. They are often informal and loosely organized, but may be carrying on a tradition. These few examples also illustrate that human goodwill can overcome practical limitations—as individuals with small, unstable incomes are still willing to give to others. While often overlooked, philanthropy continues to take place across all strata of Indian society.

4

Corporate Giving

In short, we will move our business from the transactional to the transformational. We are seeing that creating shared value is a powerful business strategy that can deliver both profit and social impact. In the long run, it is perhaps the most sustainable form of corporate philanthropy.

Anand G. Mahindra
Chairman and Managing Director
Mahindra Group

Charitable giving in India has traditionally been a personal matter, and Chapter 3 illustrates how people of all social classes and castes practice philanthropy on an individual and family level. In some ways, families in India represent micro-socioeconomic systems that are strongly entrenched in their parochial or religious communities, as they primarily give to the indigent in these communities. Larger donations by wealthy entrepreneurial families are more than often channeled into the most preferred activity: temple building.

Corporate India, still largely family owned and managed, also actively partakes in charitable works. With a few major exceptions (the Tatas, Murugappas, Birlas, and Godrejs), families and companies have generally targeted their philanthropy to take care of their employees' needs, ranging from education to health-care needs. Because many Indian businesses are family controlled, there is often an overlap between family philanthropy and corporate philanthropy.

In the past three decades, however, Indian corporate philanthropy has started to shift away from traditional forms that were inward and narrowly focused to forms that are more outward and broadly focused. For example, many corporations have recently rechanneled their giving toward local neighborhoods and the poor living in the vicinity of their factories or office buildings. More and more, corporations are also focusing their philanthropy on the amelioration of local environmental problems and preservation of local historical buildings or artifacts.

Globally, corporate philanthropy is a growing phenomenon, especially with the advent of large multinational corporations, and it is increasing in scope and diversity under the mantle of CSR. In many developing countries, wealthy corporations are now expected to engage in CSR to address local needs (Logsdon et al. 1990; Wang and Qian 2011). A recent review of the literature on the research of corporate philanthropy by Arthur Gautier and Anne-Claire Pache in the *Journal of Business Ethics* (Gautier and Pache 2013) finds that only a few decades ago, such corporate giving was considered "an illegitimate practice" (Davis 1973; Friedman 1970), whereas today, it is considered illegitimate not to do so (Seghers 2007). Further, Gautier and Pache (2013) find that corporate philanthropy is now pervasive in small- and medium-sized enterprises worldwide, not only large multinationals.

History of CSR in India

CSR, practiced in full force by many large- and medium-sized enterprises and by most multinationals, is not a new phenomenon in India. It has appeared in many guises since businesses first arose. Businesses have long engaged in philanthropy and charity, ranging from old practices of giving alms to beggars and holy men approaching storefronts, to religious offerings with the expectation of accruing blessings for their businesses. Merchants' charitable practices also involved keeping money and resources aside for the needy, providing relief in times of natural calamities, building temples, and planting trees.

According to the prevalent Hindu Vedic philosophy, the principal role of money was to serve the needs of society, thus donating to the welfare of others was perceived as the best use of money. Depending on the caste and class of the merchants, motivations varied and were often influenced by religious beliefs of practicing daan (donation, alms, and service without pay) among Hindus, zakat among the Muslims, and *tithing* among the Christians. CSR in India is still influenced by these traditions, which linger especially in the psyche of businesses that are family owned.

According to Muniapan and Dass's (2008) research on Indian Vedic texts, business is perceived as a "legitimate and an integral part of society" and "it should create wealth for the society through the right means of action. '*Sarva Loka Hitam*' in the Vedic literature referred to 'well-being of stakeholders.' This means an ethical and social responsibility system must be fundamental and functional in business undertakings" (p. 415). Muniapan and Dass assert this makes business sense because a corporation that pursues ethically and socially responsible actions "would sustain long-term advantages and obtain profits." They point the reader to the following quote from the Vedic literature:

> May we together shield each other and may we not be envious towards each other. Wealth is essentially a tool and its continuous flow must serve the welfare of the society to achieve the common good of the society. (Atharva Veda 3-24-5)

The embedding of deeply spiritual values in Indian philosophy underpinned the practice of CSR, which was localized and largely motivated by religious beliefs.

The colonial rule of the British beginning in the late 1800s changed India's economic, social, and political systems—and the way Indian businesses practiced philanthropy. Colonial rule during the two world wars encouraged trade and growth of industry in India. Under the influence of the British colonial rulers, a few families from native merchant communities such as the Jejeebhoy, Tata, Birla, Bajaj, Godrej, Shriram, Singhania, Modi, and Mahindra founded homegrown industries (Sharma 2009). The British encouraged the wealthy and elitist merchant classes to espouse British institutions of philanthropy, and incentivized their philanthropic efforts by offering knighthood and lightening their tax burdens (Sundar 2000).

The early philanthropic efforts of elite merchants resulted in the construction of hospitals, colleges, and orphanages, as well as the promotion of art and culture. The efforts to emulate their colonial rulers, in large part, was driven by a desire to be treated as equals, secure the rulers' goodwill, and enhance their own reputation among the local population (as illustrated in the case study that follows). Their later efforts involved setting up trusts and endowments to support education (building schools and universities) and health care (hospitals and clinics) on a long-term basis—forms of philanthropy that were a result of British influence.

During the struggle for Independence, many of these industrialists promoted a variety of social reforms such as the removal of 'untouchability' and 'widow-burning.' They were also enormously influenced by Mahatma Gandhi's concept of trusteeship wherein the wealthy are regarded as trustees of their assets (including their knowledge and skills), provided they conduct themselves in an ethical and socially responsible way. The concept required trustees to manage their assets in the best possible way, take only a part of the profit for themselves, and dedicate the remaining profit for the betterment of the society (Upadhyaya 1976).

From Indian Independence in 1947 onward, businesses responded actively to their role in nation-building and promoting social and economic development. Business leaders, who had taken on roles as freedom fighters pre-Independence, continued to support many of the social reforms proposed by Gandhi as social activists at the local and national level. As India progressed to an independent democracy, many of the indigenous industrialists who had worked for Independence were seen as partners of the government in promoting national welfare and nation-building.

Gandhi's theory of trusteeship was instrumental in the foundation of formal CSR in India. His goals were to ensure both social and economic development went hand in hand. Sharma (2009) writes that:

> Gandhi felt that the capitalist[s] [should] be treated as trustees of the assets vested with them—provided they conduct themselves in a socially responsible way. This demanded that they manage the assets in the best possible way, take a part of the profit to sustain themselves and dedicate the remaining profit for the uplift of the society. (p. 1519)

Indeed, nation-building and promoting socioeconomic development also became the foremost goals of India's ruling party during the 20th century—this included the removal of the caste system and the development of rural areas.

The early successful Indian industrialists, such as Mr J. R. D. Tata, Mr Birla, and others, were instrumental in institutionalizing social responsibilities within their businesses. The Tata group became a leader in this respect. In 1951, Mr J. R. D. Tata alerted the country on the risks of uncontrolled population growth, and advocated for increased family planning education especially among the rural poor. As a result of his advocacy, many chambers of commerce throughout India began actively encouraging its members to participate in the efforts for agricultural reform, rural development, and family planning.

Jawaharlal Nehru, the first prime minister of a newly Independent India, was acutely aware of the social welfare needs of the nation. He made economic development a priority for the government through public sector undertakings, often referred to as public sector units (PSUs), and laid out a clear path for economic development. Using PSUs as an instrument for domestic economic growth, the government played a large hand in the economy. This state-sponsored economic development saw the rise of PSUs in various sectors such as heavy industries, mining, steel, shipping, aviation, petroleum, and equipment manufacturing. The PSUs were conceived and operated according to India's socialist ideals and the stated purposes of promoting the public good and paying attention to the reduction of inequities in society. As such, PSUs can be seen as the earliest manifestations of CSR in India to which large enterprises subscribed.

Over the years, "PSU operations have extended to a wide range of activities including manufacturing, engineering, steel, heavy machinery, machine tools, fertilizers, drugs, textiles, pharmaceuticals, petro-chemicals, extraction and refining of crude oil; services such as telecommunication, trading, tourism and warehousing; and a range of consultancy services" (Deloitte and Touche 2010: 3).

In this mixed economy, the government ran many of the key industries as PSUs. The prime minister openly and explicitly promoted a "statist" model of CSR in the 1950s, which focused on community and worker relationships. The model was protected under labor laws and newly adopted management principles, and was accompanied by a mandate to pay attention to job creation, employee pensions, and other benefits. Furthermore, PSUs were required to act responsibly in the communities in which they were located. This trend of PSUs showing strong commitment to social causes and undertaking socially responsible businesses continued despite the trend toward privatization that followed. PSUs such as Bharat Heavy Electrical Limited (BHEL), National Thermal Power Corporation (NTPC) Limited, and Oil and Natural Gas Corporation (ONGC) Limited thus sustained a long tradition of social responsibility, and made a significant impact on the development of poorer and undeveloped regions in India through their efforts to reduce mass unemployment and provide healthy working conditions, job security, health-care benefits, education benefits, and pensions to their employees.

The rise of PSUs gave a boost to the early industrialists who, by helping the government promote its development policies, became large and profitable enterprises with lucrative government contracts. During this time, the social responsibilities undertaken by PSUs influenced the corporate sector. Records from the 1960s show reports and seminars organized around the social responsibilities of business. The 1965 conference was chaired by Lal Bahadur Shastri, the second prime minister of India, and was attended by leading politicians, industrialists (private sector, public sector, and PSUs), policy makers, and trade unionists. It issued the following declaration on the social responsibilities of businesses:

> [A business has a] responsibility to itself, to its customers, workers, shareholders and the community.... [E]very enterprise, no matter how large or small, must, if it is to enjoy confidence and respect, seek actively to discharge its responsibilities in all directions ... and not to one or two groups, such as shareholders or workers, at the expense of community and consumer. [A] business must be just and humane, as well as efficient and dynamic. (Mohan 2001: 110)

The conference records further show a strong focus on a multi-stakeholder approach with business regarded as a "corporate citizen...[who] is esteemed and judged by its actions in relation to the community of which it is a member, as well as by its economic performance" (Mohan 2001: 110). The influence of Mahatma Gandhi's philosophy of trusteeship is also prevalent in the records, which promote voluntary codes of conduct that focus on long-term gain rather than short-term profits, with a mandate to work with the government in the task of nation-building. This required 'public meetings' with multi-stakeholder dialogue, and necessitated a social audit for an assessment of firms' corporate social performance. Finally, employers were exhorted to ensure that the basic needs— housing, sanitation, education, and health care—of their employees and their communities were met.

Despite Prime Minister Jawaharlal Nehru's optimistic expectations for the role of PSUs in nation-building, rural economic development, and social responsibilities, things went awry. Politicians used PSUs as easy channels to create jobs for their constituents and give out political patronage, rendering the PSUs inefficient, overstaffed, and bureaucratic. As PSUs became more entangled in politics and plagued with corruption and management inefficiencies, many pushed for the privatization of PSUs in the late 1980s and 1990s (Sharma 2009). Nevertheless, Indian PSUs did and continue to make a major contribution to the development of undeveloped or underdeveloped regions. For a period after Independence, PSUs successfully increased employment and provided employees with reasonable jobs that gave them economic security and benefits such as pensions, health care, and education (Sharma 2009).

Family Businesses and Corporate Philanthropy and Beyond

Family businesses, small and large, dominate the business scene in India; according to one estimate, 85 percent of all Indian businesses are family owned. Because family culture is highly enmeshed in Indian business culture, families often play a very active role in the businesses' decisions regarding charitable giving. Typically, a business supports some self-initiated charitable endeavor through a fixed percentage of its surplus income and/or other investment income.

Very often, family members—primarily women and nonworking family members—were encouraged to take an active part in the trusteeship role, and were expected to take up various philanthropic initiatives toward helping the poor and underprivileged in the community. 'Sewa,' meaning 'service to others,' is a core tenet of Indian scriptures, and it was thought to bring success to both the business and the family. Thus, family members took an active part in the businesses' philanthropic activities; despite little or no training, they were involved in the direct disbursement of philanthropy, often in the form of cash donations, scholarships for education, and health care to the indigent (Ramachandran 2010).

Many large business conglomerates, especially those established before Independence, prospered and were highly involved in philanthropy. At the turn of the century, many business leaders gradually transformed their informal and ad hoc philanthropy to more formal structures by setting up trusts and endowments. These trusts were used to support schools, colleges, hospitals, orphanages, and the arts. As the struggle for Independence took a stronghold under the increasing influence of Mahatma Gandhi's philosophy and practice, the leading industrialists of India became freedom fighters and actively participated in social reform movements (Mohan 2001). These included the fight to abolish the practices of untouchability and promote equity through women's empowerment and education.

Family businesses (Tata, Godrej, Birla, etc.) and nonfamily-owned businesses (Hindustan Lever, Larsen & Toubro, etc.) were highly involved in these efforts. On a larger scale, the Birlas donated to the freedom movement, the Godrej family donated to the Tilak Fund for the abolishment of untouchability, and the Tatas and the Murugappas donated to the establishment of hospitals and schools. On a smaller scale, the Usha Martin Group, makers of wire ropes, donated to help Jharkhand villagers—a region where the company had its roots (Ramachandran 2010).

As they prospered, many previously family-owned businesses transformed from being run by family members to becoming professionalized. Larger business were less likely to be run by the families who owned them, and more likely to be run by professional managers who were accountable to the shareholders. As a result, the way that corporate philanthropy was practiced and managed also saw a change. The businesses' practice of philanthropy was professionalized, and more family foundations and trusts (and NGOs) were set up to provide relief to poor communities (Mohan 2001). In many of these cases, family members often continued to take an active part in deciding the range of philanthropic activities, although they recruited nonfamily and qualified professionals to develop structure, systems, and processes for successful execution and management of these philanthropic activities (Ramachandran 2010). Furthermore, they demanded higher accountability and transparency from the organizations and NGOs they funded.

Many large- and medium-sized businesses engage in philanthropic activities through the creation of family foundations and NGOs, and it is not unusual to see some family members participate as trustees. Nevertheless, with increased professionalization by managers, decisions regarding philanthropy are being taken out of the family arena and relegated to departments or managers either in the public relations, marketing, or social responsibility departments. Furthermore, the mantra of efficiency that is paramount in businesses' success was applied to their philanthropic practices, resulting in a strong preference for projects that were tangible with measurable outputs in the short-to-medium term.

The use of metrics and strategic planning has transformed corporate giving from its traditional roots to another business venture for corporations. Furthermore, many Western-based tenets of CSR that see businesses as being socially responsible actors have entered into

India. These CSR practices include instituting a triple bottom line in annual reports that show the firm's contribution not only to shareholder financial value but also to social and environmental initiatives. The introduction of the social and environmental bottom lines gave an impetus to corporations to become more strategic and encompass longer-term impacts in their CSR agenda. The triple bottom lines, it was argued, would eventually make the company sustainable in the future and ensure its profitability and shareholder value in the future. Indeed, CSR was recognized as essentially instrumental to corporations early on, as seen in the statement by Friedman (1970):

> It will be in the long run interest of a corporation that is a major employer in a small community to devote resources to providing amenities to that community or to improving its government. That makes it easier to attract desirable employees, it may reduce the wage bill or lessen losses from pilferage and sabotage or have other worthwhile effects.

From a purely financial shareholder perspective, investments in social demands that could produce an increase of the shareholder value are rational and should be undertaken. CSR can ensure businesses a reputational advantage and, in the long term, increase its financial bottom line, which Jensen (2000) calls 'enlightened value maximization.'

Since the 1990s, CSR practices in India have evolved into a more direct engagement of business in mainstream socioeconomic development, which was largely motivated by both public and government expectations. Indeed, a 1997 survey of 650 randomly selected companies from the top 2,000 companies across India—conducted by the Social and Rural Research Institute of the Indian Market Research Bureau—found that most CEOs acknowledge that companies have a social responsibility. A majority of them (81 percent) had actively supported social activities on an ongoing basis and with long-term commitment.

Thus, one can argue that some form of CSR has been practiced by Indian businesses for a long time—just under different frameworks. Corporate giving evolved from the trusteeship model promoted by Mahatma Gandhi, and the statist model by Prime Minister Jawaharlal Nehru of PSUs, to the CSR model that has resulted in the professionalization of corporate giving and adoption of global principles of CSR and triple bottom lines (Sharma 2009; Sundar

2000). A recent trend in CSR is the rights-based approach, especially in the global marketplace (Cassel 2001). The UN Global Compact, which includes principles in the areas of human rights, labor, and the environment, is considered a basis for such an approach to CSR being undertaken by businesses worldwide.

CSR in India: Four-model Summary

Kumar et al. (2004) summarized the historical and current trends of India's experience with CSR, and presented four models of CSR in the Indian context (see Table 4.1). First, the CSR model historically encompassed corporate philanthropy and the Gandhian ethical/trusteeship model, which was particularly prevalent in family-run firms; the dominant mode of giving was donations in cash or kind, followed by community investment in trusts, and provision of essential services related to health and education.

Table 4.1:
Four models of CSR

Model	Economic and Social Context	Focus	Champions
Ethical/ Trusteeship	British colonial rule Independence movement	CSR is a voluntary commitment by companies to public welfare and nation-building	Mahatma Gandhi
Statist	Socialist and mixed economy Large public sector and state-owned companies	State ownership and legal requirements influence CSR	Jawaharlal Nehru
Liberal	Economic privatization and deregulation professionalization	CSR limited to the needs of private owners (shareholders)	Milton Friedman
Stakeholder	Globalization Citizen and stakeholder activism	CSR responds to the needs of stakeholders, customers, employees, communities	R. Edward Freeman

Source: Adapted from Kumar et al. (2004: 8). Prepared by the authors.

With strong government intervention post-Independence, the statist model came into existence. The prime example is the dominating presence of PSUs in the heavy industry and services sector. Changes in the economic landscape, from a highly regulated market to a liberalized environment, led to a growing and prosperous economy, and influenced CSR activities. Then came the period of globalization with the rise of multinationals. During this period, there was increased input from active stakeholders (workers and the community), whose interests were hitherto ignored. Concerns of multi-stakeholder groups and their demands eventually influenced corporations to address larger community-based issues and issues of 'sustainability' with a focus on social equity, environmental protection, and human rights.

CSR Trends

According to the World Bank, Indian PSUs' spending on CSR from 2009 to 2010 was about $700 million, while Indian companies' CSR spending for the year 2009–2010 was $7.5 billion. In an attempt to understand the factors that presented themselves as the drivers and barriers of these CSR efforts, Arora and Puranik (2004) conducted surveys across different organizations and their various stakeholders. The findings, first and foremost, reveal an increase in the number of companies undertaking CSR activities as compared to previous decades. This was attributed to "an enabling corporate environment that is more conscious of the implications of involvement of business in CSR activities with specific reference to the Indian context" (p. 94).

In most firms, the CSR initiatives came from the CEOs, except in the case of PSUs where the impetus was government-established directives, which required PSUs to undertake CSR activities. Interestingly for privately controlled corporations, the principal driver in undertaking CSR was a philanthropic motive, which was then followed by a reputation-enhancing motive. Building employee morale and behaving ethically were less likely to be cited as motives. For PSUs, the motives for government regulation lay in socialist ideals of the public good and nation-building. As expected, the CSR activities were more present in older firms with larger revenues than smaller firms or more recent start-ups.

Stakeholder (workers, company executives, and the general public) surveys found that most Indians thought the main goal of business should be:

> providing good products and cheaper prices, ensuring that operations are environmentally friendly, treating employees fairly without any discrimination based on gender, race, or religion, and applying labour standards globally. More than 60% of the general public feel that companies should also be held responsible for bridging the gap between the rich and the poor, reducing human rights abuses, solving social problems, and increasing economic stability. (Kumar et al. 2001: 19)

Interestingly enough, despite the general public's high expectations of firms' CSR activities, CSR is not the standard by which the public judges the firm; firms are more likely to be judged on their brand quality and the reputation of the firm.

Some barriers to undertaking CSR activities were the government's bureaucratic, unclear, and ineffective policies combined with poor records of monitoring, complicated tax systems, and poor infrastructure (Prakash-Mani 2002). Other surveys stressed the difficulties that came with the evolution of CSR activities from the passive philanthropy model to newer modes of CSR, especially those dealing with gender parity, human rights, and environmental standards—as these are more complex undertakings that require more effort and risk-taking than a cash donation.

Government and CSR in India

The Indian government has directly and indirectly played a role in the development of CSR both in the public and private arena. In the private sector, the government has played a direct role through the state-run PSUs. It has formal guidelines, including legislation on the CSR activities of PSUs, what constitutes CSR, and what percentage of profits PSUs should devote to CSR. For example, the Voluntary Guidelines issued in 2009 and revised in 2011 by the Ministry on corporate governance and CSR—the National Voluntary Guidelines on Social Environmental and Economic Responsibilities of Business— put forth what 'business responsibilities' are in the context of PSUs.

The Government of India created an all-inclusive proposal for the contribution of businesses toward social well-being and made clear its expectations. For example, the guidelines require that the financial budget of CSR and sustainability activities is based on the profitability of the company. If the after-tax profits of the company (in the previous year) ranged from INR 100 crore ($16.36 million) to INR 500 crore ($81.78 million), companies should designate 2–3 percent to CSR; and if the after-tax profits are above INR 500 crore, 1–2 percent should be designated to CSR. Loss-making companies are not required to allocate funds for CSR activities in the years when they incur losses.

Furthermore, if companies do not spend the allocated budget, it must be carried over to the next fiscal year; companies must disclose reasons of not utilizing their full CSR budget. There exist additional guidelines with respect to the CSR projects that companies undertake in regard to emergency relief, development of backward districts, and environment sustainability. The document also outlines the governance relationships between all of the stakeholders, and requires that all PSUs put in a section showing their CSR activities in their annual report.

In light of the increasing number of highly profitable corporations that have emerged since economic liberalization, the Government of India has decided that these enterprises should also be required to contribute to the public good and nation-building, especially in the underdeveloped parts of India. Indeed, the guidelines for the PSUs served as a forerunner to the design of Section 135 of the Companies Act recently introduced by the government (Government of India 2010).

The Companies Act, 2013 Clause 135, which was passed in August 2013 after much debate by Parliament, requires profitable companies, including PSUs, with revenues of INR 1,000 crore ($163.57 million) or more—or net worth of INR 500 crore or more or net profit of INR 5 crore ($817,860) or more—to engage in CSR. They are required to spend a minimum of 2 percent of their average net profit over the next three years annually on CSR activities. This is a mandatory CSR spending rule effective from the fiscal year 2014–2015 onward. According to *Forbes India*, The Companies Bill, Clause 135, will impact nearly 3,000 companies (Ernst & Young 2013).

Although the companies will retain the right to choose which projects to support, the project must come from a list of eligible CSR areas defined by the government as:

eradicating extreme hunger and poverty; promotion of education; promoting gender equality and empowering women; reducing child mortality and improving maternal health; combating human immunodeficiency virus, acquired immune deficiency syndrome, malaria and other diseases; ensuring environmental sustainability; employment enhancing vocational skills; social business projects; contribution to the Prime Minister's National Relief Fund or any other fund set up by the Central Government or the State Governments for socio-economic development and relief and funds for the welfare of the Scheduled Castes, the Scheduled Tribes, other backward classes, minorities and women; and such other matters as may be prescribed. (Seddon 2013)

The government has considered several ways of enforcing this legislation, including a financial penalty on those profit-making companies that underutilize their CSR budget allocation. The government has authorized that all underutilized funds will go to a central fund controlled by a board of members to use for designated purposes. The government is further committed to "transparency and disclosure," and requires disclosure of all CSR activities; thus, this allows the general public to be final arbitrators of the mandated CSR activities undertaken by companies.

However, as pointed out by some commentators,

more than half of the profits after tax available from companies on the 2012 Economic Times 500 list of India's largest listed companies are in industries that face limited competition to meet critical needs (such as shipping or refining), don't depend on everyday goodwill for their brand (such as steel or cement), or simply have a reputation that dwarfs attention to CSR (such as mining). What's more, three-quarters of India's companies are family-owned or promoted, according to Chandrajit Banerjee, Director-General of the Confederation of Indian Industry, and it's hard to see how disclosing failure to meet CSR spend at the Annual General Meeting of this audience would be a threat. (Seddon 2013)

Conclusion: Forces of Change

While corporate philanthropy has existed for many centuries in some form or another, this chapter focused on the corporate philanthropic trends in India pre- and post-Independence. Under the influence of cultural and religious imperatives, the context for corporate philanthropy and philanthropy in general has flourished. Although the forms of philanthropy have changed over the years and have been influenced by government policies, there has been a constant source of largesse from the corporate sector to the public good. This concluding section focuses on the forces that have influenced corporate philanthropy, and briefly summarizes the changes in the traditional practices of Indian corporate philanthropy. During the pre-Independent era, religious imperatives mostly compelled businesses to practice philanthropy. In addition, many business leaders were influenced by British philanthropic cultural practices of building schools and hospitals, and emulated the practices to gain favor in the eyes of the colonial rulers. After gaining Independence, the task of nation-building and Mahatma Gandhi's philosophy became the key forces that propelled charitable corporate behavior. In addition, the central government's nation-building agenda put in place PSUs with built-in social responsibilities, which in turn influenced corporate leaders' philanthropy.

With economic liberalization in the 1990s, corporate India flourished and there was unprecedented growth in corporate wealth for the first time since Independence. Many businesses prospered and were left with large surpluses. At the same time, this growth meant that family members could no longer run family-owned businesses on their own, and families increasingly turned to professional management for expertise. As a consequence, the philanthropic activities of family businesses were also institutionalized; professionals were brought in to manage trusts and family foundations. Thus, the nature of Indian corporate philanthropy changed, from being ad hoc and informal to more formal and strategic. In addition, there was a need for accountability from the managers, which required metrics to measure outcome and impact to ensure efficiency. Corporate philanthropy started being seen from a business perspective and considered an 'investment' that would enhance companies' long-term sustainability and reputation in the community.

Globalization trends led to an increased number of multinational corporations, many of which brought over corporate philanthropic practices to India from their home countries. There was increased public pressure on businesses to adhere to those practices of socially responsible behavior. As a result, many of the multinationals'

CSR practices—including the creation of triple bottom lines, making strategic choices, and the practice of transparency and accountability—were adopted in the Indian context. As Indian corporations made foreign investments and acquired foreign companies, they further integrated their standards to global standards (such as the UN Global Compact).

With an increasing awareness of global climate change and the effects of rapid growth on pollution indicators, corporations have come under the microscope about their practices. Many large corporations whose wealth increased several thousand-fold are seen as irresponsible citizens as they contribute to climate change. The influence of consumers and other stakeholders has grown exponentially. India's media-savvy and educated population is growing, and there is rising scrutiny and public pressure. Many Indians are aware of the growing contribution of businesses to climate change, and, not surprisingly, many have responded through their CSR practices. Thus, we see more and more companies focusing on the environmental bottom line in their CSR activities.

The Government of India has played an important role in guiding corporate philanthropy through their requirements for PSUs. In addition, the government expects corporations to not only contribute to the public good by paying taxes but also be invested in social and economic development. By making corporate donations tax deductible, the government gives fiscal incentives to business to be 'good citizens.' With the unprecedented growth in the wealth of corporations since economic liberalization, however, the Government of India has passed Clause 135 of the Companies Bill, which requires that qualifying companies spend a prescribed formula-based amount on CSR, report on these activities, or explain why they failed to do so. This has raised the ante on CSR activities of PSUs and businesses. Some estimates suggest the law will directly impact at least 2,500 companies, including the top 100 companies across several sectors, and generate an estimated $2 billion in CSR spending.

Today, individuals worldwide have raised their expectations of corporations. The Government of India sees partnering with businesses as a way to strengthen their own efforts to develop underdeveloped regions across the country.

Case Studies

Case Study 1. Getting a Rise Out of Philanthropy in Pre-Independent India: The Case of Jamsetjee Jejeebhoy

In precolonial India, charity was oriented toward reinforcing the community's religious and cultural values, and was practiced by individuals and families to gain religious merit and an upstanding reputation. Parsis, who are of Iranian descent and make up the Zoroastrian religious sect in India, prudently used charity to establish their standing in Bombay and in the Indian community at large. By administering relevant charitable projects such as the building of rest houses, water tanks, wells, housing colonies, fire temples, and towers of silence (Palsetia 2005: 202), the Parsi elite effectively gained reputations as generous 'merchant princes' as well as political control in their communities.

And then came the imperialist British, who indelibly changed the landscape of Indian charity. The Parsi community, eager to "appease, shape, and fashion stable moral bonds with the British in the interests of trade, family prestige, and social and religious life" (Haynes 1991:108), quickly adopted British cultural forms of charity by shifting the focus of public projects to education and medical services. By the 19th century, Parsi charity went beyond its traditional reach to support British causes in both India and abroad (Hinnells 1985: 317–325). In the midst of these changes and the many benefits derived from the new forms of giving, the Indian Parsi merchant Jamsetjee Jejeebhoy proposed the first large-scale charitable project in collaboration with the British (Palsetia 2005: 203).

An analysis of Jamsetjee Jejeebhoy's rise to prominence and of his use of philanthropy offers a unique perspective on the role of the indigenous elite in redefining the British–Indian relationships as well as in reshaping the culture of Indian cities by adhering to imperialist norms. From being a Batliwala (dealer in bottles) to starting his own opium shipping empire, Jejeebhoy truly ascended from the bottom up as a merchant. By the 1850s, Jejeebhoy's success in the opium trade and his contacts with British, American, and Chinese traders cemented his position as one of the key *shetias*, or Indian community elites, who served as points of contact for the British. The British valued and cultivated their relationships with shetias, who could be trusted to keep their communities under control. In many ways, Jejeebhoy's rise to prominence is analogous to the rise of Bombay and the Indian merchant class that made a place for itself within the colonial society.

Aware of public philanthropy's potential to augment the role of the Indian merchant and cognizant of the flaws of the existing medical system, Jejeebhoy proposed a partnership with the government to begin a charitable project that would improve medical services in the community. The proposed project was the construction of a large-scale hospital that Jejeebhoy offered to fund so long as the British contributed an equal share, an agreement Jejeebhoy hoped would make him an equal partner in the eyes of the British, who preferred to view the shetias as assistants.

As the project took off, it became more and more clear that equal-footed collaboration would be unfeasible due to the cultural differences between Jejeebhoy and the British. Many of Jejeebhoy's suggestions for the hospital involved segregation by caste and class per Indian tradition. The British were horrified at a suggestion so inimical to the prevailing mode of European philosophy regarding medicine and care, and they reduced Jejeebhoy's role in the committee to something marginal. Still, Jejeebhoy persevered against the odds to remain a part of the process and represent indigenous opinion by appealing to higher authorities and also donating the land on which the hospital would be built. When a new committee was formed six years later, Jejeebhoy was invited to join and help oversee the actual construction of the hospital. The hospital was named after Jejeebhoy, and the sick were separated by caste and gender as he had first suggested. However, the British intervened and made clear that the hospital had to meet the requirements they laid down, and again diminished Jejeebhoy's role to that of a donor who was expected to support all British decisions with unwavering loyalty. Thus, Jejeebhoy's vision of British–Indian collaboration in philanthropy was slow in coming and far short of the partnership he had initially intended.

In 1844, Jejeebhoy was the first Indian to be knighted, and a marble statue of him was raised shortly after to commemorate his many contributions to philanthropy. When he passed away in 1959, the public eulogies suggested that Jejeebhoy had reached a prominent status in colonial society because of his philanthropy. Without a doubt, Jejeebhoy was the first to follow a model of building reputation and augmenting political influence in British officialdom through Western-style philanthropy, which prompted similar actions from other shetias. This not only benefited the social landscape—with many Parsi shetias building libraries, hospitals, and schools—but also enhanced British hegemony in India (Palsetia 2005).

Case Study 2. Tata Group

THE TATA GROUP, PRE-INDEPENDENCE TO POST-INDEPENDENCE: TRACING THE RISE OF ONE OF INDIA'S LARGEST CORPORATE PHILANTHROPISTS

Setting the Stage
With nearly a 150-year history, over 100 operating companies worldwide, 455,000 employees, and a combined market capitalization of $109 billion under its belt, the Tata Group is indisputably a key player in the Indian economy.

Tata has a massive presence not only in the corporate world but also in the arena of CSR. As the given statistics satisfactorily justify the claim that Tata is an economic force to be reckoned with, this case study will primarily focus on how Tata has grown to be a top leader in CSR by tracing its history to present time.

The history of what would become the Tata Group actually began before Jamsetji Tata himself founded the empire in 1868. The story really began when his father Nusserwanji Tata broke the familial tradition of joining the Zoroastrian priesthood to launch his own trading business, Tata & Co. After graduating from Elphinstone College in 1858, Jamsetji joined his father's trading firm despite the sociopolitical tensions that dampened Indian economic endeavors following the Sepoy Mutiny of 1857. Soon after Jamsetji joined the firm, he was sent to Hong Kong to set up another branch of the company. In just four years, he successfully expanded his father's business in China and Japan.

The year 1868 was a year of transition for Jamsetji, as he left his father's company to start his own. He bought and made large profits from cotton mills, which produced cotton cloth that was sold all over India as well as to countries in the Orient and the Middle East. Notably, Jamsetji was one of the first to link industrial progress with nationalism as a supporter of Mahatma Gandhi's 'trusteeship' principles. As such, the public soon identified Tata's industrial power with Indian nationalism. In line with nationalist sentiment, Jamsetji renamed one of his mills, originally named Dharasmi Mills, to Swadeshi Mills—derived from Sanskrit 'swadeshi,' which translates to 'of one's own country'; and Swadeshi mills eschewed using non-Indian raw material (Tata Group 2014a). Jamsetji Tata "saw his industrial empire as part of the wider story of India's astonishing development" (Francis et al. 2010: 115).

From the pre-Independent years, Jamsetji was known for pioneering more humane conditions for the workers in all of his companies. He is credited not only for instituting the eight-hour workday, paid leave, and retirement pensions (Goldstein 2008) but also for providing medical facilities and accident compensations. He set the bar for workers' welfare so high that other companies who wished to be known for their employee welfare measured themselves by the 'Tata' standard. However, not all of Jamsetji's charitable ventures were devoted to the welfare of his companies' employees. He was a philanthropic visionary who comprehended the larger potential of wealth, and wanted to use it on behalf of the Indian people during his lifetime. In 1892, he set up the J.N. Tata Endowment Trust—one of the earliest trusts to be set up for secular causes—to provide Indian students with scholarships to study abroad.

Since Jamsetji's passing, the Tata empire has remained under the control of the Tata family and the Tata Trust. More importantly, his sons Sir Dorabji Tata and Sir Ratan Tata inherited their father's industrial prowess, nationalism, and philanthropic spirit and continued Jamsetji's legacy.

Today, Tata philanthropic trusts hold 66 percent of the shares in Tata Sons, one of the promoter holding companies of the group. The accrued wealth from this asset helps finance the trusts' support of a multitude of causes aimed at uplifting society in the areas of education, health, and art and the harnessing of civil society. The Sir Dorabji Tata Trust and its Allied Trusts, Sir Ratan Tata Trust (SRTT), and Navajbai Ratan Tata Trust are the principle trusts of the Tata Group; together, they form India's largest philanthropic group.[1]

Sir Dorabji Tata Trust and Allied Trusts

Sir Dorabji Tata, the older son of Jamsetji, set up one of India's oldest philanthropic trusts in 1932. Later, this Trust was augmented with ally trusts and became conjunctly known as Sir Dorabji Tata and Allied

[1] http://www.tata.com/ourcommitment/articlesinside

Trusts (SDTT). These trusts offer monetary assistance and grants to three levels of society: individual (usually merit or means based, mainly in the areas of health & education), institutional (mainly in the areas of learning and research), and, lastly, cultural. The emphasis on education once again related to notions of nation-building. Examples of institutional support in Mumbai include the Tata Institute of Social Sciences (TISS), the Tata Memorial Centre, and the Tata Institute of Fundamental Research. The third level of society that benefits from the Dorabji Tata Trust consists of NGOs with a focus on culture. The trust supports natural resource management and livelihoods, urban poverty alleviation and livelihoods, education, health, civil society, governance and human rights, media, and the arts and culture.

The model of the SDTT has evolved over time. Up to the 1970s, SDTT mainly focused on institutions, and then shifted to social causes as India's GDP grew. Up to the early 1990s, many NGOs approached SDTT informally for grant requests, but that transitioned in 1997 to a more formal approach with guiding reports used to determine action. Since the mid-2000s, SDTT has followed a proactive model based on research, seeking out NGOs with which to partner and thus also share risk. Feeling that SDTT was too spread out across all sectors, SDTT also narrowed down its focus for a more pronounced impact. The respect that many companies have for Tata's approach to philanthropy can be seen when companies, pressured to engage in CSR but unsure of who to select as recipients, blindly give to the same NGOs that SDTT supports.

The Allied Trusts comprises smaller trusts: some with their own limited mandates, while many are broadly oriented in their support. One example of a smaller trust with a narrower focus is the Lady Tata Memorial Trust, which was established by Sir Dorabji Tata in 1932 in memory of his wife, Lady Meherbai, who died of leukemia. This trust specifically sponsors research in the area of leukemia. Another example is the Lady Meherbai Tata Education Trust, also established in 1932, which gives grants to female scholars who wish to pursue higher education in the areas of social work and public health.[2]

The Sir Ratan Tata Trust and Navajbai Ratan Tata Trust
The concept of helping the less fortunate was especially dear to Sir Ratan Tata, who took the time to support and partake in several charitable initiatives. Prominent among these was a provision of

---

[2] http://www.tata.com/ourcommitment/articlesinside

funds over a period of 10 years to Gopal Krishna Gokhale's Servants of India Society, which worked to empower and transform the downtrodden masses into active members of Indian society. Gokhale was also instrumental in procuring INR 1.25 lakh from Sir Ratan Tata to support Mahatma Gandhi's fight in South Africa to safeguard the rights of the Indians there.

In his 1913 will, Sir Ratan Tata left the bulk of his fortune to form a trust that would provide funds with priority given to education- and industry-related causes. Hence, the SRTT was officially established in 1919 with a corpus of INR 8 million after Sir Ratan Tata's death. The organizations that have benefited from the funds have had to be subjected to periodic audits; such provisos are considered vanguards in philanthropy created by one clearly ahead of his time. In 1919, the Sir Ratan Tata Foundation funded a Chair at the London School of Economics devoted to studying the causes of poverty and possible solutions to alleviate poverty. The foundation donated £1,400 per year until 1931 toward this Chair. Furthermore, Sir Ratan Tata was responsible for contributing INR 75,000 to finance the archeological excavations in Patna that revealed several valuable artifacts between 1913 and 1917. A connoisseur of beautiful art, Sir Ratan Tata traveled around the world and collected paintings and collections of jade, china, and pottery. In his will, he left a great part of his collection to the Prince of Wales Museum in Bombay, where many of these contributions can be seen in the Far Eastern Section today.

In the earlier years, the trust concentrated its giving in the Bombay region. Though individual grants were initially popular, especially in the chosen areas of education and medical relief, institutional grants became the preferred method of helping over time as the trust built in the various modes of institutional giving. This was partly the result of advice from Mr S.M. Markham of the Carnegie Trust in 1932 on how to focus Tata Trust's grant-making; Markham suggested working in three- to five-year policy plans, larger grants, and projects toward national welfare (Francis et al. 2010: 111). One of the earliest ventures of the trusts was the Sir Ratan Tata Industrial Institute, which in 1948 provided jobs for needy women at a time when such openings were rare. The TISS was established even earlier in 1936 as the Sir Dorabji Graduate School of Social Work. In 1944, it was renamed TISS, and 20 years later, it was accepted as a university. TISS continues as an institution of excellence in higher education and, through its areas of study, contributes to an understanding of the role of civic society. The Navajbai Tata Trust was established in 1974 and works with SRTT to give grants to institutions that make a visible difference for the community.

CONCLUSION

Indian philanthropy was traditionally guided by religion and nationalism; in the case of the Tatas and their trusts, it is clear that nationalism especially played an important role. As philanthropy evolved in India during the 20th century, older traditional forms (including informal, one-on-one, ad hoc, and religiously motivated) existed alongside new philanthropic traditions (Sundar 2000: 129). While Jamsetji Tata came to be seen as the father of modern Indian philanthropy (Sundar 2000: 130), all the Tata trusts were pioneers in India to "use wealth as a *catalyst* for development" (Sundar 2000: 186). A number of nationally important institutions are testaments of the Tata trusts' pioneering spirit: the National Centre for the Performing Arts, Indian Institute of Science, JRD Tata Ecotechnology Centre, the Tata Blood Bank, and the Tata Department of Plastic Surgery at the J. J. Group of Hospitals and the Demographic Centre at the Institute of Population Studies, Mumbai.[3] During the 1990s when the Tata Group was growing within India's expanding economy, the trusts gained even more wealth and designated it to a range of causes across education, health, arts and culture, rural livelihoods of communities, and public initiatives, expanding beyond the Mumbai region (Francis et al. 2010: 112). The Tata trusts are widely acknowledged as not only the largest philanthropic group in India with a rich history but also as the indisputable key players in modern Indian philanthropy.

Case Study 3. Amin Welfare Trust

The Amin brothers, Ikbal and Iftikar, were just everyday businessmen who ran a successful tannery business called Super Tannery, where leather is tanned and then used in the manufacture of fashion shoes that are exported around the world. Although they gave to the occasional charity, they never considered involvement beyond

---

[3] http://www.tata.com/ourcommitment/articlesinside

cursory giving. All of this changed when communal riots began occurring in their region at the start of the new century. When Ikbal, the younger brother, heard the tragic stories of the victims who came to the Amin family asking for help, he was moved to take action. For about two months, Ikbal lived at one of the government-arranged camps alongside displaced people, and helped many of them relocate and make a living. During those two months, Ikbal saw firsthand the reality of the poverty that plagued his city as well as the disadvantages that poor people experienced in obtaining basic amenities. It was only when Ikbal came out of his comfort zone that he became aware of the state of deprivation in which large sections of society lived. Ultimately, Ikbal realized that the lack of education was at the heart of the problems. Thus, he embarked on the next chapter of his life with a vision to help future generations of poor people by empowering them with education.

In 1993, Ikbal and his brother formed the Amin Welfare Trust "with the sole objective of extending help to the poor and needy, deprived and underprivileged class of society." The mission statement of the trust is "promoting hope in life." Super Tannery—60 percent owned by the brothers and 40 percent owned by public holders—provided the funding for the trust's projects. The two brothers and the shareholders reached a consensus that 10 percent of the annual net profit be donated to the trust without any further permission. Whenever the costs of the trust necessitated a 3–4 percent increase in the designated fund, the shareholders consented to cover the extra costs.

When the brothers surveyed the potential students for their forthcoming school, they realized that most of the slum children were severely undernourished. Thus, they decided that health welfare of the poor was an even more urgent need. In 1995, the trust spent INR 4 lakh to buy a small piece of land and another INR 15 lakh to build the ground floor of a hospital in the densely populated region of Kanpur, where tuberculosis was rampant especially among the impoverished population. The hospital was named 'The Chest Hospital' in order to let people know that it specialized in treating tuberculosis. Unfortunately, the name deterred patients from coming to the hospital because tuberculosis carried a serious stigma in the community. Once the hospital was renamed to Amin Charitable Hospital, it became popular and clientele increased.

The year 1997 was an important year for the Amin Trust as it received FCRA approval, meaning it could accept donations and additional funding from foreign countries. Funding also came from local sources. One donor was a father who gave INR 10 lakh to build the second floor of the hospital in memory of his young son who died in an accident. While some donors sponsored the treatment of a specific patient, others paid for the development of more services, such as dental and physiotherapy services. The brothers assert that very few donors have received tax breaks for their donations. Most donors are compelled to give for personal reasons, whether it is in gratitude of a saved child or in memory of a loved one. Altogether, donations play a huge role in the hospital's ongoing success in Kanpur. What began as a one-story building with one doctor who served on an outpatient basis, the hospital has grown into a three-story building with 12 doctors who attend to over 200 patients a day, providing a range of medical services from ENT to gynecology.

When I met with the brothers, they told me a touching story of a young boy with a mouth disfigurement whose life changed, thanks to the hospital. Before receiving treatment, the boy had wandered around with his father to beg for money and usually kept his mouth covered with a handkerchief; sometimes, the father would pull off the handkerchief to elicit sympathy and donations from passing pedestrians. One time when the boy and his father were begging near the hospital, one of the staff invited them in to see if the boy could be helped. The doctors agreed that a surgery could restore the face but at a price the father could not afford. A massive appeal was sent out to all of the other tanners, as these were the people that the brothers associated with regularly. Within an hour, donations poured in to make the surgery possible. Drawing on the boy's rib, the doctors reconstructed the boy's jaw and face successfully. With this transformation, the boy was able to pursue a better life. The hospital continues to treat all kinds of ailments and charges little or no money depending on the resources of the patients.

While building the hospital went according to plan, building a school proved to be a far more difficult process. The trust bought a small plot of land to build a school, but its plans were overturned when the land mafia simply took over. Unhindered, the Amin brothers relocated the construction of the school on land they had bought for their holiday farmhouse. Still, they lacked the 'big fat seed capital' for the construction of the school. The trust dealt with this issue by applying for and receiving a one-time grant of US$165,000 from the Islamic Development Fund. With land and start-up capital under their belts, the brothers had the confidence to start building the school. However, construction was halted as soon as it began because the brothers had not applied for the requisite permissions for such construction. It took over a year to attain all the necessary permits and permissions, but every obstacle was eventually resolved and the trust has since built three different kinds of schools:

1. Super International School: This not-for-profit school caters to the middle class and offers a quality education for a reasonable fee; surplus funds are put into the development of the school.
2. Amin Girls High School: Located in the slums, this school educates about 500 girls from the area today at a minimal cost of INR 50, 70, and 100 per month according to income ability. The school also assists and sponsors bright students who cannot afford to pay the fees. At the request of foreign donors, the school now offers English medium classes starting at the nursery school level; the plan is to gradually introduce English at the nursery school level and add English to a subsequent grade each year while ensuring that the teachers are qualified to teach English, thereby working toward a successful transition. With English added to the curriculum, student fees have inevitably increased, but this problem was resolved with an increase in diaspora funding. The hope is to grow the school and eventually admit 1,000 girls over the next three years.
3. Nai Roshni (or New Light) Schools: These small primary schools are scattered across poor slum areas, and are run by young girls who have completed their own schooling and are able to provide space in their own homes as classes for children. These young teachers are compensated fairly by the minimal fees students pay. A unique aspect of these schools is that no child is turned away based on his/her financial circumstance. Moreover, all of the children are given nutritious biscuits and fruit every day. Initially, the trust established eleven Nai Roshni schools, but had cut down to seven schools in order to provide schooling more logistically. Rather than have two schools fairly close to each other, the trust closed down the school with less students and had these students transported to a nearby school. Ultimately, these primary schools prepare

students for mainstream schools. Positive results are already visible, as about 151 young students have entered mainstream schools where they continue to receive support in the form of books, school uniforms, and extra tutoring. The Amin brothers hope the Nai Roshni schools will extend education opportunities to students who would otherwise go uneducated.

The trust was fortunate to earn the attention and confidence of United States Agency for International Development (USAID) and State Innovations in Family Planning Services Agency (SIFPSA), which provided about INR 15 million in funds. With the generous support of these two international agencies, the trust initiated several projects starting 1997, many of which still function today:

1. Integrated Counseling and Testing Center (ICTC): This center offers HIV test kits, provided by the Indian government, to patients who come of their own free will or come with the recommendation of a medical provider. If the test is positive, the center counsels the patient to seek help from other NGOs, and educates the patient on the modes of HIV transmission.
2. Family Health Project for the Industrial Worker: This project receives US funding that is channeled through the Indian government. Mainly, it provides family planning information and services, and sponsors the Mother Child Health Project. Amin Trust works with SIFPSA on the Mother Child Health Project to encourage mothers to deliver their children in hospitals and receive appropriate follow-up services and vaccines.
3. The Integrated Nutrition and Health Project: This project is funded by CARE International and administered through the field-workers of Amin Trust and United Nations Development Programme (UNDP), who work closely with local communities, private companies, resident welfare associations, and government departments. The main purpose is to help local communities gain access to basic services that contribute to an improved quality of life.
4. The RACHNA Project: Funded by CARE International, this project raises awareness of HIV/AIDS through Amin field-workers who have informed and educated six villages with information material through meetings and plays.

5. The CHAYAN Project: Also funded by CARE International, this project raises awareness of HIV/AIDS specifically among tannery workers, and offers information on reproductive and child health.

Alongside these projects, the two brothers are involved in several smaller schemes dedicated to improving the health and safety of people in nearby villages. They continue to work with welfare workers trained by international health agencies on short-term projects on an ongoing basis.

5

Diaspora Philanthropy[*]

Introduction

The word "diaspora" comes from the Greek words "to sow" and "over," and was used to describe the "sowing" of Greek colonies in faraway places. The word is also related to involuntary expulsion with a sense of loss for the homeland coupled with a desire to return. Diasporas—whether they are made up of individuals who voluntarily left for faraway lands or were formed as a result of involuntary expulsions—try to maintain a sense of attachment with their homelands. Diasporas refer to a settled community, rather than temporary migrants with the intention of returning to their country of origin. As Sheffer (1986: 3) puts it, "Modern Diasporas are ethnic minority groups of migrant origins residing and acting in host countries but maintaining strong sentimental and material links with their countries of origin—their homelands."

Most emigrants maintain some ties with their countries of origin, whether through friends and families they left behind or through local institutions such as schools or places of worship in which they had been active. These ties to people and places help assuage the pain of dislocation and distance. The desire to maintain such ties often propels visits, the exchange of news, and gifts of money to people and organizations with whom ties are maintained. Understandably, these ties weaken over successive generations as emigrants form deeper bonds with their host countries through the slow but definite process of acculturation (Gans 1992; Kumar et al. 2008).

The Indian diaspora is estimated to be around 27 million people worldwide, with 2.7 million residing in the US. The American Community Survey of the US Census Bureau reports that the Indian population in the US grew at a rate of 53 percent between 2000 and 2007, and is among the fastest growing ethnic groups in the

*Much of the materials in this chapter come from research conducted by Professor Devesh Kapur and his colleagues and we are grateful to him for sharing his research.

(Bakshi and Baron 2011). Members of the Indian diaspora make up nearly 8 percent of America's physicians and surgeons, 7 percent of its IT workers, and 3 percent of its engineers. On average, diaspora Indians as a group have one of the highest median household incomes in the country (Richwine 2009).

Globally, we find the Indian diaspora ubiquitous, from the fifth-generation descendants of indentured labor in the Caribbean, to the fourth-generation descendants of traders from British colonial times in Africa, and to the second-generation descendants of professionals in the US and Canada. Emigrants from India work in varied fields and these occupations range from IT engineers in the US to construction workers in the Middle East (Agarwal 2012).

In developing countries such as India, diaspora philanthropy represents a fair share of philanthropic resources that are used to address a wide range of social and public issues. This chapter reports on the philanthropic donations made by the Indian diaspora, followed by three case studies on diaspora individuals who engage in structured philanthropic efforts in India.

Migration Flows

There have been significant waves of emigration from India since the early 1800s. Indeed, nearly 30 million Indian workers were shipped throughout the British Empire on labor contracts for a hundred-year period starting in 1834 (Humphrey 1993). According to Kapur et al. (2004), this first major wave of migrants went as indentured laborers, mostly to the British colonies of Sri Lanka, Malaysia, and Myanmar (Burma). Under the kangani/maistry recruitment method, British employers exported Indian labor to British colonies, and were authorized to use enforceable, written labor contracts, but laborers were legally free to leave. Further, unlike traditional indentured labor, laborers brought with them their kin and family. Indian contract labor was also exported to other European colonies (Mauritius, Trinidad and Tobago, Guyana, as well as Reunion Island, Guadeloupe, Martinique, and Suriname) to work on plantations that had previously used slave labor from Africa. Over the last hundred years, this diaspora's ties with India have weakened, with their affiliations generally limited to religion and culture.

The next major wave of migration went primarily to East and South Africa to work as merchants, traders, and civil servants for the colonial governments. The majority of these migrants was from Gujarat and Punjab, and they were economic migrants in search of better opportunities. By the end of World War II, the number of Indians in East and South Africa had increased significantly. As merchants and traders, Indians in Africa occupied a middle position between the British colonial rulers at the top and the African majority at the bottom. Today, this group's ties to India are also weak, but stronger than those of the first wave of migrants, as they are fewer generations removed from their forefathers.

To assist in postwar reconstruction, in the 1950s, a large number of unskilled and semiskilled Indian workers from Punjab and Gujarat moved to the UK. This group of migrants consisted of Indians from mostly lower-to-middle socioeconomic groups, and from laboring and trade professions. This wave of migrants was largely halted during the 1970s due to the 1972 Immigration Act. Their ties with India are stronger than the previous migrants as they are even fewer generations away from the initial migrants. Nevertheless, their philanthropic predispositions are not aimed toward India (Kapur et al. 2004) but often more so toward their host countries.

As the UK closed its doors to Indian migrants in the 1970s, the Middle East, US, and Canada opened their doors. It is important to note that the migrants attracted to the Middle East versus those attracted to North America were significantly different. With the increase in oil prices during the 1970s, large numbers of Indians migrated to Middle Eastern countries to meet the demands for labor. As with previous waves of migration, the majority of migrants was unskilled or semiskilled and took low-paying jobs. As the policies of Middle Eastern countries made permanent settlement impossible, this group of migrants was inherently temporary. After working for a period of time, many returned to India, although many of the skilled migrants tried to move to countries such as Canada, Australia, and New Zealand. The philanthropy of this group has for the most part focused on sending money back to families and home communities.

Starting in the 1960s, many Indian emigrants left for North American countries, in particular the US, because the 1965 passage of the Hart–Celler Act opened the doors to immigrants from Asia, Africa, and the Middle East (Massey 1981). Similarly, the introduction of a points system in Canada in 1967 liberalized immigration laws for immigrants with education and skills, leading to a large influx of Indians in Canada (Bloom et al. 1995). Post-1965, migration from India to the Middle East also persisted to meet the demand for labor in construction and related industries, but the majority of that group was unskilled or semiskilled. In contrast, Indian immigrants to the US and Canada were educated professionals and students seeking profitable professions and permanent homes in their host countries. This wave of immigration was followed by another wave in the 1990s of educated immigrants, who came to work in the growing IT industry on work visas; they are loosely identified as the 'knowledge' diaspora (Chacko 2007). Many of these immigrants came under temporary visas, and most returned to India later as successful entrepreneurs. The first generation of immigrants from 1965 onward, who became financially successful, were more likely to engage in diaspora philanthropy because (a) they had the resources to do so, and (b) they had stronger ties to the home country than did the next generations of immigrants (their children or grandchildren). Clearly, this group's ties with India are the strongest; thus, its philanthropic inclinations are also directed toward India.

Diaspora Giving

In the fiscal year 2008–2009, nearly 24,000 NGOs received over $2.3 billion in donations from foreign sources, a 12 percent increase from the previous year. Of this, the US diaspora's giving amounted to nearly $740 million, making it the largest source for diaspora giving, followed by the UK and Germany. This is not surprising given that the Indian diaspora in these countries tends to be better educated, more skilled, and in better-paying jobs. If we compare the flow of donations of diaspora Indians to NGOs with the flow of remittances to citizens, we find that the latter account for $49.3 billion while direct philanthropy to NGOs accounts for less than 5 percent of all the funds flowing to India from the US (Bakshi and Baron 2011).

Diaspora philanthropy among Indians tends to be directed toward one's immediate circle of relatives and friends, showing the extent of personal and family attachments Indians maintain even after emigrating. In times of natural disaster or emergencies—such as the Kargil war (1999), the cyclone in Orissa (1999), and earthquakes in Gujarat (2001)—philanthropic aid becomes more pronounced. In 2002, the American India Foundation (AIF) raised $7.5 million from members of the Indian diaspora living in the US. Of the $7.5 million, $1 million went to the victims of the 9/11 terrorist attack in the US, and the rest went to relief efforts following the devastating earthquakes in Gujarat (Anand 2004).

Donations are also made on an ongoing basis, not in direct response to natural disasters or emergencies but in response to the challenges of poverty in India. These donations are often motivated by visits home to India or media articles on the inabilities of the government to meet the welfare needs of the population. The visits home give diaspora Indians a chance to experience firsthand some of the pressing needs in India, as well as opportunities to practice their philanthropy. Often, diaspora donors' social networks in India, including extended family members and friends, help weed out causes and institutions that are untrustworthy. The networks also provide them with some form of accountability from afar. Thus, diasporas' long-standing ties to the home country motivate diaspora philanthropy and make it easier for immigrants to channel their philanthropy to the appropriate recipients.

Diaspora philanthropy among first-generation immigrants is driven by a wide variety of motivations and goals. Some diaspora donors have direct connections and give because they are asked to and can guide their philanthropy to a particular cause or recipient. Others rely on the media or their networks of friends and family at home to identify particular causes or recipients. Other diaspora donors may choose to donate through intermediaries, either for convenience or to achieve greater impact. Intermediaries are NGOs, community-based associations, faith-based groups, and professional networks. Internet-based philanthropic platforms such as GiveIndia (see case study in Chapter 6) also facilitate diaspora funding by connecting donors to recipients. Due to the global mobility of talent, there is an increasing number of highly successful first-generation diaspora members worldwide, and the Internet is making it possible to reach these dispersed immigrant populations and nurture their connections to their home country despite the distance.

Diaspora donors can give in a variety of ways; the two most frequent donations are those of money and time. For the latter, donors return to their home countries and volunteer their time and efforts, especially their professional experience and technical expertise. As such, many diaspora Indians are known to return to India on a regular basis to teach or apply their professional skills in the fields of medicine and technology. Monetary donations, small or large, can be given directly to specific recipients, NGOs, foundations, or to projects such as the construction of a school, hospital, or village well. One such example appeared in a *The New York Times* article that covered the story of an Indian immigrant couple who lived in New York. Mr Om Sharma, a taxi driver, and his wife, Krishna, a nurse at Bellevue Hospital Center, who had contributed $2,500 annually for the last 20 years to run a school in India (Dugger 2000).

Some of the most common motivations for immigrant communities to donate to causes in their native countries are sense of attachment and the feeling of "giving back to their motherland." Benedict Anderson's (Anderson 1991) concept of nations as 'imagined communities' based on commonalities shared by citizens no matter how close or far they live from one another might explain why Indian immigrants are willing to support causes in India regardless of their citizenship in different countries. For example, in 2008, a charitable foundation was set up by the Canadian Association of Physicians of Indian Heritage that gave these physicians an opportunity to work together and collectively help eradicate disease, hunger, and poverty in India and elsewhere.

Religious groups act as especially important bridges between immigrants and their nations of origin by reproducing their culture and helping solidify their sense of belonging (Handy and Greenspan 2009). These bridges are a means of actualizing the notion of "flexible citizenship" (Ong 1998), and the practice of diaspora philanthropy reinforces this notion. The Bochasanwasi Shri Akshar Purushottam Swaminarayan Sanstha (BAPS) case study that follows illustrates this type of group.

It is indeed a natural disposition for diasporas to want to engage with the communities they left behind. This is facilitated by easy access to information and people via the Internet. Furthermore, NGOs are active in their fund-raising and often target nonresident Indians deliberately in their appeals for valuable human and financial capital. In addition, actions undertaken by the government to facilitate foreign money transfers serve to increase diaspora giving, although the process still remains cumbersome (Mehta and Johnston 2011).

Since its formulation in 1976, the FCRA has been responsible for regulating incoming money from foreign sources to NGOs in India.

NGOs that want to accept foreign funding are required to obtain certification from the government, which they can obtain only after showing that they have existed for more than three years and have a specific cultural, economic, educational, religious, or social focus. The funds received by the organization must be used only for the specified purpose. The rationale for regulating foreign sources was to disallow funds for activities that were considered "detrimental to national interest." Despite this motive, the regulations are difficult to implement. The FCRA in its current form is considered to be unfavorable to donors and NGOs, as they add additional transaction costs. To add, the process of obtaining the necessary certification is heavily bureaucratic and cumbersome, and increases the likelihood of Indian NGOs not seeking diaspora funding. In light of this, some civil society groups have questioned the motives behind the FCRA, claiming that the act's language and application make it easy for authorities to target organizations that are seen as threats to political interests.

Also worth noting is the power of incentives—such as tax credits or offsets in the country of residence—in motivating diaspora philanthropy. Many NGOs in India are allowed to accept foreign donations, and give donors a tax exemption in their countries of residence. This was not always the case. Historically, the Indian government viewed foreign funding and philanthropy with suspicion because funds from diaspora populations have played a significant role in shaping the power relationships and political contours within the country; thus, the Government of India has shied away from taking funds from foreign sources and is still strict about foreign contributions today (Dusenbery and Tatla 2010).

Although the Indian government today is still reluctant to accept foreign funds from international aid agencies due to their "quid pro quo" approach, it views foreign funding and philanthropy from the diaspora with less suspicion as diaspora funds rarely come with strings attached. In 2000, a high-profile committee was asked by the government to research and write an extensive report on the Indian diaspora. Based on the recommendations of this report, an annual conference called the PBD is held every year to facilitate networking opportunities. The program explicitly encourages the Indian government and Indian organizations to engage with "the global Indian." The program also honors Indian emigrants who have had a significant impact on India, and communicates new policies concerning overseas Indians. It aims to harness the intellectual and financial capital as well as the business and philanthropic investments of the diaspora. In 2005, the government set up the Ministry of Overseas Indian Affairs (MOIA) with the mission to connect the Indian diaspora community with its motherland (Agarwal 2012).

Mechanisms That Facilitate Diaspora Giving

There are a variety of motivations behind the philanthropic giving of money, time, or other resources that vary between individuals and circumstances. Researchers investigating the motives of donors find a spectrum that ranges from self-interested ones to altruistic ones. These motives are more generally characterized by Bekkers and Wiepking (2011) as eight mechanisms facilitating giving, based on a literature review of more than 500 articles. They structure their review around the central question of why people donate money to charitable organizations, and categorize the following mechanisms as the most important forces that motivate charitable giving—including awareness of need and solicitation, costs and benefits, altruism, reputation, values, and efficacy. Subsequently, these will be explored in the chapter.

Awareness of need is a dominant precondition for philanthropic activity, as it moves individuals to action. The needs of people in India are particularly vast. Emigrants do not forget the endemic poverty of their homeland and, after securing successful livelihoods in Western countries, seek to give back to the poor in India. The awareness of need—accentuated by the differences in living conditions in India and the new countries of residence—combined with the availability of resources motivate the diaspora to contribute to the development in India (Staub and Baer 1974).

Furthermore, awareness of need is increased by solicitations for charitable contributions, which are often facilitated by social and mass media. Simon (1997) shows that extended media coverage of an earthquake has a strong positive relationship with private contributions. This media coverage is positively correlated to the number of beneficiaries (or those affected) and to the psychological distance between potential donors and beneficiaries (Adams 1986; Simon 1997). Bielefeld et al. (2005) found that in the presence of high levels of income inequality, donations were higher. Thus, emigrants who have a connection to their home countries are more motivated to give if their home countries have high levels of income inequality and high rates of poverty and are constantly covered by mass media for negative reasons.

Given that most donations are made in response to solicitations, the way in which potential donors are solicited may govern the success of solicitations. In fact, some studies reveal that almost 85 percent of donations is made in response to solicitations and that increased solicitations augment the probability of donations. Solicitations are usually done via fund-raising letters, e-mails, or personal requests, and may originate directly from intended beneficiaries or indirectly from NGOs on behalf of the beneficiaries. Also, solicitations may be targeted to a particular segment of the population or to the public at large. In the case of diaspora donations to India, all methods described are used, with targeted donation appeals made through organizations whose membership is largely composed of diaspora Indians. Internet-based platforms such as GiveIndia (see case study in Chapter 6: Trends) also facilitate diaspora giving.

Financial incentives also play a role in facilitating people's philanthropic behavior. When there is a tax benefit to the donor, the cost of the donation is lower and giving increases. A large number of studies by economists have estimated the effects of tax price on donations. While tax benefits may reduce the costs of giving, donors must still account for the inevitable costs that come with giving (Peloza and Steel 2005). For one, the gift itself costs money, but also the transaction costs involved in finding the right recipient and ensuring that the money went to the right cause can cost donors. Often, the donor receives other incentives that make giving more attractive. These may include gifts such as cookies, mugs, or T-shirts, or access to gala dinners, lectures, operas, or special concerts. Other non-tangible benefits that come with acting altruistically are feelings of joy, or what some scholars call a 'warm-glow.' There is evidence that pro-social spending, which includes charitable donations, is correlated with greater well-being (Dunn et al. 2008) and health.

Donors also make donations to enhance their own reputations. Many studies by social psychologists show that donating to charitable causes contributes to the donor's own self-image as an altruistic, empathic, or influential person, and often is responsible for alleviating feelings of guilt and satisfying a desire to show gratitude.

Unsurprisingly, most donors want their donations to make a positive difference and are less likely to donate if they think their contributions will have no impact. Especially among diaspora donors—who cannot easily monitor the donations they make to their home countries—there is a greater need for understanding the efficacy of their donations, which leads them to give to larger, well-known, and trustworthy organizations, or to channel their money through relatives and friends who would be there on the ground ensuring the efficacy of the donations. While some diaspora donors donate through NGOs, many remain skeptical of NGOs' ability to ensure donations go to the intended recipients. To add, high fundraising and administrative costs are negative signals to donors, and lower donors' perceptions of NGOs' efficacy. To address donors' fears, NGOs try to display their efficacy and legitimacy through increased transparency of financial records, leadership donations, and matching donations.

In summary, diaspora donors, like other donors, are more likely to donate if they have confidence that their donations will go to the intended causes or recipients directly or indirectly through NGOs, and that their donations will make a positive impact. Donors are motivated by personal values to give; however, the amount they give often reflects the personal net benefits they receive from the donations.

NGOs and Philanthropy

Vyas' study (2013) of Indian diaspora members in the northeastern region of the US found that many first- and second-generation immigrants who spend their vacations in India return with a profound desire to help the development efforts and to alleviate the ubiquitous poverty they see in India. Clearly, what they see and experience firsthand during their visits to India make an indelible impression. Over the last decade, diaspora donors have become more interested than ever in creating social change in India, and are making large donations of money and time.

The main ways the donations are transferred from the Indian diaspora to India are through informal family and personal networks, religious congregations, and faith-based intermediaries, international NGOs (e.g., Save the Children), as well as US-based NGOs (AIF,

AAPI Trust) and Indian-based NGOs with FRCA certifications (CRY, Seva, GiveIndia). Due to a culture of pervasive corruption in India, religious organizations in the US and India are often seen as the most dependable channel for the diaspora's philanthropic resources. Findings by Vyas (2013), Anand (2004), Khandelwal (2002), and Handy and Greenspan (2009) stress the importance of faith-based organizations for the Indian diaspora in American and Canadian cities.

Many of the North American-based Indian religious organizations are connected to organized religious organizations in India (such as an ashram, guru, or diocese). They have multiple goals, including raising awareness among the children of emigrants, building their religious and cultural capital, and raising funds to support activities and capital campaigns to build physical buildings for their faith-based organizations, where religious services and community gatherings can be held. As scholars have noted, many immigrant congregations adopted the congregationalist models of North American churches, where the places of religious worship also function as community centers, where outreach services are performed and where members are encouraged to engage in social welfare programs outside of the congregation, including in the home country. Many of these religious organizations are fairly big and have significant budgets (Agarwal 2012).

According to Vyas (2013), many members of faith-based organizations in the US return to India during their vacations to volunteer their skills and time to tackle poverty in India—often through trips organized by the organizations. For example, a 1,000-member Telugu-language Seventh Day Adventist Church in Silver Spring, Maryland, collects funds from its congregation members to support schools, colleges, and medical facilities in Andhra Pradesh and Telangana in India. Its members also return to India to visit these facilities and volunteer their time (Newland et al. 2010).

Diaspora Indians, using existing tax laws in the US, have set up foundations and NGOs with the explicit purpose of sponsoring and encouraging diaspora philanthropy and channeling funds for social and economic development in India. In 1992, The American Association of Physicians of Indian Origin (APPI) established a charitable foundation designed to:

> ...provide an infrastructure support system for needy patients in India with two main goals: first goal was to commit their time and resources

to support the clinics for the indigent; and our second goal was to monitor effectively the clinics' progress and be accountable for the overall success of the project.

According to its website, the association currently runs 15 clinics in India that serve over 20,000 patients every year. In sum, more than a million patients have received medical care since its establishment.[1]

A well-known Indian diaspora philanthropic foundation is the AIF, which was founded in 2001 after a devastating earthquake in Gujarat to be the collective arm leading the relief and rehabilitation efforts. It now raises funds in the US and allocates them "to catalyze sector-wide change across India and uplift some of the country's most impoverished communities." In 2013, the foundation raised over $7 million. Today, the foundation continues to work directly with over 200 NGOs to create sustainable livelihoods, deliver education programs, promote health for mothers and children, and train health-care professionals. To add, AIF provides leadership training in underprivileged communities through its partnership with the W. J. Clinton Fellowship for Service in India.[2]

In 2003, Kapur et al. (2004) conducted a survey of 107 diaspora NGOs based in the US, and found that they had on average between 101 and 200 members with an annual budget ranging from $50,000 to $100,000. The majority of the organizations' members were of Indian descent/ancestry. The NGOs were centered on cultural activities, and engaged in economic, social, health, and education development activities as well as disaster relief in India during the last three years. Their fund-raising initiatives were limited to these activities, and the NGOs were not engaged in advocacy, the transfer knowledge, or the provision of technology training to their counterparts in India.

Members of the Indian diaspora also organize themselves around cultural, alumni, and professional interests. Alumni and professional represent over 8 percent of transnational Indian organizations (Agarwal 2012). These organizations include the AAPI, American Society of Indian Engineers (ASIE), South Asia Journalists Association (SAJA), the Northern Indian Medical & Dental Association of Canada (NIMDAC), Telugu Canada Foundation, and the Indo-Canada Chamber of Commerce (ICCC), just to mention a few. Though these associations were not founded specifically to practice

---

[1] http://aapiusa.org/about/aapicfchairmessage.aspx
[2] http://aif.org

philanthropy, many nonetheless coalesce around fund-raising events in the case of emergencies or natural disasters.

Alumni associations play a vital role in collecting and disseminating philanthropic donations for the diaspora communities as well as maintaining a network for their members. The immigration wave of the 1990s brought in many trained IT professionals to the US, especially those trained at the Indian Institute of Technology (IIT), as they were in high demand by US employers. During this period, Indians as a group obtained the highest number of H-1B visas given out to work in the US (Agarwal 2012). Many found success in the US, and in 1992, IIT alumnus Vinod Gupta established the IIT Foundation, a US-based NGO. Its funds have underwritten several initiatives at IIT Kharagpur, including the Campus Networking Project that aims to provide universal high-speed Internet access to all resident students and the very large-scale integration (VLSI) laboratory on campus with equipment and software. Recently, the foundation launched Visions 2020 with the objective of raising a $200-million endowment fund "to enable IIT Kharagpur maintain and enhance global leadership and excellence in technology education, research and innovation."[3]

Going Home

Although the numbers are not well known, there are increasing numbers of individuals from the diaspora choosing to leave the US or Canada to go back to India and start NGOs. The NGO Idealist. org helps such individuals in their transition back to India. One example is Mr Rajendra Vesana, who returned to southern India to establish the Touchwood Ecological and Social Foundation in 2006. Mr Vesana had been passionate about wildlife since childhood, and had his passion rekindled on a trip back to India in 1992. Subsequently, he made frequent return visits to learn more about wildlife and ecology in Tamil Nadu. In an interview with Allison Jones from Idealist.org, he said:

> In order to be more consistent in my efforts, I realized I would need a banner for my work and hence Touchwood was born in February

---

[3] http://www.iitfoundation.org/about/#iitf_about

2006 as an NGO. My passion kept growing until I finally realized that this was my calling. I decided to quit the corporate world in the year 2010 and head to the jungles to do my bit. (Jones 2012)

Touchwood advocates for the welfare of the indigenous people living in the jungles of Nilgiris, trains teachers for remote schools, and offers free medical clinics and English-language classes along with computer and vocational training.

Some second-generation Indians such as Zubin Sharma, a student at the University of Pennsylvania's Wharton Business School, also return to India frequently to work with poor and marginalized communities. Initially, Sharma took a semester off to work in education and grassroots development, returning later full-time to run an NGO he started. He writes:

> At the end of the summer, I decided to take a risk. I left Penn for a semester to work for the educational non-governmental organization— Pratham—in a village called Bishanpur in Bihar, India. I have enjoyed the experience not only in spite of, but also because of, the material conditions.

He was so inspired by this experience that he started an NGO called SEEKHO, which means "learn" and is also an acronym for the guiding principles of the organization and its mission: sustainability, education, empowerment, knowledge, hope, and ownership. The organization's goal is to improve education at multiple levels and impart skills "such as basic literacy, numeracy and hygiene and sanitation, that will allow children, even if they are tragically forced to drop out, to make better decisions, avoid being cheated and avert costly illness" (Sharma 2012). Seekho also hires local people to teach English, Hindi, computer, and leadership courses. This program has been very successful and has gained momentum in the neighboring villages, thereby spearheading literacy in the region.[4]

Though many diaspora Indians make significant efforts to engage in Indian philanthropy, they are met with challenges in terms of directing and distributing their contributions. As social problems in India are large and ubiquitous, it would be naïve to imagine that diaspora philanthropy—which remains largely personal and made through informal channels—can make large-scale impact.

[4] www.seekhoindia.org

Nevertheless, these small personalized efforts do impact the lives of the few they touch, and in this sense, personal diaspora philanthropy is effective. And, it is indeed the impact donors make at the personal, village, or local level that motivates and drives many donors to continue donating. Although diaspora philanthropy should not be relied upon to make large societal changes, it may provide models that can possibly be scaled up with public money or leveraged through domestic philanthropy or foundations with greater resources.

Challenges to Diaspora Philanthropy

While diaspora philanthropy is a significant and important source of philanthropic funds in India, there are several challenges in both promoting philanthropy among the Indian diaspora and reducing the transaction costs for donors and NGOs receiving foreign funding in terms of red tape and bureaucracy.

Many well-intentioned donors want to donate through Indian NGOs, but struggle to find NGOs that are eligible to receive foreign funding and are capable of delivering on the donors' wishes. Certain web platforms such as GuideStar India disseminate information on over 1,000 organizations at best; however, there is little information available about thousands of other NGOs that are eligible to receive diaspora donations. Furthermore, due to endemic corruption in India, there is an ongoing lack of trust in intermediaries and NGOs. This is exacerbated due to lack of both transparency and good reporting practices. Thus, many donors prefer giving money directly to people (recipients) they know, or ask family and friends to carry out their philanthropic intentions. If diaspora donors want their money go to developmental projects such as the construction of wells and other infrastructure in their villages, there are insurmountable bureaucratic hurdles that stand in the way—especially if the local organizations they want to donate to are not registered under the FCRA. This frustrates donors, intermediaries, and recipients alike as recipients' villages or NGOs need to have been registered as an organization for three years before they are eligible to apply for FCRA.

Several Internet platforms such as Give2Asia or GiveIndia try to make it easy for diaspora donations to go directly to organizations, individuals, and causes. As these are registered in the US as well as other countries, they are subject to some level of scrutiny. For example, GuideStar India is the country's largest, fully searchable database of comparable information on over 4,200 NGOs (with another 70,000-plus NGOs on their off-line database), aiming to provide reliable information about each NGO's mission, legitimacy, impact, reputation, finances, programs, transparency, and governance to help donors donate with confidence and make the best decisions possible.[5] GuideStar does not act as a watchdog organization, but "collects, organizes, and presents the information you want in an easy-to-understand format while remaining neutral. Providing nonprofit information to a broad audience at no cost to those users is an important part of our public service, one that we pledge to continue."

Nearly 80 percent of donors using Give2Asia are individuals and families who have some family or ethnic connection to the country to which they donate. Some examples of the kinds of diaspora donations that go to India via Give2Asia are documented by Bakshi and Baron (2011) in their report *Enabling Indian Diaspora Philanthropy*. For example, the Deshpande family foundation of Gururaj and Jayshree Deshpande based in Massachusetts supports over 80 NGOs working in the areas of livelihoods, education, health, and agriculture in five districts in northern Karnataka, where the family of Mr Deshpande comes from. Their Hubli Sandbox program takes a grassroots approach to scalable solutions, and works with NGOs, academics, organizations, and entrepreneurs to launch effective and scalable models of development. Their website reports having reached more than one million families in northern Karnataka.[6] The Deshpandes have also made large donations to the IIT (Madras), and are the founding donors of the Public Health Foundation of India (PHFI), along side the Government of India, Bill Gates, and other domestic donors. PHFI's ultimate goal is to strengthen India's public health institutions and systems' capability by training public health professionals and advancing public health research and technology.[7]

---

[5] www.guidestarindia.org
[6] deshpandefoundationindia.org
[7] www.phfi.org

Conclusion

Some scholars have critiqued diaspora philanthropy, saying that individuals often contribute on the basis of narrow regional, ethnic, or personal affiliations (Kapur et al. 2004). Given that the Indian immigrants in the US and Canada most likely came from relatively wealthier cities and regions, such as Kerala, Gujarat, and Punjab, they are also more likely to send their philanthropic donations to these areas, thus exacerbating existing inequities and distorting national priorities for development with their own favorites. Critics cite the diaspora's response to the Gujarat earthquake as an example of this issue, arguing that:

> Both the direct and leveraging effects of diasporic philanthropy meant that this tragedy received far greater resources than others. The spatial concentration on one cause was exacerbated by the concentration of resources on one activity—building houses (in Kutch today there are umpteen empty houses build by NGOs). In contrast the response to the riots was muted. And in both cases, preventive measures, especially developing and funding groups that could press for greater accountability from public officials and private builders, received short shrift. (Kapur et al. 2004: 16)

They further question the flow of donations through the diaspora's faith-based organizations that may have sectarian and intolerant goals. It would serve the philanthropic community well to "build upon the religious sentiments of the diaspora and provide them with information and analysis that helps them make more informed choices as well as a range of institutional mechanisms encompassing NGOs and organizations across all religions that offer a more constructive agenda" (Kapur et al. 2004: 16).

Does diaspora funding crowd out government spending? This question is always raised when private individuals and organizations get involved in spending on public services such as education, health, and environmental conservation. The same is true for poor countries that rely heavily on remittances from immigrants as well as philanthropic donations. Kapur et al. (2004) raise the question: "Do diasporic funds crowd-in or crowd-out other funds?" In other words, does diasporic funding substitute or complement other public and private funds? In addition, one can question whether diaspora funds should be seen as a form of insurance against natural disaster. Diaspora funds have been particularly salient during times of natural disasters such as the earthquakes in India, when the diaspora quickly mobilized to send millions of dollars to help with relief efforts and rehabilitation of affected communities. But such responses can be misplaced, and follow-up efforts become weaker when the initial shock and emotional response wear down and fewer resources are available to meet the affected communities' other needs.

Many changes are taking place among the prominent diaspora donors. Influential and rich diaspora Indians are joining the Gates–Buffett 'Giving Pledge,' which invites the wealthiest individuals and families in the world to commit to giving the majority of their wealth to philanthropy. Among the 127 members currently signed up, several of them are diaspora Indians: Manoj Bhargava, whose foundations include Knowledge Medical Charitable Trust and Rural India Charitable Trust, Vinod Khosla, and Neeru Khosla. In 2006, Neeru Khosla cofounded the CK-12 Foundation, which aims to develop open-source textbooks to lower the cost of education worldwide; Dr Romesh and Kathleen Wadhwani, whose Wadhwani Foundation has several high-impact initiatives in India, which include promoting entrepreneurial and employment skills and encouraging innovations.

For many years, the Government of India viewed foreign donations with skepticism and fear, making it difficult for Indian NGOs to receive foreign funding. Recently, however, the Indian government has made concerted efforts to attract Indian diaspora philanthropy and investments by holding annual conferences and even offering certain types of citizenship privileges to maintain the attachment of the Indian diaspora with India. It is expected that diaspora giving to India will increase in the coming years.

Case Studies

Case Study 1. Kashif Kumar

Kashif Kumar secured success as a young man in the corporate world. Trained in chartered accounting at Unilever and in management at Hindustan Lever, Kashif spent his prime years working in senior executive positions in both India and abroad. When he turned 40, he felt that he had accomplished enough and, exhausted with corporate life, decided to retire in order to devote himself to spiritual pursuits, especially the study of sacred scriptures. Just as he was getting ready to retire, the Indian industrial tycoon Raj Kapoor, whose family had lived a few generations in Hong Kong, approached Kashif for assistance. Kapoor was looking for someone who could properly train his sons to succeed him in his business as he believed that it was better for a 'professional outsider' to initiate his sons to business rather than attempt it himself. Kashif fit the bill with his professional business skills and qualifications. Initially, Kashif was reluctant to postpone his dreams of solitary study, and tried to excuse himself on the grounds that he wanted to devote the remainder of his life to studying the sacred scriptures (Vedas) and 'creating value.' In the end, Mr Kapoor convinced Kashif that there were many ways to create value, one of which was helping his sons receive proper training to carry on their father's legacy and work in the commercial world. Ultimately, Kashif accepted the challenge. He liaised between the board of trustees and the two sons, and set up a training program in Hong Kong.

Over time, he became aware of the fact that various members of the Kapoor family in Hong Kong had not forgotten their roots and were supporters of NGOs in India. However, these efforts were carried out individually and without any coordination or focus. Most often, a member of the family would be approached or felt affinity for a particular Indian NGO, and wrote a check to help. There was no follow-up or consistency in the help that was extended, which was unsurprising as the younger members of the family who had given money were educated in the West and knew very little about India or how NGOs functioned in the Indian context. As chairman of the company in Hong Kong, the senior Mr Kapoor was interested in creating a foundation through which all the individual donations could be channeled. In order to do this systematically, and with due scrutiny, he appointed Kashif to investigate the NGOs that were given assistance. First off, Kashif created a 'requests for approval' form for the NGOs that sought help. The form required the NGOs to complete a proposal and state their background. This information allowed Kashif to recognize commonalities in the donations as well as weed out what seemed to be fraudulent claims. In 2001, the Kapoor Foundation was officially set up, with a board comprising the chairman and five counselors. Input on what causes the foundation should support was garnered from all the family members, who agreed to focus on helping children in rural areas with education, health, and income-oriented initiatives in just four states, including Gujarat, the state to which the family traced their roots.

Eventually, an extensive process was set up: Kashif either approached a prospective NGO or was approached by one, after which the NGO was investigated. Kashif found that 30 percent of all NGOs had a gap between what they claimed to do and what they actually did. He called these the 'failed' NGOs. About 20 percent of NGOs were not bad, but not great. These were the 'mediocre' NGOs. However, 50 percent of the NGOs were 'good' and delivered on their promises. Once Kashif zeroed in on an NGO that was seeking help, he suggested ways that it could be further improved. Some NGOs were not open to suggestions, and preferred to stay their traditional route; these were removed from consideration. Those NGOs willing to improve received support from the Kapoor Foundation.

One of the authors of this book met with Kashif and asked him to share a few success stories of the Kapoor Foundation. These included:

1. **Wadi Program**: This program focuses on developing horticulture projects in conjunction with the Bharat Agro India Foundation (BAIF) to reduce migrations out of rural villages. It adopts two villages for a five-year cycle, during which BAIF provides villagers with crop seeds for cashews and mangoes so they can better utilize their land and export crops for profits. Also, the villagers are taught a watershed program that helps conserve water. Combined, these initiatives enhance the livelihoods of villagers and diminish migration.

2. **Vidhya Poshak**: This program funds meritorious students in the villages of Karnataka so they can pursue higher education. Though Sudha Murthy's Infosys Foundation began the initiative in 2003, Kashif found flaws in the foundation's method of working with students on a year-to-year basis. Kashif modified the program's methods by having it support students from Grade 11 onward till they complete their undergraduate studies, which increased the program's stability. To date, INR 10 crore (the equivalent of US$2,332,627.85) have been invested to help about 2,000 students graduate from university. As funding is not indefinite, Kashif is in the

process of setting up a microfinance company to give students loans that can be paid back once students graduate and find employment, with the interest rate kept at a reasonable rate during the years of study.

3. **Kanyakumari—Vivekananda Kendra Balwadi:** The Balwadi is a primary day-care program that looks after children who range in age from two to five years and whose parents work on the land. The program teaches values and interactive skills, and the children greatly benefit from the intellectual stimulus and nutritious meals that are provided. Studies have found that children who undergo this program tend to stay in school and have bright futures; there are already a number of past attendees who have achieved successful careers and contribute to the program today. Though Birla's Foundation had funded the program for many years, it sought an alternative donor and Kashif offered to take over. Kashif saw value in the way the program raised future leaders, and decided to fund the project as long as the Kapoor Foundation exists.

Kashif understands the significance of his role as "philanthropy facilitator" in the foundation, and believes every foundation should have a point person in charge of assessing each project/cause and measuring the impact the funds have made. In this way, the foundation can be assured that it has received the best "bang for its buck"—indeed, this is smart diaspora giving!

Case Study 2. Kishore M

Kishore M was born and raised in Wynnewood. As the closest mandir of the Swaminarayan movement—a modern sect of Hinduism—at that time was located in New York, Kishore M would visit the mandir occasionally but felt that he was missing a cultural connection. It was not until 1991 that Kishore M got more involved with the local Swaminarayan chapter (SC). He volunteered to set up computer booths for six months with the Cultural Festival of India (CFI) organized by SC in Edison, New Jersey. These computer booths had displays of educational software about different aspects of Indian culture, saints, architecture, and scriptures of the ancient Indian texts of the Ramayana and the Mahabharata. Back in those days, there were no multimedia or graphics software, disk operating system (DOS) was the prevalent operating system, and Windows was in its initial development phase. Thus, Kishore M had to rely heavily on C language programming with PCX toolkit for developing this educational software. He worked with another Indian volunteer, Bhave, who supplied authentic source and raw material for the content of these presentations while he tailored the software to cater to the average American. In six months, Kishore M's team was able to develop presentational software that employed multimedia and animation effects. Kishore M believed that this project was like a "crash course" for him and that he "would have never been able to learn so much in such a short time through other professional courses." This learning experience through volunteerism ultimately helped him get a job. But what motivated him most was how the religious leader Swaminarayan Sanstha Pramukh Swami Maharaj took interest in his work. He believes that this cultural gathering helped bring together many Indian immigrant youths in the US to work as a team.

Shortly after the CFI 1991, the BAPS center at Edison was set up, and the event brought about many developments such as youth development and leadership programs. Kishore M worked with a volunteer team to plan local- and national-level youth activities. The team did extensive studies on how the media and American society influenced the youth, and developed program curriculums that the youth could understand. Kishore M then focused on regional activities of the tristate area of Delaware, New Jersey, and Pennsylvania. He gave lectures and wrote articles for regional youth forums in Philadelphia, Cherry Hill, Lansdale, and other cities. Halfway through the first decade of the 21st century, the number of volunteers grew and younger volunteers started taking on responsibilities, building on the setup already developed by Kishore M and others.

Senior volunteers at BAPS felt that they needed Kishore M's energy to develop BAPS Medical services in the US, and though Kishore M had little background in medicine itself, he was flexible enough to adapt to this new voluntary role. Through his employment at a pharmaceutical company, he got involved in Medicare Part D awareness programs. He believes that "people should not be left out of benefitting from a program because they do not have information due to a language barrier. If people did not register during a stipulated time, the penalty for late registration would increase every month." Through his involvement with SC, Kishore M was able to effectively spread awareness of health insurance in the South Asian community in the Philadelphia region through presentations in native languages. He used a template that has been replicated as well as handouts that have been disseminated at other BAPS centers across North America.

In 2007, after hearing about Kishore M's voluntary efforts, the American Cancer Society approached him for assistance in reaching out to the Asian Indian community. Through his coordination, many women from the community volunteered for the American Cancer Society. The women were educated about not only annual mammogram routines but also how to take better care of themselves and their families. Through the collaboration between the American Cancer Society and SC, women could sign up for free mammograms from a local hospital.

The same year, Kishore M arranged for the Philadelphia Corporation for Aging to join hands with BAPS Charities, American Cancer Society, and St Mary's Hospital in organizing the first annual health fair at the BAPS Center, Philadelphia campus. Expanding on this, Kishore M worked with the American Red Cross to develop a comprehensive kit with a detailed checklist for organizing a blood donation program at the BAPS Philadelphia Center. This toolkit was later adopted by many other BAPS centers in North America for their blood drive programs. Thanks to the work of Kishore M and other members of his team, BAPS Charities has partnered with the American Heart Association, American Diabetes Association, and other organizations.

In response to the burden of having to travel long distances from homes, many patients faced difficulties finding accommodation during the time of cancer treatment, so winding down lodges (WDLs) were built. These lodges gave free temporary residences for needy patients undergoing cancer treatment. Kishore M volunteered to be the coordinator at WDL so that there could be a regular volunteer presence. He worked with different network groups and departments at the pharmaceutical company to organize various events at the WDL for cancer patients. He recollects, "AT the WDL, I would play games like Jeopardy and help organize music and dance nights to help cancer patients forget their pain and disease... [and lift] their spirits."

Case Study 3. Sai Chakapatam

An agnostic for most of his life, Sai Chakapatam recollects being raised to question and distrust organized religion and faith. One incident, however, completely changed his view on faith. On the ill-fated morning of September 11, 2001, in New York, Chakapatam witnessed the attack on the north tower from one of the lower floors of the south tower. While he managed to escape to safety before the south tower was attacked, Chakapatam watched in horror as people jumped off the higher floors of the building, unable to bear the heat. The haunting images would continue to disturb his psyche, and he was left in a state of consternation. Reflecting upon the event, Chakapatam said, "For many people it shook their faith in God, but for me it shook my faith in non-faith." He was left wondering why he lived while many others around him were not fortunate enough to see another day.

A few months later, a friend introduced Chakapatam to Vedic lectures at the Arsha Bodha Center in New Jersey. The lectures strengthened his belief in the brevity of life, and he came to see the futility of wealth and possessions. Chakapatam was later introduced to the Chinmaya Mission Center at Princeton, which, like its cognate Arsha Bodha Center, emphasized the teachings of the Vedas. Chakapatam believes these faith-based teachings have changed him for the better, especially in inspiring his philanthropic endeavors.

Chakapatam's daughter also got involved with the Chinmaya Mission Center, and decided to volunteer in India for a month with the center's Bal Vihar program. Volunteers would work with an organization called CORD India in Sidhbari to help the rural community. Though Chakapatam initially felt reluctant to send his young American-born daughter, as he feared she would have a hard time adjusting to the climate and rural environment, he agreed to let her go on the condition that he accompany the group as a parent chaperone.

During their stay in Sidhbari, the volunteers taught many handicapped children and young women how to earn a self-sustainable livelihood. They also participated in campaigns that helped spread awareness of government programs available to the underserved, such as the government-funded National Rural Employment Guarantee Scheme. The key focus was to educate people about long-term solutions so they could sustain themselves once the volunteers left.

Furthermore, the volunteers donated bags of beads that they had brought from the US to the poor and handicapped children. The children were taught to make bracelets and necklaces from these beads, which they could then sell for a modest living. Chakapatam's greatest memorabilia from this experience are pieces of jewelry, inscribed with the names of the children who made them.

Throughout the month in India, the local CORD center provided the volunteers with food, transportation, and even inspiration. Chakapatam and the other American volunteers were touched by the simple and grounded lifestyle of the local volunteers, especially that of Dr Kshama Metre, the director of the CORD operations. Chakapatam remarked, "I had seen how the volunteers and Dr. Metre lived there and how they work. I know that for every dollar I would send to this place, at least 62 cents would go to the needy."

Though the program was meant for youngsters, Chakapatam felt that he gained valuable insight on the plight of the underprivileged in rural India. Inspired by CORD India's work, Chakapatam organizes an annual local fund-raiser for different causes in India. With these funds, he travels on his own account to India and spends his annual vacations volunteering at different NGOs for a wide range of causes. Chakapatam says his yearly volunteer trips make the rest of the year worthwhile, and he looks forward to yet another trip.

6

Trends in Philanthropy

Introduction

In India and all over the world, people are beginning to alter their 'giving' behavior, from one oriented around charity to one oriented around philanthropy. Whereas charity tries to address an immediate need of a person or a group of persons, philanthropy seeks to affect long-term change through giving. Philanthropy thus requires an understanding of the complexity surrounding the social issues people want to resolve. Researchers have long been grappling with an understanding of 'giving' as a way to address immediate needs, and 'giving' as a way to bring about social change. Korten (1987) grappled with the same problem when he created a typology of NGO activities. Whereas the first activity met an urgent required need, the second level of giving was more sophisticated in that it involved increasing the capacities of individuals so that they learn to function independently and meet their own needs in the long run. The last three levels of activities help bring about structural long-term change and are therefore deemed as the most strategic and meaningful. The authors of the aptly named article 'Family and Corporate Philanthropy: Emerging Trends in India' (Ramachandran and Schmidheiny 2010) seem to be making the same distinction as Korten (1987) as they note the evolution from charity to philanthropy as an emerging trend. They use the same adage that Handy et al. (2006) employ to exemplify the difference between charity and philanthropy inherent in Korten's typology: "Give a man a fish, you feed him for a day, teach a man to fish, you feed him for a lifetime." They draw attention to the increasing shift in recent years from charity to philanthropy in many new activities such as preservation of art, history, as well as safeguarding the environment. This trend was noted when family businesses slowly transformed their charitable impulses into sustainable organized philanthropic initiatives, and companies started setting up CSR wings (Ramachandran 2009).

This chapter looks at various emerging trends in Indian philanthropy—in which Indians are focusing on more secular giving to achieve sustainable, longer term change. Following a brief review of seven key trends, we examine Indian philanthropy in the context of global philanthropy as well as across the BRICS, to contextualize philanthropic trends in India with what is happening in other countries. While it would be impossible, in this research, to cover each emerging trend in Indian philanthropy, some of the most important and indicative trends are explored in this chapter and illustrated by three case studies: Dasra, GiveIndia, and Kiran Mazumdar-Shaw.

Trends in Indian Philanthropy

Trend: The Growth of Philanthropic Capital

Major philanthropic players are giving more. According to consulting group Bain & Company, India's pool of philanthropic capital is growing, thanks to an increase in wealthy individuals' contributions to philanthropy from 2–3 percent of household income in 2010 to 3.1 percent in 2011 (Seth and Singhal 2011). Numerous philanthropists are giving or are pledging to give at record high levels. For example, Biocon CEO Kiran Mazumdar-Shaw has pledged to give away 75 percent of her wealth when she dies (*Forbes* 2010), and Grandhi Rao, the founder of infrastructure conglomerate GMR Group, has pledged $340 million—his 12.5 percent personal stake in the business and one-eighth of his family's share—through an irrevocable endowment to the GMR Varalakshmi Foundation (*Forbes* 2011). Others are P. N. C. Menon, the chairman of Sobha Developers, who plans to give away half of his estimated $435 million fortune (Koppisch 2013), and Rohini Nilekani, who sold $27 million worth of her shares in Infosys in 2013 to give to select social ventures (Koppisch 2014). Azim Premji, one of the leading philanthropists in the country, was the first Indian to sign the Giving Pledge[1] in 2013, when he committed to donating more than 12 percent of his stake in Wipro Limited to

---

[1] This pledge is an effort by Bill Gates and Warren Buffet to get the world's richest to give at least half of their wealth to philanthropy (*Economic Times* 2014).

the Azim Premji Foundation. Also, Azim Premji has already given 25 percent of his personal wealth to charity (Dhamija 2013). More recently Billionaire Anil Agarwal who founded and chairs Vedanta Resources has public reaffirmed his pledge to donate 75 percent of his wealth. However, he has not yet signed the Giving Pledge. So far only four Indians have signed the Giving Pledge and Azim Premji is the only one based in India. The others are Indian Americans Vinod Khosla, Manoj Bhargava and Romesh Wadhwani (Karmali 2014).

Not only are individual philanthropists giving more, but the nation as a whole is also projected to give more as private companies channel their capital into corporate social responsibility (CSR). The new Companies Act 2013 formalizes the role of CSR, set at 2 percent of post-tax profit for big companies. This regulatory change is estimated to unlock $3.7 billion in CSR total spending in 2014. Though this seems like a large availability of funds, there are many causes that are in dire need of funding such as education and the environment (Seth et al. 2014).

Trend: Interest in Impact

There is an increased effort and interest on part of philanthropists to ensure their contributions make the intended impact. Some have even started their own foundations in order to control the foundations' direction and efforts to achieve some desired result. Ashish Dhawan, a Harvard MBA and former Goldman Sachs banker, founded his own private equity firm after returning to India from the US, but gave it all up to start his Central Square Foundation. To advance the quality of primary to secondary education for the masses, his foundation focuses on training teachers, tracking the quality of teacher training institutions, and improving the education of principals. Not only that, Dhawan works with the government and a network of NGOs to create a chain of affordable schools, thereby rounding off his efforts to improve education. Other philanthropists who are taking a more hands-on approach to their philanthropic efforts include Vineet Nayar, vice-chairman of HCL Technologies, and Rohini Nilekani, founder of Arghyam. Nayar supports Sampark, a charity that works with governments to improve schools and expand water supplies. Nayar first got involved because his wife started Sampark; however, Nayar is now dedicated to the charity's efforts full-time (Koppisch 2013). Rohini Nilekani who founded Arghyam and Pratham Books—which promote sanitation and literacy, respectively—gives philanthropic grants to organizations that she believes will make a measurable difference in the areas that are important to her. In general, donors are thinking more about their potential impact before they fund a cause (Rai 2013). Many philanthropists also prefer to support projects that have a good track record of ameliorating the social issues that matter to them. Thus, there is more talk of scoping out the right organizations to support (Mangaleswaran and Venkataraman 2013).

Trend: Philanthropists Are Starting Early

Not only are philanthropists giving more and in a manner that is impact driven, they are starting to give at an earlier age. Bain's 2013 Philanthropy Report suggests that a young league of philanthropists—under the age of 40 and with less than three years of experience in philanthropy—are now entering the realm and their influence cannot be ignored. These younger stalwarts are influencing philanthropic giving in their own families. It is encouraging to see that in prominently philanthropic families such as the Agas, the Nadars, the Kotharis, and the Jindals, the values of philanthropy have been successfully passed onto the next generations. In such families, older and younger generations are working together for good causes, with the younger generations contributing enthusiasm and bright ideas that are then tempered and rendered practical by older generations that provide the experience, guidance, and funds (Ghosh 2011).

Trend: Foundations Are Preferred Channels

Foundations are increasingly seen as the most favored channel for giving because of their transparency and their focus on bringing about sustainable change in specific problematic areas. Bain's 2013 survey suggests that transparency and accountability of NGOs affect philanthropists' willingness to donate to them, so much so that more than 25 percent of donors said they would give more if impact communication improved: "This is likely to create an uplift of about 20% in donations from impact-motivated HNWIs" (Seth and Bhagwat 2013: 12). Although there is "broad consensus among donors and recipient NGOs that the work they fund or do is meaningful and leads to change" (Bain's 2013 survey shows a solid 80 percent of donors are satisfied with the effect of their contributions, and 90 percent of the NGOs are satisfied with what they are accomplishing), there is a discrepancy in how donors and NGOs connote 'success' (Seth and Bhagwat 2013: 4). For one, donors measure the 'success' of their donations by statistical outcomes—such as the percentage increase of children enrolled in school, or an increase in numbers of patients benefiting from surgeries and other treatments, and so forth. While NGOs realize donors' demands for statistical impact statements, they are bound by more qualitative constraints and are unable to communicate the complexity of gauging success in terms of numbers. Systemic change is difficult to measure, as it addresses deeper behavioral changes that are difficult to quantify (Seth and Bhagwat 2013). Fortunately, strategic philanthropy is on the rise with foundations such as Dasra that promote collaboration between philanthropists, researchers, and NGOs to take on complex social issues such as the empowerment of adolescent girls in India. Together, they are better positioned to bring about long-term social change and communicate the outcomes in a way that satisfies philanthropists (for further information, see case study on Dasra).

Trend: Increasing Use of Technology

Indian NGOs increasingly use technology to stimulate fund-raising and address donors' needs. Some Indian NGOs such as iCharity, Karmic Foundation, Ketto, GuideStar, and GiveIndia are taking advantage of technology to reach out and campaign for donations from international and domestic donors, often to great effect.

India is well wired as the world's third largest Internet user after China and the US According to India's 2011 census, 9.4 percent of Indian households have access to computers and 3.1 percent of households have Internet, with India's total Internet subscribers at 238.71 million at the end of December 2013 (Press Trust of India [PTI] 2014)—80 percent of these Internet subscribers are active users of the

Internet, indicating a huge cyber market potential (Agarwal 2013). Online donors in India tend to be urban, middle class, moderately religious, educated, and employed, and the heaviest Internet users are men under 35 and women between 35 and 44 (Special Correspondent 2013). While there is potential, this new group of potential donors is skeptical and prefers to give directly to selected causes rather than through flashy websites, according to a study conducted by GiveIndia of its users (Shier and Handy 2012: 227).

Cyber givers are usually those who take the initiative in giving rather than wait to be asked. As a sizeable portion of the population still prefers a more private and anonymous form of giving that will not harvest public acclaim, cyber NGOs are not sure how to extend their reach to all levels of the public (corporations as well as the public at large). According to a study by Bain & Company of high-net-worth philanthropists in some of India's largest urban areas, lack of transparency and accountability is the top hurdle for increasing charitable contributions online, followed by lack of awareness of channels for routing money, and unfriendly tax laws for donations (Seth 2012: 14). GiveIndia is one of the NGOs that successfully took on the challenge to ensure donors that their gifts were indeed going to the targeted recipients rather than to some nefarious NGO officials (see case study on GiveIndia).

Trend: Venture Philanthropy

Venture philanthropy is another growing trend in Indian philanthropy. Unlike traditional philanthropy, "venture philanthropy focuses on developing a deeper ongoing interaction between donor and recipient, with an emphasis on measurable results. The concept revolves around making social, ethical, and other do-good objectives part of investment decision-making" (Spevacek 2010). Venture philanthropy firms differ from other firms in that their business models measure returns for investment in terms of social benefits and not just monetary rewards. The Acumen Fund is one such venture philanthropy firm that uses a rigorous evaluation measure to decide upon the charitable project it will invest in. Primarily, it seeks to fund sustainable ideas that aim to improve the lives of those at the 'bottom of the pyramid' (the 2 billion people subsisting on $4 a day or less). In 2000, the Acumen Fund invested $1 million in a small IT firm called Drishtee Dot Com, which gives citizens access to computerized kiosks that provide critical information on health, pensions, government resources, and so on. Thanks to the funding, Drishtee Dot Com established more than 1,000 kiosks by 2006. Acumen plans to invest even more money in this firm in the future (Spevacek 2010).

Trend: Indian Women and Philanthropy

Women are giving more and are increasingly featured in articles on philanthropy. A list of the world's top philanthropists published by *Forbes* (March 6, 2010) features four Indian women:

1. **Anu Aga,** the director of Thermax, used to donate 1 percent of the company's profits to charity. At that time, she was preoccupied with the crises in her life: her young son died in a car crash. Then her husband died. These unfortunate incidences left her insecure, and her giving to social causes was irregular as she tried to make a success of running the company, Thermax, on her own. However, after meeting Bill Gates and Warren Buffet, she was inspired to develop a more consistent and focused mode of giving. In 2007, Aga established the Thermax Corporate Foundation that focuses on ensuring access to education for the many poor children in the villages and urban slums. She designated 3 percent of the company's pretax profits to fund the foundation. Today, Aga's daughter is the chairperson of Thermax and continues to expand the foundation's work (Ghosh 2011).

2. **Roshni Nadar,** the only child of HCL chairman Shiv Nadar, has always been interested in strengthening the social sector, and currently works to consolidate HCL's philanthropic initiatives under one umbrella: the Shiv Nadar Foundation. Though she is the CEO and executive director of HCL she spends a large amount of her time working with the Shiv Nadar Foundation. She is especially interested in Vidya Gyan that ensures free education for the less privileged children. Roshni is also a trustee of the Kiran Nadar Museum where she works

with her mother, Kiran, to try and bring art to the public at large. Kiran Nadar founded India's only private art museum. She donated her private art collection to form this museum that boasts a free entrance and a mandate to bring art to the general public.

3. **Rohini Nilekani** is the wife of Nandan, cofounder of Infosys. She grew wealthy by investing in the company, and used her resources wisely to set up two organizations—to which she has dedicated about $40 million in the past decade (Karmali 2013). In 2004, she started Pratham Books to reduce the cost of books for marginalized children. A year later, Rohini used a personal endowment to set up Arghyam, a public charitable organization that works in the areas of water and sanitation. In March 2013, Rohini sold 577,000 of her 8 million Infosys shares, and used the INR 164 crore to fund philanthropic ventures in areas that she favors: governance, legal services, environment protection, as well as new media. She believes that by providing money for grants, she can monitor their use and evaluate the impact they make (Rai 2013).

4. Biocon's CEO **Kiran Mazumdar-Shaw** is considered the richest self-made woman in India. Her philanthropic contributions are astounding: she donated $10 million to the Bangalore Cancer Center, and donates $2 million annually toward the health insurance of villagers in the state of Karnataka and has committed $3 million to the Hyderabad Business School, to name just a few of her ongoing donations. Kiran is featured in a case study discussed in this chapter.

Indian Philanthropy in the Context of Global Philanthropy

Introduction

In every country around the world, unique philanthropic structures and tendencies are shaped by historical, political, and economic factors. India's philanthropy story today at one level—particularly among the country's globalized wealthy elite—reflects global giving trends, while at another level—generally among the rural, less educated, or less well-off—maintains distinct Indian traditional giving characteristics. At the same time, there has been increasing global philanthropic interest in India, reflected in a rise in the number of NGOs registered under the FCRA, from approximately 30,000 to 44,000 over the past 10 years (Seth 2015). The FCRA registration makes them eligible to receive donations from foreign sources. Moreover, domestic philanthropic donations are ahead of donations in other developing countries in the world, with a larger percentage of Indians making charitable donations than other countries of similar level of prosperity (Seth 2015). For example, although India and the US have smaller adult populations, they have more adults donating money to charity, according to the 2013 The World Giving Index—published by the CAF (2014)

This section reviews the global trends that have a long history of influence in India. Like donors around the world, Indian donors seek transparency and professionalization from NGOs. We examine philanthropy in India as a reflection of the country's political and economic development status.

Influence of Global Trends

India has a deep-rooted culture of philanthropy; but just as the country has a long history of global nexuses—whether through trade or colonization—global trends have long played a role influencing domestic philanthropy. For example, when Christianity arrived in India, it played an important role in organizing charity and institutionalizing philanthropy through the construction of schools, hospitals, homes for the elderly, and so forth. British Victorian ideas regarding deserving and undeserving poor, and emphasis on private efforts to help the poor, influenced Indian elites to structure their giving. Today, as India becomes increasingly globalized, its elite travel and work abroad, and diaspora Indians maintain close ties or even choose to move back to India, global philanthropic trends influence Indian giving to a greater extent than ever before, as illustrated in figure 6.1.

Figure 6.1:

India's Philanthropy Sector is Mature Compared to Countries with Similar Profiles

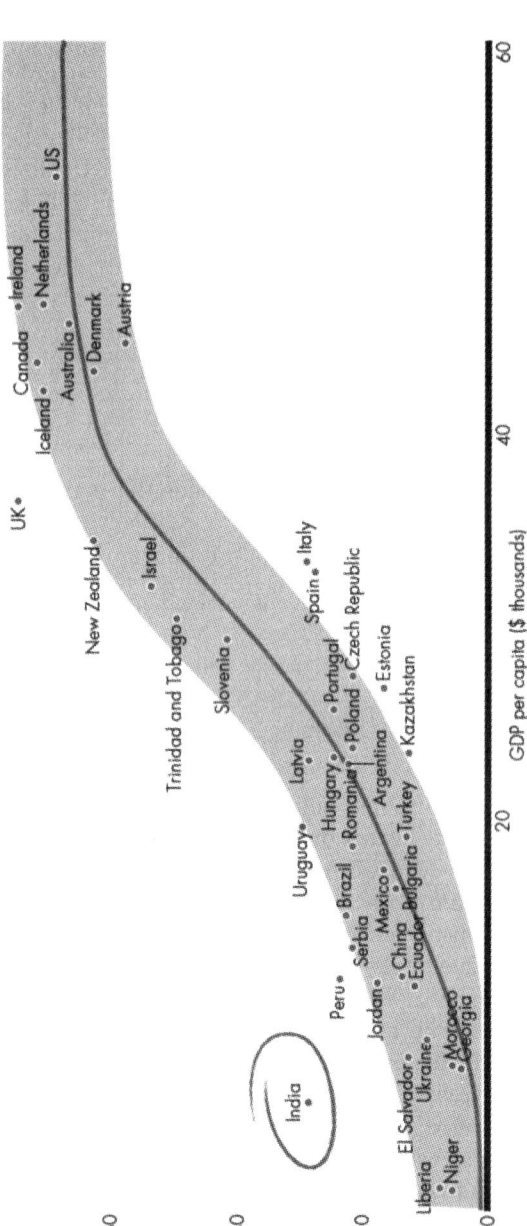

% adult population donating money (2013)

Note: GDP per capita based on country's GDP accounting for Purchasing Power Parity for year 2013.

Sources: Euromonitor; World Giving Index 2014 by Charities Aid Foundation

Source: Arpan Seth, 2015.

TRANSPARENCY AND PROFESSIONALISM

Around the world, public trust, issues of transparency, accountability, and effectiveness are universal as facilitating factors for philanthropy (Wiepking and Handy 2015). Among India's philanthropists—particularly the larger donors—transparency and professionalism of NGOs has never been so important. According to one study (which surveyed 377 donors in India), around 50 percent said they did not know a sufficient number of credible organizations or foundations through which to spread their donations—thus concentrating their giving on the few NGOs they know well and trust (Seth 2015). By contrast, with smaller donations there is less risk and thus lower desire to seek out specific information from the NGOs—consequently creating what may be considered an "apathetic" group of donors who give to a NGO mostly because friends or family did, due to guilt or a sense of need to give back (Seth 2015).

In some countries, the lack of NGO transparency and effectiveness is more a matter of public perception than an actual problem. In India, many well-run NGOs are also suspect due to the endemic corruption in all sectors, and there is pressure on government to regulate NGOs with greater care. The recognition of the need for transparency and good governance in NGOs, as an issue in itself also indicates the growing sophistication of Indian donors.

Strong government regulations that NGOs must adhere to often have a positive impact on donor trust as they make NGOs more accountable and effective (Wiepking and Handy 2015). Yet this may result in an additional administrative burden of meeting the regulations and increase the overhead costs of using professional staff. Such professionalization of India's NGO sector will lead to it moving away from volunteer-based grassroots organizations and toward more bureaucratic organizations with formal procedures, adherence to rules and regulations, and hiring paid employees who have credentialed skills.

NGOs need to become more professionalized and increase their communication with donors regarding their finances and the overheads. In turn, donors, who consider low overheads important, should also play a more active role, by not only contributing funds but also contributing their guidance, skills, time, and oversight (Seth 2015).

POLITICAL AND DEVELOPMENT STATUS

Just like news headlines around the world commenting on India's economic potential, the growth in the Indian philanthropic sector has been phenomenal; the country's ranking has improved in the World Giving Index from 134th place in 2010 to 69th place at present—from the bottom to the middle of the pack (Seth 2015). In 2010, Indians collectively donated 0.6 percent of GDP to charity—higher than other emerging markets such as Brazil (0.3 percent) or China (0.1 percent), but well below that of developed economies such as Canada (1.3 percent) or the US (2.2 percent) (Seth and Singhal 2011). In 2013, 28 percent of people in India made charitable donations, compared to 74 percent in the UK (Seth 2015).

What shapes India's particular philanthropic scale and nature are its political stability, its economic growth, its democratic government, as well as its level of development. In places of political or economic instability, NGOs struggle to operate and households are less likely to donate due to perceptions of their own financial stability (Wiepking and Handy 2015). In democratic countries, where there is a good relationship between the state and the nonprofit sector, people typically are more inclined to make donations as a good relationship between the state and the nonprofit sector signals trustworthiness (Wiepking and Handy 2015).

Fiscal incentives are also important to donors. Developed nations tend to have more generous incentives, such as in the US where donations are tax deductible from income taxes. In India, such tax incentives also exist but are less generous than in developed countries. Indeed, the tax incentive was the second most important expectation of 377 surveyed Indian donors, after the issue of transparency in application of funds (Seth 2015). Given the complexity of fiscal incentives in each country and differing tax treatments for donors depending on income levels, nature of the gift, and the purpose of the gift, it is not possible to make direct comparisons. However, as pointed out by Mark Lyons (p. 597) in Wiepking and Handy (2015) who examines the influence of fiscal incentives on philanthropy across nations, fiscal incentives do encourage donations and thus have a great impact on the robustness and scale of the NGO sector.

Across many developed nations, NGOs are implementing welfare systems, creating a sector largely dependent on financial support from the government (Wiepking and Handy 2015). While Indian NGOs are largely reliant on government funding, trust is still lacking. This may be explained by cultural values and perceptions of the role of philanthropy and NGOs: in liberal regimes—such as the US—NGOs are seen as instrumental in the provision of public goods and services, while in more welfare state regimes—such as India's—they are perceived as supplementary to the state (Wiepking and Handy 2015). Nonetheless, as the government implements the Companies Act 2013, it is estimated that it may produce $2.5–3.3 billion in corporate contributions to the philanthropy space (Seth 2015)—giving NGOs a huge boost and renewed role aligned with the private sector.

Every country struggles to find the right balance of government regulation (which can have positive impacts on increasing nonprofit accountability) without being overbearing. While some countries have voluntary third-party seals of approval (including Austria, Germany, Ireland, Israel, Mexico, the Netherlands, Switzerland, and the US), others face high levels of government regulation and control (such as China, Israel, and Lebanon) (Wiepking and Handy 2015). India is not at either extreme, but government regulation is increasing in the form of the FCRA and Companies Act 2013, mandating companies of a certain size to donate 2 percent of profits toward CSR.

Globally, the typical donor is religious, older, wealthy, and highly educated. Education boosts donations as the educated tend to have access to not only greater financial and social resources but also better understanding of the needs of others. As India's level of education and life expectancy increase, its philanthropic output is also likely to increase. At the same time, as religion remains strong in India, with high levels of trust in local temples and churches, it is likely that donations to religious causes and institutions will continue to dominate philanthropic giving.

Conclusion

India's philanthropic sector in many ways reflects global trends. India's globalized elites, historically and still today, are influenced by global trends such as demanding greater professionalization, transparency, and effectiveness from the nonprofit sector. At the same time, the relationship between NGOs and governments is changing worldwide, so too in India. And as support for NGOs from government declines, it is apparent that there is even greater need for a professional fund-raising culture to develop in India. At the same time, the need for NGOs to find private money to replace government funds is increasing.

Three key trends, reflecting global philanthropy, are starting to emerge in India, and will play a significant role in the future of India's philanthropic space. First, the visibility of wealthy donors giving away large sums of money motivates other wealthy individuals to follow their examples. While the Giving Pledge did not take off in India, there are clear signs of the country's elite competing to establish their own charitable foundations and demonstrate their philanthropic work.

Second, media attention on philanthropic activities is growing, increasing from a mere 426 mentions in the print media in 2009 to doubling the number of mentions in 2015—albeit still far from the 11,000 media reports of philanthropy in the US in 2013 (Seth 2015). Third, but not the least, is the trend toward professionalization among the NGO sector; some nascent national umbrella organizations are emerging, and are set to play an increasingly important role in creating benchmarks and standards for governance and transparency among NGOs.

India and the BRICS

The World Giving Index—published by the CAF—used Gallup's surveys of 195,000 people in 153 nations to create a picture of "giving" around the world. Predictably, the rich countries dominated the top positions. However, it was noteworthy that certain developing nations such as Guinea, Guyana, and Turkmenistan were also vying for the top positions, suggesting that one does not have to have a lot in order to be 'giving.' Even more perplexing was the fact that emerging economies such as India and China were among the least altruistic, placing at 134 and 147, respectively (Ramesh September 8, 2010). In order to put this lack of altruism in an emerging country such as India into perspective, this section examines the Charity and Philanthropy Report on the BRIC (Brazil, Russia, India, and China) countries published in 2014 (Joan E. Spero, Foundation Center). It is particularly interesting that while India has strong religious precepts that encourage giving, Indians do not "give" despite the strengthening of their economies that would give them higher incomes and increase their capabilities to give.

The US and Western countries, along with newly developed countries, are characterized by their focus on more formalized giving. While religions have encouraged giving, they have traditionally focused on more informal and direct giving that alleviates poverty, hunger, and disease. Giving remained largely ad hoc, private, personal, and often family based. Therefore, in emerging economies such as India, which are still entrenched in traditional ways of giving, formalized philanthropy remains low. Indeed, many religious concepts such as *tzedakah* and *dana* encourage anonymous giving, which then does not find its way into the accounting of the more institutionalized philanthropy that typify Western giving (Spero 2014).

However, with globalization and economic liberalization, there is the emergence of a new business class, which has accumulated vast fortunes. This is accompanied by growing inequality, especially in China and India (Shaw and Stancil 2011). The fact that some have so much and others so little in the developing world has created ripe conditions for giving, which is also emulating new models of philanthropic giving through institutions and foundations and charitable trusts. Many Western foundations served as role models and offered support to help promote local philanthropy. For example, the Rockefeller Foundation and the W. K. Kellogg Foundation are among Western foundations that help donors develop strategic grant-making, while philanthropists such as Bill Gates and Warren Buffet have launched their 'Giving Pledge' to encourage the wealthy across developed and emerging markets to use their wealth to help their societies (Spero 2014).

In each of the BRIC countries, facilitating factors such as political environment, the structures of government and bureaucracy, political culture, as well as civil society all factor in shaping the philanthropic sector. A brief scan of BRIC countries follows.

India

As a full-fledged democracy, India has a well-established civil society with many NGOs. However, many of these NGOs are small and unorganized, while the largest are religious based. India's legal and regulatory systems are archaic and complex and vary by state. Lack of accountability, transparency, as well as the complexity of tax laws all contribute to barriers to giving. The picture of charity and philanthropy in India is multifaceted. On the one hand, India has a long religious tradition of charitable giving and that continues alongside the philanthropy that emerged with the Tatas in the 19th century and the foundations that supported health, education, and other social causes into the 20th century. As the newly rich entrepreneurial class emerged, they have turned increasingly toward philanthropy. India leads other developing countries in private charitable giving "with donations estimated at between 0.3 and 0.4 percent of the GDP and with those donations growing 50 per cent between 2011 and 2012" (Seth 2011).

Organizations such as Dasra (see the case study that follows) that encourage strategic giving through their research and training services as well as their platform, Indian Philanthropy Forum, are becoming increasingly popular. Moreover, there is growing emphasis among the newly wealthy to establish and endow foundations. More importantly, this emphasis on social change puts Indian philanthropy at the forefront of BRIC countries, particularly differentiating it from the charitable giving that typifies Russia and China. In these countries, government constrains the role of foundations and civil societies, which in turn confines the role of philanthropy.

Russia

In the Communist era, the state assumed responsibility for the provision of welfare needs for citizens. With the dissolution of the Communist government in 1991, many civil societies were created with funding from Western societies seeking to strengthen democracy. However, simultaneously, other charitable organizations were created to channel illegal funds—which fueled suspicion against all civil society organizations (Spero 2014). Moreover, despite the fact that no tax breaks were provided for foundations started by rich Russians who tried to replace the government in provision of welfare, many of these organizations also advocated for democratic freedoms, which were antigovernment. Russian government officials as a result clamped down with strict regulations on NGOs, and enacted legislation that discouraged foreign funding of NGOs by insisting on cumbersome and near-impossible-to-meet reporting criteria. Predictably, foreign funding has declined, and Russian foundations now only focus on apolitical programs.

China

China's case is similar to Russia's and, in some ways, to India's—yet is unique with its own characteristics. Just as the liberalization of the economy in India led to great prosperity for some business leaders, the liberalization of China's economy starting in 1979 led to a large prosperous class while the millions of masses remained marginalized, so that by 2012 there were over 230 billionaires in China (Spero 2014). There has always been a tension between the Chinese Communist Party and NGOs that choose to function independent of the state. Like Russia, the government controls the role of NGOs, its funders, and financing, and ensures that NGOs do not promote anticommunist or antigovernment advocacy or activities.

The influence of philanthropy in the West permeates China in that the wealthy Chinese individuals also emulate their counterparts in the West. For example, in a manner reminiscent of Bill Gates and Warren Buffet, the chairman of the Hong Kong-based Hutchison Whampoa, Li Ka-shing, donated around $32 billion to his foundations that support several causes around the world. Li wished to motivate other wealthy compatriots by setting an example—and indeed a number of mainland wealthy entrepreneurs followed suit. The philanthropic sector in China is growing, and the China Foundation Center that was established in 2010 is a professionally run foundation that acts as an umbrella organization with a watchdog role; it provides information as well as rates the 27,000 Chinese foundations using a well-established list of indicators.

Brazil

Historically, giving in Brazil has been informal and religious based. The Catholic Church was powerful and influential, although in the recent decade, this influence has diminished. With forces of globalization and economic liberalization, significant fortunes were created for a small group of business magnates, resulting in a concentration of wealth among the elite and that typifies wealth distribution in the region. The strong influence of the state and the church has since given way to civil society organizations and foundations that are trying to tackle the many new societal challenges.

Several new family-owned corporate foundations have mushroomed in Brazil, especially since 2000, as a result of the globalization trend in CSR. This trend created the impetus for giving among the wealthy business owners. Some of these new corporate foundations created to dispense funds under the CSR premise are moving beyond the traditional charitable giving to a more strategic giving that typifying the trends of global philanthropy. They often direct their own programs or partner with NGOs or government. Both private and corporate foundations operate some of the country's most popular programs in education and social services (Spero 2014). Thus in many ways, the traditional paternalism that wealthy landowners practiced in Brazil for their workers, by providing for their basic needs, has been extended through CSR and includes other forms of strategic philanthropy.

Though the modes of philanthropy emerging in the BRIC countries differ, we are able to detect some common themes. In moving away from traditional and direct provision of charity, they focus on more multifaceted ways of giving such as promoting training, education and social services redresses inequalities, and income disparities. It is important to note that whereas in democracies such as India and Brazil, programs such as advocacy for human rights are common, this is not so in China and Russia, where there are stronger government regulations. In all the BRIC countries, the family-owned corporations are popular by which the wealthy elite control the philanthropic agenda, although they may often partner with NGOs and government.

In summary, while increasing wealth is creating funds for philanthropy in the BRIC countries, there is growing inequality in the wealth distribution and the countries' governments are failing to adequately provide for their poorest citizens. Thus, these countries are similar; there is a growing wealthy elite that wishes to redress these inequalities and provide for the more marginalized members of society as well as to address global concerns. They are influenced by global trends in philanthropy such as CSR and the 'Giving Pledge' and are increasingly creating foundations and charitable trusts through which they practice their philanthropy. While they may largely control the philanthropic agenda, they are more restricted in Russia and China, as government regulations often curtail their activities.

Conclusion

Though much has stayed the same in India's realm of 'giving,' a lot has also changed. Older, traditional forms of giving directed toward friends, family, and religious causes persist, but many new forms have also emerged. Especially noteworthy is the ongoing shift from charity- to philanthropy-oriented giving, which indicates that people are engaging in more thoughtful and pragmatic giving that attempts to bring about long-term sustainable change, though there is still giving aimed at addressing immediate welfare needs. Giving is also becoming formalized as more people donate to NGOs and foundations via online mechanisms.

The group of givers consists of all kinds of individuals—from the people who give what little they have, to the rising heroes of philanthropy who are giving away vast amounts of their often newfound wealth, encouraged in part by Western philanthropists such as Bill Gates and Warren Buffet. Families are giving en masse and creating trusts and foundations to manage their giving. Corporations are also becoming more involved in philanthropy, as CSR is not only mandated by government legislation but also expected in the communities in which they operate. Some corporations have successfully publicized their CSR work as a way of advertising their brand and values, while others have managed to use it as a rallying platform for their employees. Corporate philanthropy has generally been so beneficial to both the donor and the recipients that it will likely grow in coming years. Diaspora giving is also on the rise, as people who have left India are now looking to give back to their country of origin.

What unites these various groups of donors is a growing desire for measurable impact. Though they are willing to give more generously than ever, donors are also insisting that their money make a difference that is sustainable and can be monitored and evaluated. They are therefore directing their funds to organizations such as Dasra, GiveIndia, and other venture philanthropist organizations. What sets these philanthropic organizations apart is their insistence on vigilance and thorough research to ensure that the chosen social issues are addressed in the most efficient manner so that the resulting improvements can be monitored and measured. As these trends gain momentum, it will be interesting to track the impact of focused giving on those who are at the receiving end. It is hoped that all of these trends in philanthropy will bring about long-term, sustainable change so that India becomes a better place to live for all members of society.

Case Studies

Case Study 1. Dasra: A Public Charitable Trust—Venture Philanthropy with a Twist

> We view the Dasra model as being the best strategic model we have seen applied as it brings together philanthropy money with great causes.
>
> **Lynna Chandra**
> Absolute Impact Partners

Dasra considers itself "India's leading strategic philanthropy foundation working with philanthropists and social entrepreneurs to create large scale social change"[2]—a closer look at Dasra's work confirms that it does just this. Dasra has created a platform that brings together philanthropists, the leaders of the corporate and social sectors, and think tanks to strategically guide philanthropic efforts toward important social causes. In short, Dasra identifies social entrepreneurs who are already making their mark in social impact, and connects them to Dasra's management gurus and philanthropists who are looking to fund worthwhile causes. Dasra first hones in on social issues worth supporting after careful consideration of reports provided by Dasra researchers; it then short-lists effective NGOs that are working to mitigate the social issues that Dasra has chosen. Dasra then connects the chosen social entrepreneurs with philanthropists through the Dasra Giving Circle that serves as a fund-raising platform.

Dasra is the brainchild of Deval Sanghavi who was born and raised in the US. After working with an Indian NGO briefly during his student years, Sanghavi became interested in social issues in India. Later, Sanghavi worked as an analyst at Morgan Stanley, where he met his future wife and partner Neera Nundy, and together they founded Dasra, which means doing wonderful deeds in Sanskrit

[2] www.dasra.org

(Mulvany 2006). Early on, the founders realized that two factors impede the success of social entrepreneurs and their NGOs: lack of management skills and funds for projects. Thus, Dasra set out to connect social entrepreneurs of selected NGOs with HNWIs as well as hands-on support in management (with accountability built in) for a period of three years. This helps the NGOs streamline their processes and scale up (Swasti 2011).

Dasra records an encouraging change in Indian philanthropy: at present, 80 percent of funds come from domestic sources—a reversal of things just one decade ago. Dasra uses 15 percent of total grant for its own running expenses and the other 85 percent to support NGOs.[3] Dasra brings together philanthropists and social entrepreneurs and works with them to bring about large-scale social change in India. Sometimes, donors will fund a particular aspect of Dasra that interests them. For example, eBay's founder Pierre Omidyar committed funds to help Dasra scale up and increase its research operations (Bukhari 2013, personal conversation).

Dasra has streamlined a process that involves key players to synchronize their efforts to produce optimal results. For example, Dasra compiles and circulates the Dasra Research Reports, which contain ample information about key social issues as well as organizations that tackle these issues. Moreover, the Dasra Portfolio Program offers intensive assessments of these organizational efforts. This program involves four weeks of review as Dasra personnel study organizations that deal with the selected social issues. Initially, 80–100 organizations are reviewed and eventually 10–15 of these organizations are short-listed as worthy of support. A more intensive review of the chosen organizations involves critically evaluating and assessing their financial management and legality— this review takes four weeks, after which three to four organizations are short-listed and reviewed for another four weeks. A detailed analysis of each organization's programs is then presented to the Dasra Giving Circle. The Dasra Research Reports act "like a calling card which includes a theory of change as to how the Dasra team believes that that the chosen problem can best be tackled" (Bukhari 2013). In order to produce the most comprehensive reports, the Dasra research team digs deep to understand the underlying causes of the social issues it hopes to combat. For example, the problem of ensuring access to education for the many marginalized children

[3] www.dasra.org

has been widely identified as one of the key social issues in India. A cursory glance would suggest that one could resolve the problem by adding more schools and augmenting the educational infrastructure. However, the Dasra team looked beyond the surface and concluded that the educational infrastructure was less of a problem than was the quality of education, including teacher training and the curriculum.

Dasra's Giving Circle involves philanthropists who are on the lookout for high-impact funding activities. An annual Indian Philanthropy Forum gathers philanthropists to meet leaders and practitioners who are already generating high-impact programs that can be compounded with additional funding. At the forum each year, Dasra announces two exceptional NGOs to receive INR 4.5 crore in funding revenues as well as 250 days of hands-on assistance in management for the next three years. The management teams that Dasra provides are like management consultants that work with the NGOs for the long haul, assisting them to achieve their targets.[4]

Alison Bukhari—Dasra's senior advisor to philanthropists situated in the UK—provides a practical example of the workings of Dasra's fourth Giving Circle launched in July 2012 (Bukhari 2012). Philanthropists from India as well as other parts of the world had gathered in order to work on a social issue that they all favored: the empowerment of adolescent girl in India. Bukhari recalls the difficulty in getting this Giving Circle together because the social issue is so elusive and the results of the intervention are difficult to measure. Despite obstacles, a circle of enlightened philanthropists convened and drew on funding from international donors to bridge the funding gaps. This meeting came on the heels of Dasra's latest report "Owning Her Own Future: Empowering Adolescent Girls in India," which had been commissioned by Kiawah Trust, a family foundation (sometimes a trust can commission a report as long as the issue of interest is aligned to the broader goals of Dasra). The report highlighted adolescent girls in India as 'an invisible and often powerless group' who are denied what adolescent boys in India often take for granted: autonomy, mobility, and economic opportunity. Such inequality persists because certain social practices based on tradition trap and limit these young women. The report identified Bihar, Rajasthan, and Uttar Pradesh as the areas that are the most backward and traditional. Specifically, over half of the adolescent

[4] www.dasra.org

girls in these areas wed before age 18 and are often victims of domestic violence; 95 percent drop out of education in secondary school. The report pointed out the need to focus on adolescent girls as a separate group from the general category of women in which they are often subsumed, as girls are particularly vulnerable. The realms that influence the development of adolescent girls are the home, school, and place of work, while conduits through which adolescent girls can be empowered include self, peer groups, families, and communities. The Government of India also displayed interest in this issue and helped locate NGOs that work in this field in the cited backward regions. Eventually, Dasra chose 100 NGOs and then 10 final NGOs for best practices after going through its usual research processes.

Philanthropists from India and other parts of the world make up Dasra's Circle of Giving. Bukhari (2013) emphasizes that this combination of international and Indian donors is important because Indian donors are better positioned to employ a more culturally sensitive approach, while international donors can provide knowledge and expertise into the diverse modes for resolving a problem. For example, international donors may choose schools as the logical place to impart the required sex education. The local donors, however, know that Indian schools would shy away from such discussion. In this situation, Dasra recommended the NGOs impart sex education through youth groups that meet after school.

After consulting with the NGOs that worked to empower adolescent girls, Dasra identified five cornerstones for the empowerment of adolescent girls:

1. Delaying marriage/pregnancy
2. Staying in school longer
3. Improving sexual and reproductive health
4. Increasing income-generating capacity
5. Promoting girls' agency

After mapping out NGOs with high impact in empowering adolescent girls and zeroing in on the NGOs that would give philanthropists the biggest 'bang for their buck,' Dasra set out to work with the chosen philanthropists, the government, and the NGOs to make the desired social impact.[5]

[5] www.dasra.org/pdf/Dasra-Empowering-Adolescent-Girls-OHF.pdf

Generally, INR 45 lakh are garnered for each project from the Circle of Giving. Bukhari (2013) informed one of the authors of this book that the Circle of Giving consists of a mixed bag of philanthropists: some are repeat philanthropists contributing to several causes, while others are from middle-income families interested in donating to one specific social issue. What connects the philanthropists is the need for 'smart giving.' They recognize Dasra as an intelligent facilitator that connects the demands of NGOs with the resources of philanthropists. Moreover, they realize that Dasra will enable them to optimize social impact, as it has already worked out a tried and tested method of how to best tackle the social problems. More importantly, once Dasra has successfully synchronized the synergies of the philanthropist, the researcher, the social entrepreneur, and Dasra's management team to successfully resolve a given problem, Dasra measures and presents the impact that is made so that its strategic partners can appreciate the long-term change they helped bring about.

Case Study 2. GiveIndia

GiveIndia was launched in 2000 as an online conduit that connects donors to their favorite NGOs. GiveIndia's mission is "to promote an efficient and effective giving culture that provides greater opportunities to the poor in India" with a vision for "a strong 'giving' culture where Indians donate 2% of their income every year to give the poor a chance. This should result in a vibrant 'philanthropy marketplace' to ensure that the most efficient and effective nonprofits get access to the most resources" (GiveIndia 2011). Its modus operandi, influenced by business schools' return-on-investment model, perceives each potential donor as an investor in promoting social good (GiveIndia 2011). The organization regularly goes through a self-examination:

> We evaluate GiveIndia on the basis of three parameters. One is the amount of money we are able to channel. Second is the number of donors we are able to engage. Every individual donor chooses what he wants to do through GiveIndia, and therefore we can't measure the impact at the end destination. Third is the diversity of people who are choosing to give through GiveIndia. It is interesting to note that they are drawn from various classes and ethnicities. (Mehta 2009)

In practice, potential donors go to the GiveIndia website[6] where they can conduct an online search and select a social issue or NGO that matters to them. Within the parameters of the chosen issue or NGO, they are able to zero in on their favored recipients, such as young girls between the ages of 10 and 16 (to provide educational opportunities) or a group of ailing women (to provide funds so they can get surgeries). The website also provides ample information on different organizations, causes, success stories, tax benefits, and donation options to help donors make their choice. The donation can be structured as a one-time gift, a series of multiple gifts, or a monthly gift. The donors also receive updates about how their donations were used to help others. This enhances donor satisfaction, NGO credibility, and GiveIndia's transparency.

Between 2011 and 2012, GiveIndia raised INR 240 lakh for 245 NGOs across India. Perhaps among its greatest successes is its ability to reach out to diverse strata of society. In 2004, GiveIndia established a payroll giving program, which today has 110 companies signed up with over 38,000 active employees. In 2010, it launched the First Givers Club as a platform for high-net-worth donors, channeling INR 20 crore to a variety of projects. GiveIndia was fortunate to establish a connection with ICICI Bank early—this connection facilitated quick registration under the FCRA, a feat that typically takes several years for NGOs to achieve. This enabled GiveIndia to accept foreign donations earlier, and gave it a head start.

GiveIndia is more than just a conduit that receives and forwards donations. As an umbrella organization, GiveIndia audits and evaluates all organizations that are recipients of funds donated through its website. Thus, GiveIndia assures not only that the funds will reach the relevant NGOs but also that the NGO use the funds wisely. GiveIndia undertakes an extensive screening process, sometimes lasting up to 12 months, to determine the legitimacy of the NGOs they are affiliated with. GiveIndia scrutinizes the organizations' annual reports and financial records, conducts audits, and visits the organization sites to ensure that every NGO affiliated with GiveIndia is legitimate, efficient, and not corrupt.[7] This process clearly shows that GiveIndia caters to the interests of donors rather than those of NGOs; as a result, GiveIndia has earned donors' trust and a reputation for legitimacy. More importantly, GiveIndia sets aside very little of the donations to meet its own operative costs.

[6] www.giveindia.org
[7] For further information, see http://www.giveindia.org/t-certified.aspx

Further, GiveIndia relies on innovative technology to cater to the needs of both small and large donors. For its payroll giving program, GiveIndia has invested almost INR 1 crore in IT so people can sign in and out online, and have this information processed and sent to companies in a file to be uploaded into their payroll processing software (Mehta 2009). GiveIndia's model of operation is the focus of much research. The organization has managed to use latest process technologies to keep transaction and administrative costs low yet work efficiently. The findings could have practical implications for other similar programs struggling with sustainability.

A study conducted by Shier and Handy (2012) found that donations off-line easily outnumbered online donations. Those who donated money online through GiveIndia donated approximately INR 5,700, while those donating off-line reported donating on average INR 6,200. Of the respondents who did donate online, 67 percent had donated through GiveIndia. This study indicates that there is an emerging market of online donors and that GiveIndia is adequately engaging these donors. Moreover, when those who donated to GiveIndia were surveyed, they reported overall satisfaction and little apprehension about the risks (Shier and Handy 2012). The organization directs donors to the list of NGOs and the social issues that each of them works with. This allows readers to become aware of the many NGOs as well as the social issues that NGOs deal with before they decide on the NGO and the area in which they hope to make a difference (Mehta 2009). By making connections between donors and organizations, GiveIndia helps support the development of a giving culture within India.

Case Study 3. Kiran Mazumdar-Shaw

Kiran Mazumdar-Shaw was born and raised in the garden city of Bangalore, and enjoyed a middle-class upbringing as the daughter of a brewmaster at the United Breweries Ltd, the largest brewery in India. Kiran attended Bangalore University, graduated with a double major in biology and zoology and planned to become a doctor. However, she could not follow the career path because she did not like the sight of blood. Instead, she followed her father's suggestion to pursue a career as a brewmaster, and moved to Australia to study the biology of beer at the University of Ballarat. Despite the fact that

Kiran had never been away from her family before and was the only female in her class, Kiran thrived in the unfamiliar circumstances and enjoyed her studies. She returned to India in 1975, confident and more independent, only to find that there were no opportunities for a female brewmaster. She considered leaving for Scotland to accept a brewmaster position there when Biocon—an enzyme-producing company, approached her. The original founder of Biocon (a Scotsman) had heard about her from the Australian head of Biocon whom she had known at the University of Ballarat, and made her an interesting offer: a 70 percent stake in the company. After accepting the position and receiving training, Kiran began making enzymes from papaya and catfish, as well as enzymes for fermenting beer. Initially, she worked out of her garage, but the company grew rapidly, as did her prominence in the domain of business.

By 1979, Biocon was the first Indian company to export enzymes to the US and Europe. By 1985, Biocon had grown more complex and successful. However, everything was not proceeding as smoothly on the organizational front as Kiran had hoped. Despite her efforts to create a flat organization that paid fair wages and provided a harmonious environment in which workers and management could communicate and work together, the workers' union revolted. After giving them sufficient warning, Kiran gave the workers their severance pay and automated their work. The establishment changed the educational requirements for applicants and, as a result, became leaner and more efficient. In 1989, her partner sold his company to Unilever. Over the next decade, Kiran continued her pursuit of making Biocon India's largest enzymes company, and was successful in developing many specialty enzymes, building scale, and providing these products to customers in the US and Europe. When Unilever divested its specialty chemicals business to Imperial Chemical Industries (ICI) in 1998, Kiran decided to buy out the Unilever share in her company and became the sole owner of Biocon.

To take her commitment to innovation into the international market, Kiran started a new company, Syngene, to develop drug components for international pharmaceutical companies. Kiran was the first to start this trend, and many companies have followed suit to export various components for drugs. Biocon has since been developing its own pharmaceuticals along with generics. Today, it is Asia's leading contract research organization (CRO), and provides multilevel research for more than 120 multinational companies in various parts of the world. As India's largest biopharmaceutical company, Biocon is focused on affordable innovation to enhance access to health care. It has pioneered the development of recombinant human insulin and analogs in India, and has also developed many other novel biologics for cancer and autoimmune diseases. Kiran's ultimate objective is to get a novel 'Made-in-India' drug by Biocon to make it big on the international stage—a realistic possibility given the amazing research being done by scientists at Biocon.

By 2000, Kiran realized that the enzyme business was very limiting and would not allow her to fulfill her global ambitions, thus she decided to strategically shape the company's business model toward becoming a pharmaceutical company.

With a view to leverage the company's strengths in fermentation technology and recombinant proteins, Kiran decided to start with statins and insulins. By 2004, Biocon had evolved from a maker of enzymes to a biotech pharma company with an annual revenue of $122 million. The company went public in March of the same year and had a stock market value of $1.2 billion on the day of listing. To date, Biocon remains the only biotech company to be publically listed in India.

The year 2004 was also the year Biocon launched India's first indigenously developed recombinant human insulin, INSUGEN, and the year Kiran received the 'Businesswoman of the Year Award' from *The Economic Times*, a leading Indian business daily. Kiran was titled 'the richest self-made woman in India.' In 2005, Kiran built her company's 90-acre campus Biocon Park in Bangalore to accommodate 5,000 employees. This location continues to thrive as India's largest biotech hub.

Successful Entrepreneur to Philanthropist

Soon after going public, Kiran felt that it was time to give back to the community in an organized and strategic manner, and established the Biocon Foundation in 2005. Since then, Kiran has donated some $33 million to philanthropic causes, including diagnosis and research of diseases and patient care (Raghunathan 2013). She wanted to use her expertise to provide health-care coverage to marginalized groups in society who have little or no access to decent health care. The Biocon Foundation has set up several primary health-care centers in various villages in Karnataka that offer preventive and curative health to lakhs of patients. In addition to health care, the foundation focuses on three vertical pillars: health, education, and civic infrastructure.

One of us (authors) was driven to the village of Huskur, about a 20-minute drive from the Biocon office, where there was a conversation with Kiran and some of her staff. A three-room clinic— which housed a doctor's consultation room, a small laboratory, and a pharmacy—formed part of Biocon Foundation's integrated outreach strategy focused on social change and rural empowerment through health interventions. The foundation has been working with communities through integrated health-care programs that provide micro-insurance (Arogya Raksha), health delivery, and health education. There are nine Arogya Raksha clinics in the state of Karnataka, including the one in Huskur. Biocon Foundation's Arogya Raksha health micro-insurance scheme includes free medical consultation, low-cost medicines, surgeries, and hospitalization, all for an affordable premium of INR 180 per annum. The idea of insurance was, at first, a hard sell in the villages. The people in the village had difficulty with the idea of paying money in advance to cover potential medical crises and costs. They could not fathom how insurance could help them save so much in medical costs in case of medical crises and subsequent hospitalization and surgeries. Today, the idea of health insurance is slowly catching on in the villages: now there are large groups of people enrolled in insurance schemes just as there are a large number of primary health-care clinics. These physical structures played an important role in convincing villagers to join the insurance scheme, as they felt they were getting something for their money. The Government of India had also started a similar insurance program that charged INR 120 a year, which allowed patients to use the facilities of government hospitals. However, there were not many takers for this insurance scheme as people were reluctant to go to government hospitals because of their low-quality services. Therefore, Dr Devi Shetty[8] (a cardiac surgeon, philanthropist, and

---

[8] Dr Shetty has been a partner and advisor to Kiran in most medical schemes involving philanthropy. Dr Shetty's hospital, Narayana Health City, founded by him in 2002, delivers the finest cardiac care at the lowest price. Kiran through Mazumdar-Shaw Cancer Center (MSCC) has aimed to create a similar affordable model for cancer care. *The Wall Street Journal* calls Dr Devi Shetty 'the Henry Ford' of heart surgery because of the assembly-line type of surgeries carried out every day. Alternatively, the low cost of fine cardiac combined with compassion earns Narayana Health the moniker 'Narayana is where Wal-Mart meets Mother Theresa' (Anand 2009). A third of his patients are involved in low-cost insurance plans that the group has been trying to popularize. The economies of scale allow the hospital to charge the low costs because they perform so many cardiac surgeries in a day.

long-term friend of Kiran) suggested that an increase in the amount to INR 180 a year, which would allow patients access to a network of public and private hospitals and clinics.

The Arogya Raksha Yojana scheme is a unique health-care model under the aegis of Biocon Foundation. Kiran believes that this model, if properly implemented, can enable universal health care in India. This e-health and telemedicine technology involves the setting up of a novel diagnostic machine within primary health-care centers in the villages. These diagnostic machines will be linked to hospitals in cities, thereby enabling immediate diagnosis and e-consultation with a specialist. The diagnostic machines can conduct multiple tests and store patient records. The process starts when the machine electronically registers patients by taking their pictures and assigning patient numbers while noting their blood pressure, blood sugar, and hemoglobin levels. The entire process is captured on smart cards, ensuring transparency and accountability. The rural youth can be encouraged to buy into these primary health-care centers with loans from the Canara Banks. In return, the youth can manage these health-care centers and receive a percentage of patients' fees from the Indian government. Thus in one fell swoop, the poor can have access to affordable health care while the marginalized youth have opportunities for entrepreneurship. Kiran hopes that Biocon can coordinate and facilitate the cooperation of the government as well as sympathetic banks and willing entrepreneurs to make this vision of affordable universal health care in India a reality.

Cancer research and treatment are also close to Kiran's heart. After watching a close friend suffer through the treatments and eventually die of cancer, Kiran was determined to do something about this predatory affliction. The year 2004 proved to be a watershed year: Biocon went public and the stock soared. Kiran was secure, confident, and wealthy in her own right, and was more than ready to fulfill her promise to find ways to combat cancer and alleviate the sufferings it caused.

A large part of her donations to philanthropic causes has been spent on cancer diagnosis, research, and relief. Central to these efforts is the 1,400-bed MSCC that was built in 2009. Kiran aims to blend good-quality cancer treatment at MSCC with affordable care. MSCC runs as a for-profit business for those who can afford the treatments, while low-income patients get subsidized or free treatments depending on their income levels. MSCC takes a systematic approach, starting with a tumor board where each case is evaluated by a team consisting of a radiotherapist, medical oncologist, pain specialist, speech and swallowing expert, financial expert, and sociologist. The board determines the treatment regimen for each patient. Within the vast field of cancer, the Biocon Foundation runs special programs for oral cancer as India has the most occurrences of oral cancer—which can be attributed to the popular habit of chewing betel nuts and tobacco as well as 'gutkha', a sweet mix of tobacco, betel nut, and palm nut. However, the problem with oral cancers is that by the time they are recognized, they are often in the last stages. Therefore, the Biocon Foundation partnered with the Mazumdar-Shaw Foundation to devote time and effort to the early diagnosis of this form of cancer. The foundation has trained community workers to go into high-risk communities and take surveys of betel and tobacco consumptions habits, as well as pictures of suspicious-looking lesions. Oncologists at the MSCC diagnose these images and subsequently suggest treatments. The success of these efforts has led the foundation to scale up the project. So far, over 7,500 people in the villages of Karnataka have been screened for oral cancer.

Kiran has also set up the Mazumdar-Shaw Center for Translational Research (MSCTR) at MSCC, where scientists are constantly looking for ways to understand the progress of various forms of cancer as well as the best ways to respond to it at every stage. Kiran has invested nearly INR 400 million for this state-of-the-art cancer center. The visit to the health center at MSCC revealed up-to-date and impressive facilities, alongside with hands-on research with ongoing patient care and surgery.

Kiran's positive energy and style of active philanthropy has attracted senior medical leaders from all over the world, including doctors from India who have practices in the UK or the US. Many of the returning leaders, who are in their sixties, even take cuts in their salaries when they return to India to work with Kiran. More recently, some younger doctors are also returning to practice medicine to benefit Indian society, for example, Dr Paul Salins, a cranio-maxillofacial surgeon, artist, medical director, and vice president of the MSCC. Impressive was his sensitivity and intelligence that has allowed him to make great strides in both patient treatment and research. He had studied and practiced in the UK and was attracted to the philosophies of Dr Shetty and Kiran, who were trying to provide affordable high-quality health care. Dr Shetty explained the reasons why he was so attracted to MSCC as a hospital where he believed that he could actually make a difference.

The hospital has been created to ensure that every patient, regardless of class or ethnicity, is welcomed through its doors. All kinds of insurance are accepted, and when there is none, the tab is picked up by the Mazumdar-Shaw Foundation. The hospital is multidisciplinary and has every kind of specialty ranging from head and neck surgery, dermatology and genetics, to neonatology and obstetrics. More importantly, it has the latest cutting-edge technology facilities funded through Kiran's personal philanthropic initiatives. Therefore, unlike other facilities, the physicians are not lacking in funds. Their research is not driven by grant writing, but is immediately relevant to patient care and the advancement of scientific knowledge. Every Thursday, all of the core doctors meet and discuss every aspect of patient care. This mode of collaborative care prevents corruption and ensures that the best heads decide on patient care. Unlike other hospitals that have commercial targets to meet, MSCC can focus solely on delivering the best patient care. Moreover, the hospital has an agreement to work with physicians and patients from underserved areas and teach them the latest techniques in various specialties.

MSCTR, funded by Kiran, translates scientific ideas to benefit the patient in every manner possible, from finding ways to bring down the cost of a drug to better modes of treatment. MSCC has an outreach program that helps in procuring cheaper drugs or finding ways to make up for the shortfall in availability and affordability of a required drug. Moreover, a vocational center teaches other members of the family skills for employment when the breadwinner is hospitalized and unable to earn.

The MSCC has been able to function as the world's largest cancer care hospital and provide optimum health-care services to large numbers of people while contributing to hands-on cancer research, thanks to the well-designed facilities of the medical center. The floors in the hospital are huge, measuring to about one acre each. In the center of each floor are multiple open islands; each island has a certain group of specialists around it, and it is where hands-on research is carried out and collaboration is encouraged. Dr Salins makes me aware that it is a luxury to devote so much space to research instead of money-generating hospital beds. He is glad that patient care and research are the foci of all physicians, and all the activity in the hospital attests to this fact.

At the end of our meeting, Kiran told me about the Bangalore Political Action Committee (B.PAC) started in February 2013—she was greatly concerned about the quality of political governance in India. B.PAC focuses on getting better governance by encouraging citizens to engage with the political system, and works to dissipate general apathy (the rich are believed to be too busy enjoying themselves, the middle class too busy working, and the lower classes are not sure what is going on). B.PAC informs people about the political system and encourages people to vote. The efforts seem to have paid off, as voter turnout jumped 15 percent in the latest elections, thanks to the many initiatives undertaken by B.PAC and its allies. The B.PAC Civic Leadership Incubation Program (B.CLIP) has encouraged political leadership at every level of the society through education in public policy and ongoing workshops. In the last election, B.PAC produced a report card on political candidates vying for leadership through an evaluation of political candidates on a nonpartisan basis. Kiran hopes that B.PAC's efforts will encourage citizen involvement in the political process and cultivate future leaders from the lower echelons of society.

So how does one sum up the philanthropic contributions of a dynamic leader such as Kiran, who has used her enormous fortune and resources to make a difference in the lives of others in many ways? Kiran articulates her own worth succinctly: "As an entrepreneur who is driven by a sense of purpose to make a difference to global healthcare, I take pride in saying that Biocon is contributing to affordable innovation, which goes to the core of ensuring a global right to healthcare." And yet this summation does not touch on her civic contributions in politics and education. (Biocon Foundation has produced a math workbook 'Chinnara Ganitha' for public schools that helps students establish a strong foundation in math through simple instructions that appeal to young children. Teachers are being trained to use this book correctly.) Given Kiran's wide-ranging philanthropic contributions, it is difficult to sum up the offerings of this dynamic leader.

Conclusion

*Garibo ki suno—wo tumhari sunega—tum ek paisa doge—wo dus
lakh dega*
(Listen to the poor and He [the creator] will listen to you
If you give the poor one coin, He [the creator] will give you back a
million coins)

Thus goes a popular Bollywood song. The imperative to give is deeply
rooted in not only Indian culture but also other facets of Indian
life. For one, the major religions of India have played a crucial role
in driving charitable acts by cementing the importance of giving
within the religions' traditions, as well as societal obligations, and
responsibilities (Rolnick 1962: 440). Also, the notion of noblesse
oblige has driven the elites and the rich since preindustrial times to
help the less fortunate in times of need by doling out grains and other
resources. Moreover, family, kin, and community networks provided
welfare through private acts of charity that met the immediate needs
of those who were in desperate straits.

Thus, the welfare of the less privileged was often dependent on
the charity of religious institutions, informal social organizations,
and others who were better-off (Sundar 2000). And long before
CSR became a buzzword, the early merchants of India were
funding important social causes such as the construction of religious
structures, provision of education, and upkeep of the community, so
as to enhance their reputation and legitimacy. Through the execution
of family responsibilities and obligations of the elite, as well as the
strategic giving of those in commercial activities, a form of basic
philanthropy that was both secular and religious existed long before
philanthropy was deemed a subject of formal study.[1]

---

[1] We have used the terms 'philanthropy' and 'charity' interchangeably in the book as
this is the popular usage of the terms. However, we have clarified at different junctures
that Western development literature is leaning toward a distinction between 'charity,'
which was the traditional form of giving that usually catered to the immediate welfare
needs of the recipients in an informal manner, and 'philanthropy,' which is the more
modern strategic and formal manner of giving that is geared to achieving long-term
measurable change. However, because this distinction is still in its early stages, we
use the two terms interchangeably in accordance to popular usage, as many of our
interviewees have stayed with traditional terminology.

With the advent of colonial rule, British attitudes began influencing Indian modes of giving. British colonials mocked and criticized indigenous forms of charity as ostentatious, wasteful, and superstitious, and contrasted these forms with British charity that was portrayed as more rational and effective (Sharma 2009). Concurrently, rich Indian families were encouraged to move away from purely religious and traditional kinship forms of giving and toward more structured and institutional forms of giving by Indian leaders who wanted to promote indigenous development.

Thus, throughout the 18th and 19th centuries, giving in India became more structured and directed toward social development, education, health care, and poverty relief to emulate British and Christian forms of charity. It especially became fashionable with the Indian elite to leverage philanthropy to gain channels of access to the British, influence the development of civic society, and forge recognition and new public roles for themselves. Jamsetjee Jejeebhoy (1783–1859) is a fine example of someone who successfully followed an anglicized mode of charity, as he gained knighthood for constructing hospitals and institutions that catered to the development of society.

The turn of the 20th century saw the rise in popularity of socialist ideas and the subsequent move away from religious and traditional giving to more secular and organized giving (Sundar 2000). More importantly, the base for giving widened, meaning that 'giving' became more democratized to include the general members of society and was encouraged by broader society as a social good for all.

As indigenous industries burgeoned in India, coinciding with the growing momentum of the nationalist and Independence movement, the country grew more modern and a small number of individuals more wealthy, and this translated into more institutionalized modes of giving that became the hallmarks of corporations. This was also the period that Mahatma Gandhi's notion of "trusteeship"—in which the wealthy should hold their wealth in trusts and use it for the service of broader society—empowered corporations to play an important philanthropic role throughout nation-building and Independence.

The government of a newly Independent India had great plans for its economic development, following a more socialist model. A few decades later, however, it became apparent that India had not taken off economically as envisioned earlier. Business was frustrated by the many government regulations, and economic stagnation followed. Poverty levels rose, but the government was not able to provide welfare for those who most needed it. During this time, the government tried to encourage charitable giving by granting tax exemptions to those who donated to causes that the government acknowledged. These regulations, however, have fluctuated over time—sometimes quite generous in allowances for donations, and sometimes tying the allowances in so much red tape that they become counterproductive.

When India opened its economy to the world in the early 1990s and reversed its policies of self-sufficiency, it encouraged foreign investment, global technology, capital, and markets. India's economy grew by 7 percent from 1993 to 2001, and the upward trend continued through the 2000s (Malik 2013). The unprecedented economic growth in India has produced some of the world's wealthiest business leaders. According to *Forbes*, India had, in terms of US dollars, 48 billionaires in 2012 and 55 billionaires in 2013, in addition to 158,000 millionaires (O'Sullivan and Kersley 2012: 49). This gave rise to a brand of philanthropy related to giving by HNWIs that at one level emulated philanthropic practices in the West, of forming foundations and professionalizing their philanthropy, but also practiced the more traditional forms, such as building temples.

Among them are billionaires who are heroes of philanthropy, such as Azim Premji who has signed the Giving Pledge.[2] Other notable Indian philanthropists include Kiran Mazumdar-Shaw, who donates half of her annual dividends from her firm Biocon; she has disclosed to *Forbes* that she has pledged to give away 75 percent of her wealth over her lifetime. Several billionaire philanthropists have started their own foundations, while others work through the numerous NGOs in India. While there is a lot of money within India and the impact of wealthy philanthropists—such as Azim Premji, Kiran Mazumdar-Shaw, and Rohini Nilekani—is encouraging, their efforts are not the norm in private Indian philanthropy; in many ways, these individuals are exceptional. And it is perhaps the collective efforts of countless individuals across all societal ranks that will contribute most to India's development by engaging in individual philanthropic acts or through local NGOs.

The Indian diaspora is another enormous source of funds being channeled into India to help with development projects. Like

---

[2] This pledge is an effort by the Bill Gates and Warren Buffet to get the world's richest individuals to give at least half of their wealth to philanthropy.

corporations engaged in CSR, diaspora donors are also concerned with the management and impact of their funding. One of the key trends in philanthropy is that people are shifting away from giving to solve immediate welfare problems to giving that can affect long-term, sustained developmental change. Measurement and evaluation are now watchwords for donors who wish to ensure their giving produces the desired impact. Organizations such as Dasra are the perfect mediums to meet donors' expectations. After choosing and researching specific social issues, Dasra meets with philanthropists and organizations that are already working to resolve the chosen issues. These NGOs are approached, and if they agree to work with Dasra in the planned fashion, they are given management support and the long-term finances to affect social change in a measurable way. GiveIndia is another philanthropic organization that mediates between online donors and NGOs that it has already vetted. Unlike other channels, GiveIndia follows up on all funds for due diligence and to ensure that they are used to bring about the expected change.

Alongside the growth of private philanthropy by HNWI in recent years and diaspora Indians, CSR among corporations in India is also emerging as a popular trend that encourages corporations to give away some of their earnings to better the lives of the communities in which they make their profits. Though many Indian corporations had taken it upon themselves to work toward the betterment of their communities long before CSR was popularized, the recent Companies Act 2013 will take corporate spending on communities to a new level, as it requires very large and profitable companies to spend at least 2 percent of their average net profits toward CSR. Many of the companies will comply by channeling their funds to one or more of the 3.3 million NGOs that dot the Indian landscape. The concern is that these NGOs may lack the skills and management to execute the high-impact development projects the companies expect.

What-ifs

In examining the constantly changing nature of philanthropy in India, it is exciting to ask where these trends may lead—and how far could Indian philanthropy go? Along these lines, we speculate, by bringing up ideas, how the practice of philanthropy might evolve in the future:

1. What if HNWIs did not set up their own separate foundations, but rather pooled their resources into one large foundation? What if they got together and formed giving circles to be even more impactful due to their collective philanthropy?
2. What if communities were real stakeholders in the philanthropy they received? If philanthropists increasingly responded to community and recipient needs—as opposed to giving based on personal passions and experiences—through engagement and research combined with greater recipient ownership over funds, might philanthropy be channeled more efficiently?
3. What if India's social sector organizations were professionally trained, organized, and robust enough to maximize the large amount of funds entering the philanthropic space as a result of the Companies Act 2013 (which mandates large companies to channel 2 percent of their profits toward CSR)?
4. What if wealthy landlords, farmers, and small industrialists—who are often located in India's second-tier cities and currently route most of their charity through religious groups—were tapped to expand their philanthropic impact? Given that most enterprises in India are small or medium in scale, what if their philanthropic and socially responsible activities were better understood and organized?
5. What if all philanthropists agreed to collectively battle corruption in India?
6. What if cyber philanthropy was boosted in India? In India, seven out of eight Internet subscribers access the Internet from their mobile phones, according to the Telecom Regulatory Authority of India (TRAI). This may make donating even more accessible to India's growing middle class, and has the potential to tap into a huge potential pool of donations through regulated, professional online fund-raising platforms.
7. What if those who practiced philanthropy at the bottom of the pyramid were engaged in learning how to do so strategically at the grassroots level?

Looking Ahead

In looking at Indian philanthropy and how it may develop in coming years, there is cause for both hope and caution. Given that India's economic liberalization that enabled dramatic growth of private wealth is relatively recent—dating back to the 1990s—India most likely needs another generation that grows up in a robust middle class before widespread philanthropy takes off. It will also take some time before many of the new Indian foundations go global, although there is plenty to keep them occupied within India for now.

There is room for more experimentation, and greater need to find the right balance between status quo and risk-taking. Perhaps in part because many Indian philanthropists take the successes or failures of their foundations personally, they are not comfortable with failure, which is an important tool for learning in social development. Nonetheless, organic platforms that bring philanthropists together and facilitate discussions are emerging, following on the heels of earlier initiatives such as the annual Dasra Indian Philanthropy Forum and the Azim Premji-led meeting in Bangalore in 2012. These offer an opportunity for Indian philanthropists to consider how they can go beyond achieving numerical benchmarks to bring true leadership to the philanthropic space. Philanthropists are beginning to realize that while increased donations are important, it is even more important to develop an infrastructure that channels the donations and resources strategically to bring about long-term, sustainable change.

In an increasingly market-dominated society, there is a continuous eroding of government funding for social programs and a greater reliance on philanthropic donations. Many organizations receiving funding from foreign governments find that such policies affect them as countries cut back aid provided through national funds.

One such example is that of the Canadian government's recent closure of its Canadian International Development Agency (CIDA) organization. CIDA, formed under the liberal government of Pierre Trudeau in 1968, had a mandate to "support sustainable development in developing countries in order to reduce poverty and contribute to a more secure, equitable, and prosperous world" (CIDA-ACDI 2011). The Conservative government, under Stephen Harper, announced in 2013 that CIDA would be merged with the Department of Foreign

Affairs and International Trade (DFAIT); and while Canada's foreign aid will continue, the nature of the aid will change to reflect national priorities such as focus on encouraging economic growth through support of local industries. This is a shift away from the 45 years of multidimensional aid founded and promoted by CIDA that created an era of Canadian compassion to the world.

Drawing on the personal experience of one of the authors, one case is that of CORD, a division of Chinmaya Mission Halton Region, a successful nonprofit located in Ontario, Canada. CORD was affiliated with the CIDA that funded its efforts at empowering rural women in a desolate region and drawing them out of their cycle of dependency by ensuring that they learned the skills to either work for other organizations or start their own enterprise (Handy and Kassam 2007). CORD was especially renowned for its ability to build organizational and operational capacity of village groups to run their own activities in an integrated, participatory, and sustainable manner, while augmenting their income and enabling natural resource management by the villagers. CORD became a flagship NGO, thanks to the funding and efforts of CIDA. Alongside the giving of grants, CIDA encouraged local fund-raising in order to ensure awareness of the projects. CIDA's strategy was to match any funds that were raised—and so, like many other NGOs, CORD eventually received double the amount of any money raised locally. The partnership between CORD and CIDA was mutually beneficial. CORD received the much-needed funding, and CIDA was very pleased with the progress that CORD was making, and even invited CORD's director and founder, Dr Kshama Metre, to North America to talk about her successful strategies of empowering women to break their cycle of dependency and earn enough for themselves and their families. With the recent changes to CIDA and receding government/ international funding, CORD has had to rely on other philanthropic organizations. Consequently, CORD-Ontario's fund-raising efforts are now focused in developing countries, and these funds are used to underwrite the funds lost through CIDA. Sadly, while funds are replaceable, the long-term and enduring social and cultural capital that CIDA's staff provided is lost.

A number of steps could be taken to advance the Indian philanthropic sector. Currently in India, there is little training for development professionals who are focused on philanthropy and NGO work that is not ancillary to other degrees such as social work.

Advancing the sector requires more educational programs that train individuals in philanthropy. The sector would then benefit with professional managers and executives who could take more calculated risks and innovate the Indian philanthropic sector. Fundamental to the progress of the philanthropic sector is research, monitoring and evaluation, and greater analysis and reflection on what approaches and tool work best in the Indian context, and why. The various philanthropic-support organizations in India would also benefit from trained professionals, as well as the impact of the philanthropy undertaken and its sustainability.

Even as the amount of philanthropy in India grows, there is still a marked preference for philanthropic focus in certain areas—particularly health and education, which is seen as the panacea for India's problems, and dates back to the colonial period (Sundar 1996: 414). Less philanthropic attention is devoted to socially or politically sensitive, controversial, or rights-based issues, such as disability, mental health, sexual preferences, sex education, sexual abuse, arts, traditional crafts, natural resource management, consumer rights, and legal aid, to name a few.

While it has been argued that "It would be naïve… to think that increased funds from philanthropy, whether domestic, foreign, or diaspora, will 'solve' India's poverty problem" (Kapur et al. 2004: 205), it is clear that philanthropy plays an important societal role, and it is important to collaborate across sectors and focus on the best way to leverage philanthropic funds. From the government's side, greater trust in private foundations and consistency in tax outlook and policy could encourage more structured giving. Private acts of giving can also be made more public to inspire (or shame) others to give more, and both positive and negative experiences should be shared as lessons for others to learn from. The media can play a role in spreading these lessons. Further, business-leader philanthropists should openly discuss their visions of society and philanthropic values, the role they will play in realizing their visions, and the resources they will make available toward them (Sundar 2000). As the structures that define the philanthropic field in India are not yet as entrenched as they are in developed donor nations, there is a great opportunity for India to develop innovative and impactful approaches to philanthropy.

It is undeniable that India faces immense poverty and a growing wealth gap. At the same time, there are increasing numbers of people and organizations—from all socioeconomic backgrounds—that are determined to improve the lives of others and cause positive social change. Their philanthropic efforts are gaining momentum, and it will be exciting to see how the promise of philanthropy in India is realized in the practice of philanthropy in the years to come.

Bibliography

Adukia, Rajkumar. 2005. Handbook on Laws Governing Formation and Administration of Charitable Organizations in India. Available at www.caa.in (accessed October 9, 2015).

Agarwal, Sanjay. 2010. *Daan and Other Giving Traditions in India*. Delhi: Account Aid.

Agarwal, Sanjay and AccountAid. 1999. "Non-Profit Company." *AccountAble*, March. Available at http://www.accountaid.net (accessed October 9, 2015).

———. 2005a. "Accountability and Hindu Dan." *AccountAble, April*. Available at http://www.accountaid.net (accessed October 9, 2015).

———. 2005b. "Accountability and Islamic Charity." *AccountAble*, May. Available at http://www.accountaid.net/ (accessed October 9, 2015).

———. 2005c. "Accountability and Christian Charity." *AccountAble*, June. Available at http://www.accountaid.net (accessed October 9, 2015).

———. 2005d. "History of FCRA." *AccountAble*, August. Available at http://www.accountaid.net (accessed October 9, 2015).

———. 2013. "Society, Trust or Company." *AccountAble*. Available at http://www.accountaid.net/ (accessed October 9, 2015).

Agarwal, Rina. 2012. Tapping the Indian Diaspora for Indian Development. Available at https://www.princeton.edu/cmd/working-papers/2012TransnationalMeeting/2012-India.pdf

———. 2015. "Tapping the Indian Diaspora for Indian Development." In *The State and the Grassroots: Immigrant Transnational Organizations in Four Continents*, edited by Alejandro Portes and Patricia Fernandez Kelly, 84–110. New York: Berghahn Press.

Agarwal, Surabhi. 2013. "Do India's Online Numbers Stack Up?" *Business Standard*, December 10, 2013. Technology Features. Available at http://www.business-standard.com/article/technology/do-india-s-onilne-numbers-stack-up-113121001148_1.html (accessed October 9, 2015).

Agrawal, Madhusudan. 2011. "Love Warrior on A Tricycle: Story of Raghu." *Service Space*. Available at http://www.servicespace.org/blog/view.php?id=2312 (accessed October 9, 2015).

Ahmed, Hasanuddin and Ahmedullah Khan. 1998. Strategies to Develop Waqf Administration in India. Research Paper No. 50. Jeddah: Islamic Research and Training Institute, Islamic Development Bank.

Ammerman N. 1997. "Organized Religion in a Voluntaristic Society." *Sociology of Religion* 58 (3): 203–215.

Anand, Geeta. 2009. "The Henry Ford of Heart Surgery." *Wall Street Journal*, November 25. Available at http://online.wsj.com/news/articles/SB125875892887958111 (accessed August 13, 2014).

Anand, P. 2004. *Hindu Diaspora and Religious Philanthropy in the United States*. New York: Center on Philanthropy and Civil Society.

Anderson, B. 1991. *Imagined Communities: Reflections on the Origin and Spread of Nationalism*. London: Verso.

Anderson, Leona. 1997. "Generosity of Householders, Generosity of Kings: Situating Philanthropy in South Asia." In *Philanthropy and Cultural Context*, edited by Philo Hove and Soma Hewa, 185–202. Lanham, New York and Oxford: University Press of America Inc.

———. 1998. "Contextualizing Philanthropy in South Asia: A Textual Analysis of Sanskrit Sources." In *Philanthropy in the World's Traditions*, edited by W. Ilchman, S. Katz and E.L. Queen, 57–72. Bloomington: Indiana University Press.

Andreoni, James and John Karl Scholz. 1998. "An Econometric Analysis of Charitable Giving with Interdependent Interfaces." *Economic Inquiry* 26: 410–28.

Aravamudan, Gita. 2010. *Unbound.* pp. 198–2010. New Delhi: Penguin Books.

Arora, B. and R. Puranik 2004. "A Review of Corporate Social Responsibility in India." *Development* 47 (3): 93–100.

Arvind, Gaysu. 2009. "Local Democracy, Rural Community, and Participatory School Governance." *Journal of Research in Rural Education* 24 (2): 1–13.

Babu, Venkatesha. 2006. "The Importance of Being Kiran Muzumdar." *Business Today.*

Bakshi, Nishita and Barnett F. Baron. 2011. "Enabling Indian Diaspora Philanthropy." Available at Give2Asia. http://give2asia.org/documents/Give2Asia-IndiaDiasporaGiving-Report.pdf (accessed October 9, 2015).

Barnes, Taylor. 2010. "Difference Maker: After Seeing Mumbai's Slums Bulldozed, He Now Works to Save and Restore Them." *The Christian Science Monitor*, August 30, 2010. World. Available at http://www.csmonitor.com/World/Making-a-difference/2010/0830/After-seeing-Mumbai-s-slums-bulldozed-he-now-works-to-save-and-restore-them (accessed October 9, 2015).

Basu, Soma. 2013. "Chai and Love." *The Hindu*, August 28, sec. Features—Society. Available at http://www.thehindu.com/features/metroplus/society/chai-and-love/article5067984.ece (accessed October 9, 2015).

———. 2014. "Making a Difference: Food to the Lonely." *The Hindu*, January 1, sec. Metroplus—Society. Available at http://www.thehindu.com/features/metroplus/society/making-a-difference-food-to-the-lonely/article5526172.ece (accessed October 9, 2015).

BBC. 2011. Thousands flock to funeral of Indian Guru Satya Baba, April 27. Available at http://www.bbc.co.uk/news/world-south-asia-13204914 (accessed October 9, 2015).

Bekkers, R. and P. Wiepking 2011. "A Literature Review of Empirical Studies of Philanthropy: Eight Mechanisms that Drive Charitable Giving." *Nonprofit and Voluntary Sector Quarterly* 40 (5): 924–73.

Bennett, Roger. 2003. "Factors Underlying the Inclination to Donate to Particular Types of Charity." *International Journal of Nonprofit & Voluntary Sector Marketing* 8 (1): 12–29.

Berk, Tony. 2011. HelpAge India Generates Instant Fundraising Reports, Streamlines Donation Processes with Oracle CRM On Demand, August18. Available at https://blogs.oracle.com/cx/entry/helpage_india_generates_instant_fundraising (accessed October 9, 2015).

Bhargava, A. 2010. *Hindu American Seva Charities—Call to Serve Briefing Report for President Obama.* The White House Office of Faith Based and Neighborhood Partnerships.

Bhownick, Nilanjana. 2014. "India is Home to More Poor People than Anywhere Else on Earth." *Time Magazine*, New Delhi, July 17.

Blackwood, Amy S., Katie L. Roeger and Sarah L. Pettijohn. 2012. *The Nonprofit Sector in Brief: Public Charities, Giving and Volunteering.* Washington, DC: The Urban Institute's Centre on Nonprofits and Philanthropy.

Bloom, D.E., G. Grenier and M. Gunderson 1995. "The Changing Labour Market Position of Canadian Immigrants." *Canadian Journal of Economics* (Canadian Economics Association) 28 (4b): 987–1005Bornstein, Erica. 2009. "The Impulse of Philanthropy." *Cultural Anthropology* 24 (4): 622–51. doi:10.1111/j.1548-1360.2009.01042.x.

———. 2012. *Disquieting Gifts: Humanitarianism in New Delhi.* Stanford Studies in Human Rights. Stanford, CA: Stanford University Press.

Brooks, A.C. 2003. "Religious Faith and Charitable Giving." *Policy Review* 121: 39–50.

Bukhari, Alison 2012. "Collaborating Internationally to Empower Indian Women." *Alliance Blog*, July 31. Available at http://www.alliancemagazine.org/blog/collaborating-internationally-to-empower-indian-women/ (accessed October 9, 2015).

———. 2013. Personal Conversation. Dasra, London.

Bundhan, Rebecca. 2013. "Mumbai's Bhendi Bazaar: A Slumdog Millionaire Overhaul." *The National*, September 8.

Business India. 2013. Bhendi Bazar Redevelopment Project Gets Govt Nod, October 20. Available at http://www.business-standard.com/article/economy-policy/bhendi-bazar-redevelopment-project-gets-govt-nod-113102000345_1.html (accessed on January 11, 2014).

CAF. 2011. "World Giving Index 2011: A Global View of Giving Trends". Charities Aid Foundation. Available at https://www.cafonline.org/pdf/world_giving_index_2011_191211.pdf (accessed October 9, 2015).

———. 2012. "World Giving Index 2012: A Global View of Giving Trends." World Giving Index, Charities Aid Foundation. Available at http://www.cafonline.org/PDF/WorldGivingIndex2012WEB.pdf (accessed October 9, 2015).

Cantegreil, Mathieu, Dweep Chanana and Ruth Kattumuri, eds. 2013. *Revealing Indian Philanthropy.* London: Alliance Publishing Trust. Available at http://www.ubs.com/content/dam/ubs/global/wealth_management/philanthropy_valuesbased_investments/indian-philanthrophy.pdf (accessed October 9, 2015).

Cantrell, J.E., E. Kyriazis, and G. Noble. 2014. "Developing CSR Giving as a Dynamic Capability for Salient Stakeholder Management." *Journal of Business Ethics* 1–19.

Caplan, L. 1998. "Gifting and Receiving: Anglo-Indian Charity and Its Beneficiaries in Madras." *Contributions to Indian Sociology* 32 (2): 408–31.

Cassel, D. 2001. "Human rights business responsibilities in the global marketplace." *Business Ethics Quarterly* 11 (2):261–274.

Census of India. 2011. "Final Population Totals". The **Registrar** General & Census Commissioner, Ministry of Home Affairs, Government of India. *Census Info India 2011.* Available at http://censusindia.gov.in/2011census/censusinfodashboard/index.html (accessed October 9, 2015).

Chacko, E. 2007. "From Brain Drain to Brain Gain: Reverse Migration to Bangalore and Hyderabad, India's Globalizing High Tech Cities." *GeoJournal* 68 (2–3): 131–40.

Chaudhari, Kalpesh. 2011. "Food for Cause." *Ahmedabad Mirror*, March 17, sec. City.

Chaves, M., and S.L. Miller, eds. 1999. *Financing American Religion*. Walnut Creek: Alta Mira Press.

Chaves, M. 2004. *Congregations in America*. Cambridge: Harvard University Press.

CIDA-ACDI. 2011. Available at http://web.mit.edu/urbanupgrading/upgrading/resources/organizations/cida-acdi.html accessed October 17, 2013.

Cnaan R.A., R.J. Wineburg, and S.C. Boddie. 1999. *The Newer Deal: Social Work and Religion in Partnership*. New York: Columbia University Press.

Cnaan, R.A., S.C. Boddie, F. Handy, G. Yancey, and R. Schneider. 2002. *The Invisible Caring Hand: American Congregations and the Provision of Welfare*. New York: University Press.

Cnaan, R.A., T. Forrest, J. Carlsmith, and K. Karsh. 2013. "If You Do Not Count It, It Does Not Count: A Pilot Study of Valuing Urban Congregations." *Journal of Management, Spirituality and Religion* 10 (1): 3–36.

Copeman, J. 2011. "The Gift and Its Forms of Life in Contemporary India." *Modern Asian Studies* 45 (5): 1051–94.

Dadrawala, Noshir. 2003. *Merchants of Philanthropy: Profiles in Good Corporate Citizenship*. Mumbai: Centre for Advancement of Philanthropy.

———. August, 2013. *Personal Conversations*. Mumbai, India: Center of Philanthropy .

Das, Gurcharan. 2002. *The Elephant Paradigm: India Wrestles with Change*. New Delhi: Penguin Books.

Dasgupta, Ajit Kumar. 1996. *Gandhi's Economic Thought*. Routledge Studies in the History of Economics. London and New York: Routledge.

Dastur, Nicole. 2009. Bollywood Walks for Shabana. *Bombay Times*, October 29.

Davis, K. 1973. "The Case for and Against Business Assumption of Social Responsibilities." *Academy of Management Journal* 16 (2): 312–22.

Deloitte and Touch. 2010. Public Sector Enterprise in India–Catalyst for Growth. Member of Indian Chamber of Commerce: Deloitte Touch Tohmatsu Private Limited.

Deloitte and Indian Chamber of Commerce. 2010. *Public Sector Enterprises in India: Catalyst for Growth*, Deloitte Touche Tohmatsu India Private Limited. Available at http://www.indianchamber.org/policy_forms/3.pdf (accessed October 9, 2015).

Dhamija, Anshul. 2013. I have given 25% of my wealth to charity, Wipro chairman Azim Premji says. Bangalore: *The Times of India*, April 19. Available at http://timesofindia.indiatimes.com/india/I-have-given-25-of-my-wealth-to-charity-Wipro-chairman-Azim-Premji-says/articleshow/19633650.cms(accessed October 19, 2014).

Dochterman, Clifford L. 2006. The ABCs of Rotary. Rotary International. Available at http://shop.rotary.org/The-ABCs-of-Rotary/dp/B0043MXSCS (accessed October 9, 2015).

Dongre, Y. and Gopalan, S. 2008. Third Sector Governance in India. In *Comparative Third Sector Governance in Asia: Structure, Process and Political Economy*, edited by S. Hasan and J. Onyx, 227–51. New York: Springer.

Dugger, C.W. 2000. In New York, Just a Cabby. In India, a School's Hero. *The New York Times*. January 23. Available at www.nytimes.com/2000/01/23/world/in-new-york-just-a-cabby-in-india-a-school-s-hero.html?pagewanted=1

Dunn, E.W., L.B. Aknin, and M.I. Norton. 2008. "Spending money on others promotes happiness." *Science* 319: 1687–88.

Dusenbery, V.A. and D.S. Tatla. 2010. *Sikh Diaspora Philanthropy in Punjab: Global Giving for Local Good.* Oxford: Oxford University Press.

Ebaugh, H.R. and J.S. Chafetz, eds. 2000. *Religion and the New Immigrants: Continuities and Adaptations in Immigrant Congregations.* Walnut Creek: AltaMira Press.

Economic Times Bureau. 2014. India Inc honchos to talk philanthropy with Bill Gates at an event hosted by Azim Premji. *The Economic Times:* Corporate Trends, September 20. Available at http://articles.economictimes.indiatimes.com/2014-09-20/news/54135378_1_amnesty-india-azim-premji-foundation-india-inc(accessed October 9, 2015).

Editor. 2014. A Vertical Makeover. *Buildotech Magazine*, India, July 14.

Ernst & Young LLP. 2013. Corporate Social Responsibility in India: Potential to contribute towards inclusive social development. *Global CSR Summit 2013: An Agenda for Inclusive Growth.* Available at http://www.ey.com/Publication/vwLUAssets/EY-Government-and-Public-Sector-Corporate-Social-Responsibility-in-India/$File/EY-Corporate-Social-Responsibility-in-India.pdf (accessed October 9, 2015).

Eswar Kumar Belli, S. and T.S. Raghavendran. 2014. "Role of Shri Kshetra Dharamsthala Rural Development Project (SKDRDP) in Microfinance through SHGS: A Study in the Shimoga District of Karnataka." *IOSR Journal of Economics and Finance (IOSR-JEF)* 3 (2), Ver 11, 53–9, March–April.

Express News, The Indian Express. 2011. "State may refer Ambani's Wakf Land deal to CBI." *The Indian Express*, August 2.

Finke, R., M. Bahr, and C.P. Scheitle. 2006. "Toward Explaining Congregational Giving." *Social Science Research* 35 (3): 620–41.

Foley, M.W. and D.R. Hoge. 2007. *Religion and the New Immigrants: How Faith Communities Form Our Newest Citizens.* New York: Oxford University Press.

Forbes. 2012. "The World's Billionaires." *Forbes.* Available at http://www.forbes.com/billionaires/#p_1_s_a0_All%20industries_India_All%20states_(accessed October 9, 2015).

Forbes Asia. 2011. "48 Heroes of Philanthropy." *Forbes Asia,* June 22. Available at http://www.forbes.com/global/2011/0718/heroes-philanthropy-11-kaldor-zhiqiang-oberoi-heroes-list.html (accessed October 9, 2015).

———. 2010. "48 Heroes of Philanthropy," March 6. Available at http://www.forbes.com/2010/03/08/asia-heroes-charity-personal-finance-philanthropy-india.html (accessed October 31, 2015).

Francis, Jane, Alexander Jackson, and Shivani Satija. 2010. "India: Fusing the Old and the New: The Sir Ratan Tata Trust and Philanthropy in India." In *In an Age of Turner & Gates: Collaboration, Scale and Leverage Re-Imagined*, edited by Norine MacDonald QC and Luc Tayart de Borms, 109–17. London: MF Publishing.

Friedman, M. 1970. The Social Responsibility of Business is to Increase Its Profits. *The New York Times Magazine*, pp. 173–178.

Friedman, M. and R. Friedman. 1962. *Capitalism and Freedom.* Chicago: University of Chicago Press.

Gans, Herbert J. 1992. "Second Generation Decline: Scenarios for the Economic and Ethnic Futures of the Post 1965 American immigrants." *Ethnic and Racial Studies* 15 (2): 173–92.

Gautier, A. 2015. "Research on Corporate Philanthropy: A Review and Assessment." *Journal of Business Ethics,* edited by A. Gautier and A. C. Pache, 126 (3): 1–27.

Geithner, P.F., L.C. Chen, and P.D. Johnson. 2004. *Diaspora Philanthropy and Equitable Development in China and India.* Cambridge: Harvard University Press.

Ghosh, Ahona. 2011. "Act of Giving: Giving across Generations." *The Economic Times,* October 4. Available at http://articles.economictimes.indiatimes. com/2011-10-04/news/30242489_1_anu-aga-meher-pudumjee-thermax (accessed October 9, 2015).

Goldstein, Andrea. 2008. "Emerging Economies' Multinationals: Explaining the Case of Tata." *Transnational Corporations,* 17 (3) by United Nations (New York and Geneva, November). Available at http://unctad.org/en/docs/diaeiia20083_ en.pdf#page=93 (accessed October 9, 2015).

Gosvami, S. and S.K.H. Madhur. 1995. Vrindavan-Shri: Vrindavan Vikas Samiti Smarika (Vrindavan: ShriVrindavan Vikas Samiti) in Shinde, Kiran A.' What are Charitable Trusts Doing in Religious Tourism? Insights from an Indian Pilgrimage Site. *Tourism Planning & Development* 8 (1), February 2011, 21–36.

Government of India. 1961. *Income Tax Act, 1961.* Available at http://law. incometaxindia.gov.in/DIT/Income-tax-acts.aspx(accessed October 9, 2015).

———. 2010. *Guidelines on Corporate Governance for Central Public Sector Enterprises.* New Delhi: Ministry of Heavy Industries and Public Enterprises, Department of Public Enterprises, May. Available at: http://dpe.nic.in/sites/upload_files/dpe/files/gcgcpse10.pdf (accessed October 9, 2015).

———. 2011a. *Corporate Social Responsibility: Companies Bill 2011.* Available at www.mca.gov.in/Ministry/pdf/The_Companies_Bill_2011.pdf (accessed October 9, 2015).

———. 2011b. *National Voluntary Guidelines on Social Environmental and Economic responsibilities of Business.* Available at http://www.mca.gov.in/Ministry/latestnews/National_Voluntary_Guidelines_2011_12jul2011.pdf (accessed December 2, 2013).

———. 2012a. "Final Report on Non Profit Institutions in India." New Delhi: National Accounts Division, Central Statistics Office, Ministry of Statistics and Programme Implementation. Available at www.mospi.gov.in

———. 2012b. "Annual Report 2011–12". New Delhi: Ministry of Home Affairs, Government of India. Available at http://mha.nic.in/sites/upload_files/mha/files/AR(E)1112.pdf

———.2013. The Companies Act 2013. New Delhi: Ministry of Law and Justice. Available at http://www.mca.gov.in/Ministry/pdf/CompaniesAct2013.pdf

Granito, Alison. 2007. "NGO advertising: visibility counts." Available at http://www.livemint.com/Consumer/0HmL1U7doCXYDiI1dwq99J/NGO-advertising-visibility-counts.html (accessed May 6, 2015).

Guha, Ramachandra. 2012. "Give and Let Give". Hindustan Times. Http://www.hindustantimes.com/. Available at http://www.hindustantimes.com/News-Feed/Editorials/Give-and-let-give/Article1-637299.aspx (accessed September 21).

Gupta, Ashis Kumar. 2010. "Soul Curry: The Two-Rupee Miracle." *Times of India,* July 1, sec. Life and Style. http://timesofindia.indiatimes.com/life-style/

Soul-Curry-The-two-rupee-miracle/articleshow/4747553.cms (accessed October 9, 2015).

Hall, P.D. 2005. *Religion, Philanthropy, Service and Civic Engagement in Twentieth Century America in Gifts of Time and Money: The Role of Charities in America's Community*. Oxford: Rowman and Littlefield Publishers.

Hammack, David C. and Steven Heydemann, eds. 2009. *Globalization, Philanthropy, and Civil Society: Projecting Institutional Logics Abroad*. Illinois: Indiana University Press.

Handy, F. M. Kassam, S. Feeney, and B. Ranade. 2006. *Grass-roots NGOs by women for women: The driving force of development in India*. New Delhi: SAGE Publications.

Handy, F. and I. Greenspan. 2009. "Immigrant Volunteering: A Stepping Stone to Integration?" *Nonprofit and Voluntary Sector Quarterly* 38 (6): 956–82.

Handy, F. and M. Kassam. 2007. "Practice What You Preach? The Role of Rural NGOs in Women's Empowerment." *Journal of Community Practice* 14 (3), 69–91.

Handy, Femida, Meenaz Kassam, Jillian Ingold, and Bhagyashree Ranade. 2011. *From Seva to Cyberspace: The Many Faces of Volunteering in India*. New Delhi: SAGE Publications.

Harper, Malcom, D.S.K. Rao, and Ashis Kumar Sahu. 2008. *Development, Divinity and Dharma: The Role of Religion in Development and Microfinance Institutions*. United Kingdom: Practical Action Publishing.

Haynes, Douglas E. 1987. "From Tribute to Philanthropy: The Politics of Gift Giving in a Western Indian City." *The Journal of Asian Studies* 46 (2): 339–60.

———. 1991. *Rhetoric and Ritual in Colonial India: The Shaping of Public Culture in Surat City, 1852–1928*. Berkeley and Los Angeles: University of California Press.

Hinnells, John R. 1985. "The Flowering of Zoroastrian Benevolence." In *Papers in Honour of Professor Mary Boyce, Hommages et Opera Minora*, edited by H.W. Bailey, A.D.H. Bivar, J. Duchesne-Guillemin, and J. Hinnells, vol. 10, 261–326. Leiden: Brill.

Hoge, D.R. 1995. "Explanation for Current Levels of Religious Giving." In *Cultures of Giving: How Region and Religion Influence Philanthropy*, edited by Charles H. Hamilton and Warren F. Illchman, 21 (7), Spring 1995. San Fancisco: Jossey-Bass.

Hughes, P. and W. Luksetich. 2007. "Income Volatility and Wealth: The Effect on Charitable Giving." *Nonprofit and Voluntary Sector Quarterly* 37 (2): 264–80. doi:10.1177/0899764007310416.

Humphrey, M. 1993. "Migrants, Workers and Refugees: The Political Economy of Population Movements in the Middle East," *Middle East Report* 181:2–7.

Iannaccone, L.R. 1997. "Skewness Explained: A Rational Choice Model of Religious Giving." *Journal for the Scientific Study of Religion* 26 (2): 141–57.

India Knowledge@Wharton. 2011. "Religious Giving: Do Unregulated 'Temples of God' Really Serve a Higher Purpose?" Wharton School of the University of Pennsylvania. Available at http://knowledge.wharton.upenn.edu/india/article. cfm?articleid=4601(accessed October 9, 2015).

indiacsr. 2013. "Coming Soon, Stricter CSR Spend Norms for PSUs." *indiaCSR*, August 29, Financial Express edition. Available at http://www.indiacsr.in/ en/?p=12083 (accessed October 9, 2015).

Jensen, M.C. 2000. "Value Maximization, Stakeholder Theory, and the Corporate Objective Function". In Breaking the Code of Change, edited by M. Beer and N. Nohria, 37–58. Boston: Harvard Business School Press.

Jha, Veena. 2012. India Emerging: The Reality Checks. New Delhi: Academic Foundation.

Johnson, Donald Clay. 1996. "Ahmedabadi Philanthropy and Libraries." Libraries & Culture 31 (1): 103–12.

Johnson, P.D. 2007. Diaspora Philanthropy: Influences, Initiatives, and Issues. Boston: The Philanthropic Initiative, Inc. and The Global Equity Initiative, Harvard University, May.

Jones, Allison. 2012,. "Why I left the corporate world in Canada to start an NGO in India." Idealist.org, August 7. Available at http://idealistcareers.org/why-i-left-the-corporate-world-in-canada-to-start-an-ngo-in-india/ (accessed October 9, 2015).

Joshi, E.B. 1968. Uttar Pradesh District Gazetteers: Mathura. Lucknow: Government Press, Uttar Pradesh.

Juergensmeyer, M., D.M. McMahon, and E.L. Queen. 1998. "Hindu Philanthropy and Civil Society." In Philanthropy in the World's Traditions, edited by W. Ilchman and S. Katz. Bloomington: Indiana University Press.

Kapur, Devesh, Ajay S. Mehta, and R. Moon Dutt. 2004. "Indian Diaspora Philanthropy." In Diaspora Philanthropy and Equitable Development in China and India, edited by Peter F. Geithner, Paula D. Johnson, and Lincoln C. Chen, 177–213. Cambridge, MA and London: Harvard University Press.

Karmali, Naazneen. 2013. "Rohini Nilekani Sells Infosys Shares, Raises $27 Million For Charity." Forbes, March 9. Available at http://www.forbes.com/sites/naazneenkarmali/2013/08/03/rohini-nilekani-sells-infosys-shares-raises-27-million-for-charity/ (accessed October 19, 2014).

———. 2014. "Mining Magnate Anil Agarwal Reaffirms Pledge To Join Ranks of India's Most Charitable." Forbes, September 26. Available at http://www.forbes.com/sites/naazneenkarmali/2014/09/26/mining-magnate-anil-agarwal-reaffirms-pledge-to-join-ranks-of-indias-most-charitable/ (accessed October 9, 2015).

Kasturi, Malavika. 2010. "'All Gifting Is Sacred': The Sanatana Dharma Sabha Movement, the Reform of Dana and Civil Society in Late Colonial India." Indian Economic and Social History Review 47 (1): 107–39. doi:10.1177/001946460904700104.

Kaviraj, S. and S. Khilnani, eds. 2001. Civil Society—History and Possibilities. Cambridge: Cambridge University Press.

Khandelwal, Madhulika S. 2002. Becoming American, Being Indian: An Immigrant Community in New York City. Ithaca: Cornell University Press.

Knowledge@Wharton. 2011. "Religious Giving: Do Unregulated 'Temples of God' Really serve a Higher Purpose?" May 19. Available at https://knowledge.wharton.upenn.edu/article/religious-giving-do-unregulated-temples-of-god-really-serve-a-higher-purpose/ (accessed October 9, 2015).

Koppisch, John. 2011. "48 Heroes of Philanthropy." Forbes. Available at http://www.forbes.com/global/2011/0718/heroes-philanthropy-11-kaldor-zhiqiang-oberoi-heroes-list.html (accessed on December 12, 2015).

———. 2012. "48 Heroes of Philanthropy." Forbes Asia, June 20. Available at http://www.forbes.com/sites/johnkoppisch/2012/06/20/48-heroes-of-philanthropy/ (accessed October 9, 2015).

Koppisch, John. 2013. "48 Heroes of Philanthropy." *Forbes Asia,* June 10. Available at http://www.forbes.com/sites/johnkoppisch/2013/05/29/48-heroes-of-philanthropy-2/ (accessed October 9, 2015).

Koppisch, John 2014. "48 Heroes of Philanthropy." *Forbes Asia,* July 21. Available at http://www.forbes.com/sites/johnkoppisch/2014/06/25/48-heroes-of-philanthropy-3/

Korten, D.C. 1987. "Third Generation NGO Strategies: A Key to People Centered Development." *World Development* 15:145–59.

Kourula, Arno and Minna Halme. 2008. "Types of Corporate Responsibility and Engagement with NGOs: An Exploration of Business and Societal Outcomes." *Corporate Governance* 8 (4): 557–70. doi:10.1108/14720700810899275.

Krishna, C.G. 1992. *Corporate Social Responsibility in India.* New Delhi, India: Mittal Publications.

Kroll, Luisa. 2011. Forbes: *The Little Black Book of Billionaire Secrets.* Available at http://www.forbes.com/sites/luisakroll/2011/10/27/ambani-brothers-lakshmi-mittal-lose-big/

Kumar, Arun. 2012. "Is The Lord's property safe in Tirumala Tirupati Devasthanamus' hands?" *The Times of India,* Hyderabad, April 12.

Kumar, N., P. Trofimovich, and E. Gatbonton. 2008. "Investigating Heritage Language and Culture Links: An Indo-Canadian Hindu Perspective." *Journal of Multilingual and Multicultural Development* 29 (1): 49–65.

Kumar, R., D.F. Murphy, and V. Balsari. 2001. "Altered images: The 2001 state of corporate responsibility in India poll: Understanding and encouraging corporate responsibility in South Asia." New Delhi: TERI-India. Available at http://www. terieurope.org/docs/CSR-India.pdf

Kumar, R., D.F. Murphy, R. Mortier, C. Rathnasiri, and L. Guanarante. 2004. *Understanding and encouraging corporate responsibility in South Asia, Update two: Sri Lanka.* New Delhi: TERI Press.

Laidlaw, James. 1995. *Riches and Renunciation: Religion, Economy, and Society among the Jains.* Oxford: Claredon Press.

Lala, R. M. (1998). *The Heartbeat of a Trust: The Story of the Sir Dorabji Tata Trust.* New Delhi: Tata McGraw–Hill.

Lall, M.C. 2001. *India's Missed Opportunity: India's Relationship with the Non-Resident Indians.* United Kingdom: Ashgate Publishing Limited.

Levy, Ariel. 2012. "Drug Test." *The New Yorker.*

Logsdon, J.M., M. Reiner, and L. Burke. 1990. "Corporate Philanthropy: Strategic Responses to the Firm's Stakeholders." *Nonprofit and Voluntary Sector Quarterly* 19 (1): 93–109.

Lushington, Charles. 1824. *The History, Design, and Present State of the Religious, Benevolent and Charitable Institutions, Founded by the British in Calcutta and Its Vicinity.* Calcutta: Hindostanee Press.

Malik, Tanveer. 2013. Impact of globalization on Indian economy—An overview. Available at http://www.fibre2fashion.com/industry-article/8/738/impact-of-globalization1.asp (accessed October 9, 2015).

Mangaleswaran, Ramesh and Ramya Venkataraman. 2013. *Designing Philanthropy for Impact: Giving to the biggest gaps in India,* October. Chennai: McKinsey and Co.

Maple, Terrie and Richard Harrison. 2012. *India Giving: Insights into the Nature of Giving Across India.* New Delhi: Charities Aid Foundation (CAF) India. Available at https://www.cafonline.org/media-office/press-releases/2012/caf-launches-india-giving.aspx (accessed October 9, 2015).

Massey, Douglas S. 1981. "Dimensions of the New Immigration to the United States and the Prospects for Assimilation." *Annual Review of Sociology* 7:57–85.

Mauss, Marcel. 1966. *The Gift: Forms and Functions of Exchange in Archaic Societies.* Translated by Ian Gunnison. London: Cohen and West Ltd.

Mazumdar, Sudip. 2004. "First Lady." *Newsweek.*

McIntyre, Mike. 1996. *The Kindness of Strangers.* Berkley trade pbk. edition. New York: Berkley Books.

Meera, Mitra. 2007. *It's Only Business! India's Corporate Social Responsiveness in a Globalizing World.* New Delhi: Oxford University Press.

Mehta, K. and P. Johnston. 2011. "Diaspora Philanthropy and Civic Engagement in Canada: Setting the Stage." *The Philanthropist* 24 (1): 3–12.

Mehta, Nipun. 2009. "From Chain Smoking to Chain Giving: Profile of Venkat." *Service Space.* Available at http://www.servicespace.org/blog/view.php?id=2122 (accessed October 9, 2015).

Meyer, Christian and Nancy Birdsall. 2012. "New Estimates of India's Middle Class." Technical Note. Washington, DC: Center for Global Development. Available at http://www.cgdev.org/doc/2013_MiddleClassIndia_TechnicalNote_CGDNote. pdf (accessed October 9, 2015).

Mishra, Kailash K. 2002. Chaupal as Multidimensional Public Space for Civil Society in India. Paper presented in the International Seminar jointly organized by Indira Gandhi Center for the Arts, New Delhi and National Folklore Support Center, Chennai.

Mohan, A. 2001. "Corporate Citizenship: Perspectives from India." *Journal of Corporate Citizenship* 2001 (2): 107–117.

Mulvany, Clare. 2006. "Dasra- Fortifier of Deeds." Blog: *Exceptional Lives,* September 19. Available at http://exceptional-lives.blogspot.ca/2006_09_01_archive.html (accessed October 9, 2014).

Muniapan, A. 2001. "Corporate Citizenship." *Journal of Corporate Citizenship* 2001 (2): 107–117.

Muniapan, B. and Dass, M. 2008. "Corporate Social Responsibility: A Philosophical Approach from an Ancient Indian Perspective." *International Journal of Indian Culture and Business Management* 1 (4): 408–420.

Nag, Sajal. 2008. *Pied Pipers in North-East India: Bamboo-Flowers, Rat Famine, and the Politics of Philanthropy, 1881–2007.* New Delhi: Manohar.

NCAER. 2003. Domestic Tourism Survey: 2002–2003. New Delhi: National Council of Applied Economic Research and Ministry of Tourism and Culture, Government of India.

Newland, K., A. Terrazas, and R. Munster. 2010. *Diaspora Philanthropy: Private Giving and Public Policy.* Washington D.C.: Migration Policy Institute.

O'Sullivan, Michael and Richard Kersley. 2012. "Global Wealth Report 2012." Credit Suisse Global Wealth Report. Zurich: Credit Suisse Research Institute. Available at https://infocus.credit-suisse.com/app/article/index.cfm?fuseaction= OpenArticle&aoid=368967&coid=118&lang=EN (accessed October 9, 2015).

Ong, A. 1998. *Flexible Citizenship: The Cultural Logics of Transnationality.* Durham: Duke University Press.

Ostrower, Francie. 1997. *Why the Wealthy Give: The Culture of Elite Philanthropy.* Princeton, NJ: Princeton University Press. Available at http://site.ebrary.com/ id/10035828 (accessed October 9, 2015).

Palsetia, Jesse S. 2005. "Merchant Charity and Public Identity Formation in Colonial India: The Case of Jamsetjee Jejeebhoy." *Journal of Asian & African Studies (Sage Publications, Ltd.)* 40 (3): 197–217. doi:10.1177/0021909605055071.

Pappu, S.S. Rama Rao. 2004. "Hindu Ethics." In *Contemporary Hinduism: Ritual, Culture and Practice,* edited by Robin Rinehart. Santa Barbara: ABC-CLIO.

Parthasarathy, Vimla. 2011. "What Do Donors Want of NGOs? Some Empirical Evidences from Indian NGOs." *Elixir International Journal,* Elixir Mgmt. Arts 39: 5093–5097.

Partners in Change. 2004. Third Report on Corporate Involvement in Social Development in India, Partners in Change, India.

Peloza, J., and P. Steel. 2005. "The Price Elasticities of Charitable Contributions: A Meta-Analysis." *Journal of Public Policy & Marketing* 24:260–272.

Prakash-Mani, K. 2002. *Corporate Social Responsibility in the Indian Context, Sustainability.* UK: Sustainability Radar.

Press Trust of India (PTI). 2014. "Internet Subscribers in India Touch 235.71 Mn in 2013: Govt," *Business Today,* Info Tech, February 19.

Print Edition. 2011. New Sources of Aid: Charity Begins Abroad. *The Economist,* August 13. Available at http://www.economist.com/node/21525836 (accessed October 9, 2015).

Radley, Alan and Marie Kennedy. 1995. "Charitable Giving by Individuals: A Study of Attitudes and Practice." *Human Relations* 48 (6): 685–709. doi:10.1177/001872679504800605.

Raghunathan, Anuradha. 2013. "Heroes of Philanthropy: Kiran Mazumdar-Shaw's Affordable Health Care Legacy." *Forbes Asia,* June. Available at http://www. forbes.com/sites/forbesasia/2013/05/29/heroes-of-philanthropy-kiran-mazumdar-shaws-affordable-health-care-legacy/ (accessed October 19, 2014).

Rai, Archana. 2013. "With Rs 164 crore in kitty, Rohini Nilekani to chart a new course in philanthropy," Bangalore: *The Economic Times,* August 8. Available at http://articles.economictimes.indiatimes.com/2013-08-08/news/41202077_1_ rohini-nilekani-indian-institute-pratham-books (accessed December 12, 2015).

Raja, K.S. Sripada. 2012. "Philanthropic Perspectives of Hinduism." Available at http://www.learningtogive.org/religiousinstructors/voices/phil_persp_of_ hinduism.asp (accessed October 9, 2015).

Ramachandran, K. 2009. "Family and Corporate Philanthropy: Emerging Trends in India." The Daily Sabbatical. *Forbes, India,* December 4. Available at http:// india.forbes.com/article/isb/family-and-corporate-philanthropy-emerging-trends-in-india/7652/0 (accessed October 9, 2015).

———. 2010. "Family and Corporate Philanthropy: Emerging Trends in India." Forbes India magazine, May 3. Available at http://forbesindia.com/article/isb/family-and-corporate-philanthropy-emerging-trends-in-india/12682/1 (accessed July 31, 2014).

Ramachandran, K. and Thomas Schmidheiny. 2010. "Family and Corporate Philanthropy: Emerging Trends in India." The Daily Sabbatical. Forbes India, May 3. Available at http://forbesindia.com/article/isb/family-and-corporatephilanthropy-emerging-trends-in-india/12682/1 (accessed October 9, 2015).

Ramakrishnan, Hema. 2011. "Charities, Trusts to come under one law for more transparency." *The Economic Times*, India, March 23.

Ramesh, Randeep. 2010. "Charitable Giving by Country: Who is the Most Generous?" *The Guardian*, September 8. Available at http://www.theguardian.com/news/datablog/2010/sep/08/charitable-giving-country (accessed October 9, 2015).

Reddy, Nidhi M., Lalitha Vaidyanathan, Katyayani Balasubramanian, Kavitha Gorapalli, and Sharad Sharma. 2012. "Catalytic Philanthropy in India." Hyderabad and Mumbai: Indian School of Business and FSG Consultants. Available at http://www.fsg.org/tabid/191/ArticleId/582/Default.aspx?srpush=true (accessed October 9, 2015).

Report of the High Level Committee on the Indian Diaspora. 2001. "Non Resident Indians and Persons of Indian Origin Division," Ministry of External Affairs, Government of India. pp. 481–501. Available at http://shodhganga.inflibnet.ac.in/bitstream/10603/8022/9/09_chapter%202.pdf (accessed October 9, 2015).

Richwine, J. 2009. "Indian Americans: The New Model Minority." *Forbes*, February 24. Available at http://www.forbes.com/2009/02/24/bobbyjindal-indian-americans-opinions-contributors_immigrants_minority.html (accessed October 9, 2015).

Robinson, Sheila A. 1997. "Development and Philanthropy in the Context of South Asia: Moving toward Transformation." In *Philanthropy and Cultural Context*, edited by Philo Hove and Soma Hewa, 295–314. Lanham, New York and Oxford: University Press of America Inc.

Rolnick, Phyllis J. 1962. "Charity, Trusteeship, and Social Change in India: A Study of a Political Ideology." *World Politics* 14 (3): 439–60.

Rotary International. 2014. "About Rotary." *Rotary International*. Available at https://www.rotary.org/en/about-rotary (accessed October 9, 2015).

Rothermund, Indira. 1969. "The Individual and Society in Gandhi's Political Thought." *The Journal of Asian Studies* 28 (2): 313–20.

Rudner, David West. 1987. "Religious Gifting and Inland Commerce in Seventeenth-Century South India." *The Journal of Asian Studies* 46 (2): 361–79.

Sasidharan, G. 2010. "Corporate social responsibility and public relations in India." Doctoral dissertation. Available at http://scholarbank.nus.edu.sg/bitstream/handle/10635/20945/Sasidharan%20G.pdf?sequence=1 (accessed May 6, 2015).

Sawhney, M. 2003. "The Role of Non-governmental Organizations for the Welfare of the Elderly: The Case of HelpAge India." *Journal of Aging & Social Policy* 15 (2–3): 179–191.

Schervish, P.G. and J.J. Havens. 1995. "Do the Poor Pay More: Is the U-Shaped Curve Correct?" *Nonprofit and Voluntary Sector Quarterly* 24 (1): 79–90. doi:10.1177/089976409502400109.

———. 2001. "Wealth and the Commonwealth: New Findings on Wherewithal and Philanthropy." *Nonprofit and Voluntary Sector Quarterly* 30 (1): 5–25. doi:10.1177/0899764001301001.

Schervish, Paul G. 2003. "Hyperagency and High-Tech Donors: A New Theory of the New Philanthropists." Available at www.bc.edu/content/dam/files/research_sites/cwp/pdf/haf.pdf (accessed October 9, 2015).

Schervish, Paul G., Andrew Herman, and Lynn Rhenisch. 1986. "Towards a General Theory of the Philanthropic Activities of the Wealthy." In *Boston College Social*

Welfare Research Institute. Massachusetts: Boston College. Available at http://www.bc.edu/content/bc/research/cwp/publications/by-topic/theory.html (accessed October 9, 2015).

Seddon, Jessica. 2013. "The Social Net Worth." *The Caravan: A Journal of Politics and Culture,* September 1. Available at http://caravanmagazine.in/perspectives/social-net-worth (accessed October 9, 2015).

Seghers, V. 2007. *Ce qui motive les entreprises mécènes: Philanthropie, investissement, responsabilite´ sociale?* Paris: Editions Autrement.

Shackley, M. 2001. *Managing Sacred Sites: Service Provision and Visitor Experience.* New York: Continuum London.

Shariff, Abusaleh. 2010. "Economic of Religion: Spiritual Capital and Philanthropy among Muslims." In *Handbook of Muslims in India: Empirical and Policy Perspectives,* edited by Rakesh Basant and Abusaleh Shariff, 308. New Delhi, Oxford and New York: Oxford University Press.

———. 2007. "Economic of Religion: Spiritual Capital and Philanthropy amongst Muslims in India." In *Handbook of Muslims in India: Empirical and Policy Perspectives,* edited by Rakesh Basant and Abusaleh Shariff. New Delhi: Oxford University Press.

Sharma, Sanjay. 2001. *Famine, Philanthropy and the Colonial State: North India in the Early Nineteenth Century.* New Delhi: Oxford University Press (SOAS Studies on South Asia). Available at http://www.oxfordscholarship.com/view/10.1093/acprof:oso/9780195653861.001.0001/acprof-9780195653861 (accessed October 9, 2015).

Shah, Dhinal. 2011. "Floating a Trust May Help You Earn Goodwill and Get Tax Benefits Too." *The Economic Times,* India, December 6.

Sharma, Seema. 2009. "Corporate Social Responsibility in India: An Overview." *The International Lawyer* 43 (4): 1515–1533.

Sharma, Zubin. 2012. "Live a life to be thankful for: Find more time for things you value inherently." Guest Column: *The Daily Pennsylvania,* November 29.

Shaw, William and Bennett Stancil. 2011. "Implications of Rising Inequality in Emerging Markets." Carnegie Endowment for International Peace, *International Economic Bulletin,* November 17.

Sheffer, G. 1986. "A New Field of Study: Modern Diasporas in International Politics," In *Modern Diasporas in International Politics,* edited by G. Sheffer, 3. London: Croom Helm.

Seth, Arpan. 2010. "An Overview of Philanthropy in India," presented at the Indian Philanthropy Forum, March 19, Mumbai. Available at http://www.bain.com/publications/articles/overview-of-philanthropy-in-india.aspx (accessed October 9, 2015).

———. 2012. "India Philanthropy Report 2012." India Philanthropy Report. Mumbai: Bain & Company.

———. 2015. *India Philanthropy Report 2015.* Bain & Company and Dasra. Available at http://www.bain.com/Images/BAIN_REPORT_India_Philanthropy_Report_2015.pdf (accessed October 17, 2015).

Seth, Arpan and Anant Bhagwat. 2013. *India Philanthropy Report 2013,* March 5. New Delhi and Mumbai: Bain & Company. Available at http://www.bain.com/Images/BAIN_REPORT_India_Philanthropy_Report_2013.pdf (accessed October 9, 2015).

Seth, Arpan and Madhur Singhal. 2011. *India Philanthropy Report 2011,* June. New Delhi and Mumbai: Bain and Company. Available at http://www.bain.com/publications/articles/india-philanthropy-report-2011.aspx (accessed October 9, 2015).

Seth, Arpan Karan Singh, and Dinkar Ayilavarapu. 2014. *India Philanthropy Report 2014*. Bain & Company, March 7. Available at http://www.bain.com/publications/articles/india-philanthropy-report-2014.aspx (accessed October 9, 2015).

Shier, M.L. and F. Handy. 2012. "Understanding Online Donor Behavior: The Role of Donor Characteristics, Perceptions of the Internet, Website and Program, and Influence from Social Networks." *International Journal of Nonprofit and Voluntary Sector Marketing* 17 (3): 219–30.

Shinde, Kiran A. 2002. Urban environmental governance for religious tourism in selective pilgrim tours in India, Unpublished Master's Thesis, Asian Institute of Technology, Pathumthani, Thailand.

———. 2004. "Quest for Good Governance: Contribution and Potential of Religious Institutions as Stakeholders." Presented at 'The Quest for Good Governance' organized by Monash Governance Research Unit and Monash Institute for the study of Global Movements.

———. 2011. "What are Charitable Trusts Doing in Religious Tourism? Insights from an Indian Pilgrimage Site." *Tourism Planning & Development* 8 (1): 21–36, February.

Shukla, Archana. 2010. "First Official Estimate: An NGO for every 400 people." *Indian Express*, July 7. Available at http://archive.indianexpress.com/news/first-official-estimate-an-ngo-for-every-400-people-in-india/643302/ (accessed October 9, 2015).

Sidel, Mark. 2000. "New Economy Philanthropy in the High Technology Communities of Bangalore and Hyderabad, India: Partnership with the State and the Ambiguous Search for Social Innovation." Paper presented at the Rockfeller Foundation Conference 'Philanthropy and the City: A Historical Overview.' www.rockarch.org/publications/conferences/sidel.pdf (accessed October 9, 2015).

Sidel, Mark and Noshir Dadrawala. 2008. "Philanthropy and Law in South Asia: Recent Developments in Bangladesh, India, Nepal, Pakistan and Sri Lanka." University of Iowa Legal Studies Research Paper Number 08-13. Available at http://ssrn.com/abstract=1126337 (accessed October 9, 2015).

Sood, Atul and Bimal Arora. 2006. "The Political Economy of Corporate Responsibility in India." *United Nations Research Institute for Social Development* (Paper Number 18). Technology, Business and Society: 82.

SOS Children's Villages of India. 2014. "Hand in Hand with SOS Children's Villages of India." Available at http://www.soschildrensvillages.in/campaign/hand-in-hand (accessed October 9, 2015).

Special Correspondent. 2013. "India Is Now World's Third Largest Internet User after U.S., China." *The Hindu*, August 24, sec. Technology - Internet. Available at http://www.thehindu.com/sci-tech/technology/internet/india-is-now-worlds-third-largest-internet-user-after-us-china/article5053115.ece (accessed October 9, 2015).

Spero, Joan. 2014. Charity and Philanthropy in Russia, China, India, and Brazil. New York: Foundation Center.

Spevacek, Ann Marie. 2010. *The Changing Face of Indian Philanthropy*. US Aid Knowledge Services Center.

Sri Sathya Sai Baba Trust. 2003. Available at http://srisathyasai.org.in (accessed July 21, 2013).

Staub, E. and R.S. Baer. 1974. "Stimulus Characteristics of a Sufferer and Difficulty of Escape as Determinants of Helping." *Journal of Personality and Social Psychology* 30: 279–84.

Sthalekar, Siddharth. 2014. "One Last Lesson in Faith from Raghuhbai." *Moved by Love.* Available at http://www.movedbylove.org/blog/view.php?id=269 (accessed October 9, 2015).

Stibbard, Paul, Russell David, and Bromley Blake. 2012. "Understanding the Waqf in the World of Tust." *Trusts & Trustees* 18 (8): 785–810.

Studin, Irvin. 2013, March 22. "Shutting Down CIDA Reveals That Ottawa's Cupboard of Ideas Is Bare." *The Globe and Mail*, Available at http://www. theglobeandmail.com/globe-debate/shutting-down-cida-reveals-that-ottawas-cupboard-of-ideas-is-bare/article10162119/ (accessed October 9, 2015).

Sundar, Pushpa. 1996. "Women and Philanthropy in India." *Voluntas* 7 (4): 412–27.

———. 2000. *Beyond Business : From Merchant Charity to Corporate Citizenship : Indian Business Philanthropy through the Ages.* New Delhi: Tata McGraw-Hill Pub. Co.

———. 2010. *Foreign Aid for Indian NGOs: Problem or Solution?* New Delhi: Routledge.

Swasti, Ira. 2011. "For turning charity into real impact," *Inc. India,* December. Available at http://www.growthinstitute.in/emagazine/dec11/cover-story-4.html

Tandon, R. 2012. *Philanthropy in India Today: Potential for Democratic Transformation?* In Conference on Diaspora Philanthropy in India, University of Iowa, March .

Tata Group. 2014a. "Citizen Jamsetji." *Tata Sons Ltd.* Available at Available at http://www.tata.com/aboutus/articlesinside/Citizen-Jamsetji (accessed August 18, 2014).

———. 2014b. "Tata Titans." *Tata Sons Ltd.* Available at http://www.tata.com/ aboutus/articlesinside/Tata-titans (accessed 18 August 2014).

———. 2014c. "The Giant who Touched Tomorrow." *Tata Sons Ltd.* Available at http://www.tata.com/aboutus/articlesinside/AapOEYsYNwI=/TLYVr3YPkMU (accessed August 18, 2014).

The Economist. 2012. "Special Report—The World Economy: For Richer, For Poorer." *The Economist,* October 13. Available at http://www.economist.com/ node/21564414 (accessed October 9, 2015).

The World Bank Group. 2010. "Poverty Trend (by International Standards)." *Poverty & Equity: India - Country Dashboard.* Available at http://povertydata. worldbank.org/poverty/country/IND (accessed October 9, 2015).

Times of India. 2011. "TTD deposits 1,175 kg of the Lord's gold with SBI," February 12. Available at http://timesofindia.indiatimes.com/india/TTD-deposits-1175-kg-of-Lords-gold-with-SBI/articleshow/7478903.cms(accessed October 9, 2015).

UBS-INSEAD. 2011. "UBS-INSEAD Study on Family Philanthropy in Asia." Switzerland, Singapore, Hong Kong: UBS-INSEAD. Available at http://www. insead.edu/facultyresearch/centres/social_entrepreneurship/documents/insead_ study_family_philantropy_asia.pdf (accessed October 9, 2015).

UNICEF India. 2014. "9,00,000 newborn children die in India every year," December. Available at (accessed October 9, 2015).

United States International Grantmaking (USIG). 2013. "Country Information: India," current as of October 2013, *Council on Foundations*. Available at http://www. usig.org/countryinfo/india.asp (accessed May 2013)

Unnikrishnan, P.V. 2002. "Humanitarian Values in India." *Refugee Survey Quarterly* 21 (3): 150–55. doi:10.1093/rsq/21.3.150.

Upadhyaya, R.B. 1976. *Social Responsibility of Business and the Trusteeship Theory of Mahatma Gandhi*. New Delhi: Sterling Publishers.

Vertovec, S. 2000. *The Hindu Diaspora: Comparative Patterns*. London and New York: Routledge Publications.

Viswanath, Priya, and Noshir Dadrawala. 2004. "Philanthropic Investment and Equitable Development: The Case of India." In *Diaspora Philanthropy and Equitable Development in China and India*, edited by Peter F. Geithner, Paula D. Johnson and Lincoln C. Chen, 259–89. Published by Global Equity Initiative, Asia Centre, Harvard University. Cambridge, Massachusetts and London, England: Harvard University Press.

Voluntary Action Cell, Planning Commission. 2007. National Policy on the Voluntary Sector. Section 6.1. Available at http://planningcommission.nic.in/data/ngo/npvol07.pdf (accessed October 9, 2015).

Vyas, M. 2013. Valuing Volunteerism and Philanthropy: Case Study of Hindu-Faith Based Organizations in the American Indian Diaspora. Thesis Submitted to Birla Institute of Technology and Science, Pilani.

Waghorne, J.P. 2004. *Diaspora of the Gods: Modern Hindu Temples in an Urban Middle Class World*. New York: Oxford University Press.

Wang, H. and C. Qian. 2011. "Corporate Philanthropy and Corporate Financial Performance: The Roles of Stakeholder Response and Political Access. *Academy of Management Journal* 54 (6): 1159–81.

Warrier, M. 2004. *Hindu Selves in a Modern World*. London: Routledge Curzon.

Watson, Noshua. 2012. "Private Foundations, Business and Developing a Post-2015 Framework". Policy Brief Issue 25. IDS in Focus Policy Briefing. Brighton, UK: Institute of Development Studies.

Wiepking, Pamala and Femida Handy. 2015. "The Practice of Philanthropy: The Facilitating Factors from a Cross-National Perspective." In *The Palgrave Handbook of Global Philanthropy*, edited by Pamala Wiepking and Femida Handy, 597–623. Basingstoke: Palgrave Macmillan.

Wiepking, Pamala. 2007. "The Philanthropic Poor: In Search of Explanations for the Relative Generosity of Lower Income Households." *VOLUNTAS: International Journal of Voluntary and Nonprofit Organizations* 18 (4): 339–58. doi:10.1007/s11266-007-9049-1.

Wilkinson-Maposa, Susan, Alan Fowler, Ceri Oliver-Evans, and Chao F.N. Mulenga. 2005. *The Poor Philanthropist: How and Why the Poor Help Each Other*. Cape Town: Compress.

Web Resources

Archana Shukla. 2010. First official estimate: An NGO for every 400 people in India. New Delhi: *The Indian Express,* July 07. Available at http://archive.indianexpress. com/news/first-official-estimate-an-ngo-for-every-400-people-in-india/643302/2

Being Human, http://www.beinghumanonline.com

Chinmaya Organization for Rural Development (CORD). Available at http://www. rural-development.ca/who.html

CRY (Children's Rights and You), Donation page. Available at http://www.cry.org/ what-to-do/donation-gops.html

Dance in the Rain—Mijwan Sonnets in Fabrics. 2012. http://www.mijwan.org/ events-press-media/mijwan-sonnets-in-fabrics/55-dance-in-the-rain-mijwan-sonnets-in-fabrics-2012

'Donors,' www.aseema.org

GiveIndia. 2011. Our mission. Available at http://www.giveindia.org/t-abtus_mission. aspx

http://archive.indianexpress.com/news/first-official-estimate-an-ngo-for-every-400-people-in-india/643302/2

'History,' www.aseema.org

Jaipuria Bhawan, 'overview,' www.jaipuriabhawan.com

Jayranchhodedutrust, 'Knowledge Center,' www.jayranchhodedutrust.org

'Kherwadi Municipal School,' www.aseema.org

'Life Skills Programs,' www.aseema.org

'MCGM Partnership,' www.aseema.org

MWS- 'Manish Malhotra' www.mijwan.org

Koppisch, John. 2011. "48 Heroes of Philanthropy." *Forbes.* Available at http:// www.forbes.com/global/2011/0718/heroes-philanthropy-11-kaldor-zhiqiang-oberoi-heroes-list.html (accessed on December 12, 2015).

'Pali-Chimbai Municipal School,' www.aseema.org

'Santacruz Municipal School,' www.aseema.org

'Staff and Volunteers,' www.aseema.org

Index

About the Authors

Meenaz Kassam is Associate Professor at the American University of Sharjah. She has coauthored three books and several papers, including an award-winning publication. Dr Kassam's research interests include nonprofit entrepreneurship, volunteerism, and women's empowerment. Her teaching interests include environmental issues, the sociology of human behavior, and sociological theory. She is also involved in working with NGOs in various countries.

Femida Handy is Professor of Nonprofit Studies at the University of Pennsylvania. Her academic writing is on philanthropy and volunteering, and her recent coedited book, *The Palgrave Handbook of Global Philanthropy* (2015) is a comprehensive reference guide to the practice of philanthropy across 26 nations and regions across the world. Dr Handy is currently Editor-in-Chief of *Nonprofit and Voluntary Sector Quarterly*, a premier journal in the field. She has several award-winning publications and has coauthored five books and over 100 publications. She has also coauthored a children's book called *Sandy's Incredible Shrinking Footprint*.

Emily Jansons works in Corporate Social Responsibility and has a background in international development research and practice. She has done her MA from McGill University and BA (Hons) from Queen's University. At the International Development Research Centre (IDRC) in Ottawa, Canada, she conducted a research on high-net-worth philanthropy in India, resulting in several publications, including *VOLUNTAS: International Journal of Voluntary and Nonprofit Organizations*, *Alliance magazine*, and *The Hindu Business Line*. She was granted the 2012 Italian Research in Philanthropy Award from the Università Cattolica del Sacro Cuore (Catholic University of Milan) for her work on Indian philanthropy.